FREEDOM ON THE BORDER

FREEDOM ON THE BORDER

The Seminole Maroons in Florida,
the Indian Territory, Coahuila, and Texas

KEVIN MULROY

TEXAS TECH UNIVERSITY PRESS

For Sara

Copyright © 1993 Texas Tech University Press

All rights reserved. No portion of this book may be reproduced in any form or by any means, including electronic storage and retrieval systems, except by explicit prior written permission of the publisher except for brief passages excerpted for review and critical purposes.

This book is typeset in Galliard and printed on acid-free paper that meets the minimum requirements of ANSI/NISO Z39.48-1992 (R1997). ∞

Manufactured in the United States of America

Library of Congress Cataloging-in-Publication Data
    Mulroy, Kevin.
    Freedom on the border : the Seminole Maroons in Florida : the Indian territory—Coahuila and Texas / Kevin Mulroy.
        p.   cm.
    Includes bibliographical references and index.
    ISBN 0-89672-250-3 (cloth : alk. paper)
    ISBN 0-89672-516-2 (paper : alk. paper)
    1. Black Seminoles—History. 2. Seminole Indians—African influences.
    3. Blacks—Relations with Indians. 4. Seminole Indians—History. I. Title.
    E99.S28M84   1993
    975.9' 004973—dc20
                                                                92-29135
                                                                CIP

03 04 05 06 07 08 09 10 11 / 9 8 7 6 5 4 3 2 1

Texas Tech University Press
Box 41037
Lubbock, Texas 79409-1037 USA
800.832.4042
ttup@ttu.edu
www.ttup.ttu.edu

Contents

Illustrations

FIGURES

MAPS

Acknowledgments

It is a pleasure to acknowledge a number of individuals who have made important contributions to this work. Though I never met him, I owe a tremendous debt to the late Kenneth Wiggins Porter. Porter was collecting oral history in Brackettville and Nacimiento long before Indian-black relations were recognized as being worthy of academic study, and his work not only broke new ground but also set the standard for the field. He was a first-rate historian and tremendous writer, and references to his many publications will be found scattered throughout the footnotes to the ensuing chapters. Porter left behind an impressive collection of papers, including correspondence, research files, and un-published book-length manuscripts on John Horse and Wild Cat, that now are located at the Schomburg Center for Research in Black Culture in New York. My thanks go to my friend and colleague William Loren Katz and to Diana Lachatanere for facilitating my use of this collection.

My appreciation is extended to the following librarians, archivists, and curators who proved particularly helpful in locating, gathering, and sorting source materials: Martha Blaine, former Head, Indian Archives Division, Oklahoma Historical Society; DeAnne Blanton, Military Reference Branch, National Archives; Nicole Bouché, Assistant Head, Manuscripts Division, Bancroft Library, University of California, Berkeley; Laura Guttierez-Witt, Director, Latin American History Center, University of Texas at Austin; Jack Haley, former Associate Curator of the Western History Collections, University of Oklahoma; Daniel McPike, Senior Curator, Thomas Gilcrease Institute of American History and Art, Tulsa; Patricia Middleton, Reference Librarian, and George Miles, Curator of Western Americana, Beinecke Rare Book and Manuscript Library, Yale University; John Neilson, Historian/Archivist, Fort Concho National Historic Landmark; Ken Perry, Director, Museum of the Big Bend, Sul Ross State University; Dolores Raney, County Clerk, Kinney County, Texas; Tom Shelton, Library Assistant, Institute of Texan Cultures, San Antonio; Don Swanson, Chairman-Curator, Old Guardhouse Museum, Fort Clark Springs; Mary L. Williams, Park

Ranger and Historian, Fort Davis National Historic Site; and Joanne Williamson, Head, Military Records Division, National Archives.

Special thanks go to the following individuals for providing leads, challenging arguments, or insights: Gary Anderson, Professor of History, University of Oklahoma; Joaquín Arroyo-Cabrales, Instituto Nacional de Antropología e Historia, Mexico City; Amy Turner Bushnell, Lecturer in History, University of California, Irvine; the late Arrell M. Gibson, Professor of History, University of Oklahoma; Ian F. Hancock, Professor of Linguistics, University of Texas at Austin; Charles M. Neal, Jr., Medal of Honor Historical Society; Joseph A. Opala, Assistant Professor of Anthropology, University of Sierra Leone; Richard A. Sattler, Research Fellow, D'Arcy McNickle Center, Newberry Library; and William C. Sturtevant, Professor of Anthropology, The Johns Hopkins University and the Smithsonian Institution.

My deepest appreciation is extended to the following friends and associates who took time from their busy schedules to read earlier versions of the manuscript and offer constructive criticism, advice, and encouragement: Alwyn Barr, Professor of History, Texas Tech University; Rebecca Bateman, Assistant Professor of Anthropology, University of British Columbia; Joseph Holloway, Associate Professor of Pan-African Studies, California State University, Northridge; my editor, Susan Miller, Texas Tech University Press; Theda Perdue, Professor of History, University of Kentucky at Lexington; and Ron Tyler, Director of the Texas State Historical Association. Don Bufkin of the Arizona State Historical Society provided answers to my geography questions and drew the maps. Scott Braucher of the Los Angeles Times took the photographs of the present-day Brackettville group and also provided a great deal of help with reproducing some of the historic shots. John Langellier, Director of Research and Publication at the Gene Autry Western Heritage Museum, assisted greatly with dating the military photographs.

Equally generous with their time were my gracious informants. Particular appreciation here is extended to Miss Charles Emily Wilson of Brackettville, Texas, William "Dub" Warrior of Del Rio, Texas, and Ben Warrior of Sasakwa, Oklahoma, for sharing their histories with me.

Finally, I would like to express sincere thanks to my mother and late father, and the other members of my family for their continuing support of my work. Over the years, my wife Sara has provided the patient encouragement, advice, understanding, and love that has sustained me in this enterprise. As the dedication states, this book is for her.

For the slaves had learned through the repetition of group experience that freedom was to be attained through geographical movement, and that freedom required one to risk his life against the unknown. [Geography] has performed the role of fate, but it is important to remember that it is not geography alone which determines the quality of life and culture. These depend upon the courage and personal culture of the individuals who make their homes in any given locality.

Ralph Ellison, *Going to the Territory*

Introduction

This is the story of a relentless search for freedom. A burning desire for liberty provided the motivating force that would drive a courageous group of displaced Africans from the plantations of the Old South via Florida and the Indian Territory to the rugged terrain of Coahuila and West Texas. At first, freedom meant simply an escape from bondage, but ultimately it would come to embody the larger notion of self-determination. For these people, the goal would prove elusive. As history unfolded, true liberty would acquire connotations of crossing international boundaries, fighting wars, living in exile, and establishing communities on hostile frontiers.

Ethnohistorians, linguists, and anthropologists have had difficulty in agreeing upon a name for this remarkable group. *Seminole Negroes* or *Indian Negroes* were the terms preferred by nineteenth century whites, but, over the years, they also have been referred to as *Seminole blacks, Indian blacks, Seminole freedmen, Afro-Seminoles, Negro-Indians, black Indians, black Muscogulges, black Seminoles,* and, most recently, *black Seminole.* Today, Texas group members call themselves *Seminoles,* in Coahuila they refer to themselves as *Indios Mascogos,* and in Oklahoma they call themselves *Freedmens,* each conferring exclusivity and stemming from their earlier relations with the Seminole Indians. The groups' self perceptions are informative, but they certainly have not facilitated the adoption a single term to describe them.[1]

Seminole blacks remains a useful term, constituent members being Africans or their descendants, whose association with Seminole Indians played a large part in their history and the construction of their identity. As Richard Price and William Sturtevant have suggested, however, *Seminole maroons* most accurately describes the group.[2] Stated simply, these people were either fugitives from slavery or their descendants, and the communities they established closely match the classic definition of maroon societies formulated by Price.[3] Their history and their relationship with the border can be understood best in that context. Technically speaking, in Florida, the Indian Territory, and Coahuila, some of the maroons were enslaved, but Seminole slavery typically translated only into the giving of a small annual tribute to an Indian leader. Whether enslaved or free, these Africans lived apart from the Indians in remote settlements under their own leaders and controlled virtually every aspect of their own daily lives. Even after the United States abolished slavery, the Seminole black communities in Coahuila, Texas, and the Indian Territory continued to resemble other maroon societies throughout the Americas.

The Seminole blacks had a great deal in common with such groups as the Jamaican Maroons, the Ndjuka and Saramaka "Bush Negroes" of Surinam, and the Border Maroons of Saint-Domingue (or Haiti). Similarities included the building of settlements in inaccessible, inhospitable areas for concealment and defense; the development of extraordinary skills in guerrilla warfare; impressive economic adaptation to new environments; substantial interaction with Native Americans; existence in a state of continuous warfare, which strongly influenced many aspects of their political and social organization; the emergence of leaders skilled at understanding whites; and an inability, because of various needs, to disengage themselves fully from the enemy which proved to be "the Achilles heel of maroon societies throughout the Americas." Most importantly, the Seminole black communities shared with other maroon societies the internal dynamism that characterized Central and West African cultural systems. Through "functional integration," the Seminole maroons incorporated adaptations of the most useful elements of their past and present experiences into a unique and complex cultural whole.[4]

This question of terminology has deep historical roots. The problem of defining Africans associated with the Seminoles proved to be perplexing to observers, and to army officers and other United States officials since the group first came to public notice in the early nineteenth century. Were they blacks, or black Indians? Subsequent attempts by whites to classify the maroons would exert enormous influence on their history, affecting their relationship with the Seminoles and adding to the Indians' and their own perceptions that they constituted a separate and unique social group.

Beginning in the early eighteenth century, Spanish authorities granted liberty to runaways from the Carolinas and Georgia who crossed over into Florida. In return for their military support against British interests, these formerly enslaved Africans could live apart, own arms and property, travel at will, and select their own leaders. This marked the entry of Florida blacks into the world of international affairs, and the Seminole maroons subsequently would become expert in borderlands diplomacy in both the Southeast and the Southwest. The group soon would commence an extraordinary career as defenders of diverse national powers. From the beginning of the nineteenth century to the outbreak of World War I, to further group goals, the maroons fought for Spain and Britain against the United States; for Mexico against Indian raiders and Texan filibusters; and for the United States against Indian bands and border outlaws. Along the way, they would engage American forces in the most expensive "Indian" war in the nation's history as allies of the Seminoles. Often pawns in bigger games, these maroons adopted sophisticated border agendas and strategies of their own and struggled bravely to secure their fate from the wishes and whims of others.

This study uncovers a little-known aspect of the African diaspora by tracing the Seminole maroons' long search for freedom along the borders of Florida, the Indian Territory, Coahuila, and Texas. The notion of crossing borders to achieve goals is a vital aspect of their history. As runaways, they crossed over into Spanish, British, and Indian Florida. After the First Seminole War, some fled from Florida to the British Bahamas and established communities across a more tangible border, beyond the ocean. With their removal to the Indian Territory, the maroons found themselves on the wrong side of a border. Too many whites were present, and the blacks' attempts to rebuild communities failed in the face of ever-increasing American influence and interference. The year after the treaty of Guadalupe Hidalgo, a group of maroons fled to the new Rio Grande border in alliance with a band of Seminoles and a band of Southern Kickapoos. Mexico had abolished black slavery some years earlier and the maroons went in search of personal liberty. The Seminoles and Kickapoos were not subject to slavery and went for other reasons. The Indians chose to return to the United States before the American Civil War, but to the maroons, the border continued to represent the line dividing enslavement and freedom until 1865. Only after slavery had been abolished north and east of the Rio Grande did they consider recrossing the river. A border could mean different things to different groups at the same time, or different things to the same group at different times.

From whence came the strength of the maroons' resolve and the subtleties of their relationship with the Seminoles? The dynamics shaping

Seminole-black relations cannot be explained by identical interest, as some have claimed. The maroons' primary motivation remained the prospect of liberty and self-determination. Their association with the Seminoles was but one means towards achieving that end. Nor were the maroons black Seminole Indians; there is more to this story than that. Africans and Seminoles often became close allies, to be sure, but for the most part, the two groups kept themselves to themselves and maintained a social distance.

The United States army would play a dominant role in this drama, engaging the Seminole maroons in wars, overseeing their relocation in the West, employing the men as scouts, and participating in their eventual resettlement in Texas. Officers on the frontier tended to do whatever they felt was necessary to get the job done, and this helps explain why, and under what circumstances, the military first allowed the maroons to remove from Florida to the Indian Territory and later sought to persuade them to return to Texas from Coahuila. The army's activities resulted more from expediency than carefully formulated policy. Indeed, as Edward Coffman has suggested, for much of the period, the military "carried out the duties of a frontier constabulary" and pursued courses of action designed to facilitate that role.[5] After 1850, this was linked closely to the unwillingness or inability of the Department of the Interior to formulate a coherent and consistent Indian policy. As a result, ethnic groups, such as the one under consideration, often would fall victim to the ill-defined roles of governmental agencies on the frontier.

The Seminole maroons would exert an impact on the history of the southeastern and southwestern borderlands far out of proportion to their numerical strength. Indeed, the scope of their activities highlights the complexities determining the development of those regions and points to the range of African and Native American communication networks in the Southeast and Southwest. Their story furnishes considerable insight into the underlying dynamics contributing to ethnogenesis, or the birth of "New Peoples," and the development of group identity. [6] It also illustrates ways in which outsiders attempt to construct identities of others for their own purposes.

These maroons were uncompromising in their refusal to accept anything less than complete liberty. United States officials promised them freedom if they would remove to the West, but failed to keep their word. Then their former Seminole allies began to sell them out. Though in crossing the Rio Grande they entered a country that had abolished slavery, the maroons' search for self-determination just was beginning. Liberty would offer them the opportunity to make a substantial contribution to the pacification and settlement of the Mexican border country, but ironically, it also would bring displacement, exile, slave raids, foreign and Indian wars, exploitation, and destitution. For more than half a century, the Seminole maroons would seek a home of their own where they could raise families, develop thriving communities, and preserve their culture and traditions free from peril. This book chronicles the fate of that magnificent quest.

Their tale is a rich and colorful one, and one of dramatic dimensions, stretching from the swamps of the Southeast to the desert Southwest. The maroons' history of African origins, plantation slavery, Spanish and Native American associations, Florida wars, and forced removal to the Indian Territory culminated in a Mexican borderlands mosaic embracing slave hunters, corrupt Indian agents, filibusters, revolutionaries, foreign invaders, Apache and Comanche raiders, border outlaws, and Buffalo Soldiers. What emerges is an epic saga of slavery, flight, exile and ultimately, freedom. Theirs is a success story. The existence today of Seminole black communities in West Texas and Coahuila pays tribute to the proud and indomitable Seminole maroons who defied the odds and went in search of freedom on the border.

1

Florida Maroons

In 1513, Juan Ponce de León landed near modern-day Jacksonville and planted the Spanish flag in Florida soil. Spain did not occupy the peninsula immediately, however, preferring instead to concentrate its efforts on richer prizes in Mexico and South America. It was not until Phillip II established St. Augustine in 1565 that permanent Spanish settlement of Florida began. The Spaniards brought with them European diseases that ravaged the indigenous populations in the early 1600s. Beginning around 1680, moreover, the British colonists in the Carolinas sponsored Creek and Yamassee raids into the peninsula that caused more damage by killing some of the native Indians and enslaving others. In 1708, the Spanish governor reported that three hundred refugees at St. Augustine were all that remained of the original inhabitants of Florida. But during the course of the eighteenth century this void would be filled by various immigrant bands that came to be known collectively as the Seminoles.

In the early part of the century, Spaniards invited some of the Lower Creeks to settle at Apalachee to create a buffer against the British population. The War of Jenkins' Ear and King George's War of 1739-1748 drove other Indians into Florida. By 1750, Cowkeeper's band of Oconis, driven south to the Lower Chattahoochee by the Yamassee War of 1715, had established the town of Cuscowilla on the Alachua Savannah near present-day Gainesville. Around the same time, other bands of Creek extraction, including the Apalachicolas and Mikasukis, moved farther south. They settled along the Apalachicola, Lower Chattahoochee, and Flint rivers, and a confederation of Hitchiti speaking peoples began to emerge in north central Florida and the panhandle. Cowkeeper and his Alachua band attained primacy, and the lines of his descendants Payne and Bowlegs came to dominate the collective principal chieftainship of the Seminoles until their removal from Florida in the mid-nineteenth century. After 1767, Muskogee-speaking Upper Creeks began to move into northern Florida, increasing the Seminole population to around two thousand by 1790. The last of the major migrations took place after the defeated Red Sticks fled south following the Battle of Horseshoe Bend in 1814. Their numbers boosted the Seminole population to five thousand by 1822, and Muskogee became the dominant language within the confederation.[1]

The term *Seminole* first was applied in 1765 to the Alachua group and then was extended to encompass the other constituent bands of the emerging confederation. *Seminole* appears to have been a corruption of *Cimarrón*, a Spanish word for runaway or maroon.[2] This is interesting when considered in the context of the group's subsequent relations with blacks. These Indians were runaways themselves, refugees from war and oppression, exiles in a strange land. Their situation was similar to that of the Florida maroons. The constituent bands of the emerging Seminole confederation were fervent in their resistance to European influences. The Spanish and British tended to leave them to their own devices, and their economic, social, and political institutions remained much intact. The Seminoles' retention of their own notions, practices, and institutions would facilitate the incorporation of large numbers of Africans within their society and have an enormous bearing on the course of future relations between the two groups.

Only slight adjustments would be needed to include blacks. The Seminole confederation was a loose organization of associated towns enjoying a great deal of local autonomy and displaying a large measure of cultural diversity. It was to achieve such independence that most of the bands had emigrated to Florida in the first place. The constituent members came from different regions and spoke various languages. The rules of membership were, clearly, very flexible.

Native philosophy stressed harmony, balance, and a cyclical mode of existence. The Indians were subsistence farmers and hunters; they were not concerned with profits or competition. The Seminoles employed a communal land system in which the town chief, or *micco*, levied taxes from the residents in the form of agricultural surpluses. This was a remnant of the earlier *sabana* system, a form of vassalage under which Florida Indians cleared land and planted fields for their leaders and for Spanish authorities. William Bartram described the system operating among the Creeks in the 1770s. Every member of the town could enjoy the fruits of his labor, but each deposited a quantity of corn in a large

crib as "a tribute or revenue to the mico [micco]," the chief retaining
the proceeds for the public good. Payments of tribute and displays of
deference were established customs among the Seminoles, and this
would bear heavily upon the form that black slavery would assume within
the confederation.[3]

The Seminoles had enslaved other Indians before they encountered
Africans, but they associated servitude with capture in warfare rather than
an organized system of labor. They tended to view captives as replace-
ments for tribal members lost during wars, and adoption was the usual
outcome. Bartram observed some enslaved Yamassees among the Seminoles in the early 1770s. The enslaved dressed better than the Indians
they served, both men and women could marry their captors, and their
children were "free, and considered in every respect equal" to other
members of their community.[4] Though adjustments would be made
when Africans replaced Indians, Seminole slavery would continue to
adhere to native principles until emancipation.

It seems likely that Spaniards first introduced blacks to the Seminoles.
Enslaved Africans in the British colony of South Carolina had learned
quickly that Spanish Florida offered a haven for runaways. The Spanish
approach to slavery tended to be more lenient than the British, employing less rigorous codes and affording blacks a greater degree of freedom.
Those enslaved, therefore, exchanged masters gladly by escaping across
the border to Florida. Runaways from South Carolina began arriving in
St. Augustine as early as 1687.[5] Spanish officials welcomed the new
immigrants and encouraged others to flee to St. Augustine to become
Catholics, promising them asylum.[6] In November 1693, however, the
Spanish king issued an edict freeing them in the hope of attracting
others,[7] and in 1704, Governor José de Zuniga y Cerda proclaimed in
his Orders for Apalachee Province, "Any *negro* of Carolina, Christian or
not, free or slave, who wishes to come fugitive, will be [given] complete
liberty, so that those who do not want to stay here may pass to other
places as they see fit, with their freedom papers [*despachos en forma de su
libertad*] which I hereby grant them by word of the king."[8] At first, the
Spaniards reimbursed former owners, but on April 12, 1731, the Council
for the Indies in Madrid decided that from then on, they no longer would
make recompense to the British colonists or return their blacks.

In 1738, as war between Spain and Britain rapidly approached,
Governor Manuel de Montiano of Florida increased his hospitality to
runaways from the Carolinas. On May 31, he reported that he had

granted freedom to a number of blacks who had fled to St. Augustine but who then had been enslaved by Spaniards. The governor also issued a proclamation stating that from that point on, every runaway who escaped to Florida would be set free.[9] As a result, "Numbers of slaves did, from Time to Time, by Land and Water, desert to St. Augustine. And, the better to facilitate their escape, carried off their Masters' Horses, Boats etc. Some of them first committing Murder; and were accordingly received and declared free."[10]

On February 16, 1739, Montiano set aside for these fugitive Africans an armed garrison near St. Augustine called Gracia Real de Santa Teresa de Mose, which became the first known free black community in North America. A priest was assigned to the settlement to give instruction in religion, and tools were supplied to the residents until they could harvest a crop. The British colonists considered the garrison both a provocation and a source of grave danger, standing as a beacon for runaways. The participants of the famous Stono rebellion of September 1739, for example, were said to be headed for the Edisto River, the mouth of which is directly north of St. Augustine. Although an armed posse attacked and defeated these fugitives some ten miles south of Stono, this incident deeply disturbed South Carolina planters. England and Spain were officially at war by that time, and contemporaries believed that Spanish agents had instigated the insurrection. Indeed, evidence suggests that African sergeants, sent into the Carolinas by Spain to incite desertions from plantations, or revolt, had informed enslaved blacks of Fort Mose's existence.[11]

The Spaniards also used the newly freed blacks to full advantage in resisting the British invasion of 1740. Faced with the alternative of freedom or a return to chattel slavery, none would oppose the invaders with more determination than the black runaways. The Spanish fortified Mose, a strategic settlement and easily defended, with a battery of four cannon and organized its residents and the inhabitants of allied Indian villages into military companies. Of the 965 troops in St. Augustine, two hundred were armed blacks who received the same pay and rations as regular Spanish soldiers and served under officers drawn from their own ranks. Montiano employed free blacks extensively as scouts, and Africans were reported killed and captured in actions outside St. Augustine.[12] When the Spanish counterattacked Georgia in June 1742, their forces included "a regiment of Negroes. The negro commanders were clothed in lace, bore the same rank as the white officers, and with equal freedom and familiarity walked and conversed with their commanders and chief."[13]

At the very time the Seminole bands were establishing a separate political identity in Florida, therefore, their neighbors were treating Africans favorably. The Spaniards welcomed runaways from southern plantations, gave them their freedom, and asked for little in return save for their cooperation in repelling elements hostile to both parties. The way these Europeans treated their African associates well may have made an impression upon the Seminoles. The Spaniards allowed Africans to live apart, own arms and property, travel at will, choose their own leaders, organize into military companies under black officers, and generally control their own destinies. Several of the Mose men even had wives in the nearby Indian villages.[14] A separate, armed settlement of free blacks, which enjoyed the full support of the adjacent Spanish residents, had been established just outside St. Augustine, the two communities being joined in a mutually beneficial alliance based primarily upon their joint opposition to British expansionism. It seems probable that the early Seminoles would have been aware of these developments and that their initial perceptions helped determine the course of their own relations with blacks.

Spain ceded Florida to Britain under the terms of the 1763 Treaty of Paris and transferred the inhabitants of Fort Mose to Cuba. Attracted by the semitropical climate, sparse white settlement, and chronic political instability of Florida, however, runaways continued to cross the border in ever-increasing numbers. They seemingly founded maroon communities and sought military and trading alliances with the nearby Seminole villages. Africans became associated with the Seminoles in the late eighteenth century in two other ways: by capture from plantations and by purchase from whites or from other Native Americans. Those blacks also would come to reside in the adjacent Florida maroon communities.

Though it cannot be pinpointed with any degree of accuracy, the ethnogenesis of the Seminole maroons took place during the late eighteenth or early nineteenth century. The true beginnings of this ethnic group date from the time its individual members were forced to accept common values and interests to counter the threat of domination and reenslavement. The group's members would have come together as a people primarily for survival and then to pursue mutual goals. Ethnicity would have acted as a structural principle long before their society emerged clearly as an ethnic group.[15] Whether runaways, captives, or slaves of the

Seminoles, these blacks preferred to live beyond the pale and ally with Europeans and Native Americans rather than remain enslaved on Southern plantations. Of major significance to their ethnohistory, the maroons' early and close association with the Seminoles would contribute strongly to the development of their identity. Yet these people would go on to establish a culture and history of their own and in so doing define themselves, and be defined by others, as a separate and distinct entity.[16]

During the Revolution, the Seminoles engaged in attacks on American colonists' plantations as allies of the British loyalists, and captured many Africans, deeply perturbing southern whites. The planter's worst nightmare found embodiment in this cooperation between Indians and blacks, and there ensued a period of concerted efforts to divide the races. Petitions poured continually into Congress and the executive departments for the return of fugitive Africans thought to be residing in the Indian country. In order to placate the Georgians, the American government concluded the Treaties of New York (1790) and Colerain (1796) with the Creeks in an attempt to secure the return of runaways. Both parties considered the Seminoles to be part of the Creek confederacy. The Seminoles themselves did not, however, and they repudiated Creek authority to interfere in their internal affairs and determine the fate of runaways living among them.[17]

It was apparently during the late eighteenth or early nineteenth century, after Spanish authority had been restored in Florida in 1783, that the Seminoles first adopted black slavery. Nothing definite is known about the system in its formative years, detailed descriptions coming only much later. It seems likely, however, that it comprised a mixture of native practices and elements taken from the Spanish, featuring both tribute and deference, and largely independent settlements of armed blacks.

Seminole-black relations first came to light during the early nineteenth century. By 1808, Spaniards were employing Africans to trade with the Seminoles. In that year, the royal treasury in St. Augustine commissioned Juan Bautista Collins, a free mulatto, to travel to Alachua to purchase cattle from the Indians. Collins made several subsequent trips to establish relations with Chief Bowlegs, taking gifts with him, and managed to purchase a herd of 125 cattle for the Spaniards. Juan acquired considerable knowledge of Indian customs and gained the respect of the Seminoles, Bowlegs's "sister," Simency even traveling later to St. Augustine to testify on his behalf during a lawsuit.[18]

The newly-emergent Seminole maroons were recognized for the first time as a group during the events leading up to the First Seminole War. In 1812, American settlers in Spanish East Florida attempted to seize the territory for the United States. The perceived need to remove the Seminole and black threat to southern slaveholding interests, however, was at least as important a consideration to the perpetrators. During the ensuing conflict, the Seminole-black military alliance in Florida came into full view for the first time. With armed Americans laying siege to St. Augustine, the Spaniards sought the aid of the Seminoles and maroons, posting African militia among the Indians and using black translators, such as Tony Proctor, to promote the alliance. State officials mobilized the Georgia militia as a precaution against a Seminole attack, but General Floyd was quick to add, "Should they take up the cudgels it will afford a desirable pretext for the Georgians to penetrate their country, and Breake up a Negroe Town: an important Evil growing under their patronage."[19] While the Seminoles stood to lose their lands if the plot succeeded, the Africans were in danger of losing their hard-won freedom. Both, therefore, were quick to answer the Spanish appeal.

Africans subsequently played a crucial role in helping to defeat the expansionists and ensure that Florida remained in sympathetic Spanish hands. Black troops, swelled by reinforcements from Havana, formed the majority of the Spanish garrison at St. Augustine. The maroons and Seminoles caused a diversion in the patriots' rear that was responsible for reducing the number of Americans outside the city. Local blacks, joined by runaways and Africans captured from plantations, also pestered the besieging force in cooperation with the Indians. Most important of all, a force of Africans and Indians under black leadership cut the patriots' supply lines and finally raised the siege of St. Augustine.

An African and Indian force thwarted Major Daniel Newnan's subsequent attempt to destroy the Alachua Seminole settlements, and it was said that the bravest warriors were those of the black towns. In prolonging the action, the allies succeeded in causing sufficient delay for Congress to demand a halt to the campaign in Florida.[20] By the time of the East Florida annexation plot, therefore, Africans and Seminoles had joined in a close military alliance that clearly was of mutual benefit. The allies were well coordinated and effective during campaigns—altogether a formidable foe. Maroon communities also were a feature of the Seminole confederation by 1812. The blacks were armed and fought under their own leaders but were responsive to the Seminoles and clearly enjoyed an excellent understanding with the Indians.

The southerners determined quickly upon further action to remove the African and Indian menace. On February 7, 1813, a substantial force of volunteer and regular troops set out to destroy the Alachua towns, using Indian prisoners as guides. The Seminoles and blacks, realizing that they were outnumbered, fled into the swamp. The American force then destroyed two of the settlements, one being a substantial maroon community near Bowlegs's town. In the first known description of a Seminole maroon community, the American commander reported that the inhabitants had established a thriving settlement based on farming, stock-raising, and hunting:

> Tuesday, Febr. 11 was employed in destroying the Negro town shown us by the Prisoners. We burnt three hundred and eighty six houses; consumed and destroyed from fifteen hundred to two thousand bushels of corn; three hundred horses and about four hundred cattle. Two hundred deerskins were found.[21]

The actions of the invaders left a legacy of troubles. A large number of emigrant Alachua maroons and Indians established new communities on the Suwannee, perhaps named after the Bantu *nsub-wanyi* meaning "my house, my home."[22] These would play an important role in later developments. But of more immediate importance, many African associates of the Seminoles were left seeking a more secure and permanent site for a settlement. They also sought revenge.

In 1814, during the second Anglo-American war, the British were prepared to employ runaways against their former masters. Their plan was to attack from the Gulf Coast, and they landed troops at the mouth of the Apalachicola under the leadership of Colonel E. Nicholls. Nicholls then visited the Mobile district where he printed proclamations offering Africans free land in the British West Indies at the end of the war and promising they would not be delivered to their former masters. He next proceeded to Pensacola where, in late July, he hoisted the British flag beside that of Spain.

With the infusion of the Red Stick immigrants after Horseshoe Bend, the Seminoles had become more militant in their attitude towards the United States. The Red Sticks still were smarting from their recent defeat at the hands of the Americans while the Seminoles and maroons sought recompense for the destruction of the Alachua towns. Nicholls had little difficulty in rallying their support, therefore, and by late 1814, he had armed and trained over four hundred blacks and three thousand Indians.[23] On November 3, Andrew Jackson forced the British to evacuate Fort Barrancas at Pensacola. The British sailed for the Apalachicola where they deposited their African and Indian allies. There in Spanish territory on the east bank, some fifteen miles from the mouth of the river and sixty miles from the United States border, Nicholls built a fort at Prospect Bluff and manned it with blacks.

The British sailed home in the spring of 1815 after learning of the ratification of the Treaty of Ghent. Most of their former Indian allies moved off to the east leaving behind at the fort a considerable amount of arms and ammunition and more than three hundred Africans, around twenty Choctaws, and eleven Seminoles to act as its garrison, the whole headed by a maroon leader named Garçon. Nicholls had built the fort on top of a cliff at one of the commanding sights along the river, with a swamp in the rear. This protected it from the approach of artillery by land. The parapet was fifteen feet high, eighteen feet thick, and protected by nine guns. The fort was as attractive a prospect to blacks on plantations as had been the free settlement at Fort Mose, and more runaways settled beneath its ramparts. The number of Africans increased daily until their corn fields extended far along the river. South Carolinian and Georgian planters were angered by the sight of formerly enslaved blacks living comfortably and in complete freedom under the protection of a fort that also endangered their own security. United States military and naval officers only awaited an excuse to put an end to this situation.

The Spanish governor confessed his inability to suppress the danger. On May 16, 1816, therefore, Jackson ordered General Edmund Gaines to destroy the fort and return its inhabitants to their former owners. As a first step, Gaines built Fort Scott at the junction of the Flint and Chattahoochee Rivers. The navy then dispatched from New Orleans two transports, escorted by two gunboats, to supply the post with ordnance and provisions. To reach Fort Scott, the vessels would have to pass beneath "the Negro Fort." The fleet entered the mouth of the Apalachicola on July 10 and received word from Gaines that the African stronghold was to be leveled if the inhabitants opened fire. The intention was to provoke an attack that would justify the destruction of the fort.

The garrison hardly could be expected to allow men, arms, and vessels, which would be used against it, to pass by unmolested. On July 17, some forty Africans and Indians ambushed a boat's crew in search of fresh water, killing or capturing all but one. That same day, Colonel Douglas Clinch had started down the river towards the fort. When he learned of the ambush, he surrounded the garrison and called upon the blacks to surrender. They refused, Garçon hurling abuse at the enemy. Furthermore, "The negroes had hoisted a red flag, and [the] English jack was flying over it." On July 27, the gunboats came within range and exchanged shots quickly with the blacks, but "the contest was momentary. The fifth discharge (a hot shot) from gun vessel No. 154 [entered] the magazine and blew up the fort." The American forces rushed in, found two hundred seventy dead, and took sixty-four prisoners, only three of whom were neither burned nor maimed. Garçon and the Choctaw leader were two of the three unharmed, but Clinch's men turned them over to the Creek allies for execution. The military treated the prisoners before delivering them to the descendants of their families' former owners in Georgia.[24]

With the destruction of the Negro Fort, the United States forces had smashed the African power base on the Apalachicola. But the garrison had consisted almost entirely of blacks from Pensacola. The fugitives from South Carolina and Georgia plantations had settled mostly along the river. Upon hearing of Clinch's approach, they had fled eastward towards the Suwannee, where Bowlegs and his Indian and African followers had settled after being dislodged from the Alachua Savannah in 1813. The maroons then built villages along the banks of the river as far as Tampa, and reorganized. Others moved even farther to the southwest, settling in the vicinity of Charlotte Harbor.[25]

Africans and Seminoles almost immediately made reprisals along the Georgia line, killing whites and setting fire to property. In February 1817, it was reported that six hundred maroons were under arms, drilling and parading to the beat of drums with officers of their own choosing, under strict military discipline, with new recruits bolstering their numbers daily. They chose Nero, Bowlegs's principal black, as their commander, swore vengeance for the destruction of their fort, and sought an early engagement with the Americans. Throughout the summer of 1817, the Seminole blacks and Indians engaged in raiding and recruiting. During the fall, two British adventurers, Alexander Arbuthnot and Robert Ambrister, arrived at the Suwannee from the Bahamas. Ambrister stated that he had come to see the blacks righted and took over the drilling duties from Nero. The so-called First Seminole War actually broke out when Africans and Indians allied in opposition to the slave-hunting expeditions of white southerners.

Border skirmishes continued into 1818 as maroons and Seminoles raided plantations and carried off enslaved Africans and other property. Southern planters, anxious to destroy this threat to their slaveholding interests, again furnished the main incentive for further American military action. Jackson replaced Gaines at Fort Scott in March with the prime objectives of breaking up the maroon settlements that were luring blacks away from their masters, and returning runaways to their owners. Almost immediately, he led his troops into Florida and advanced on the Suwannee. The maroons had built their villages to the west of the river, a mile or so north of Bowlegs's town.[26] The warriors first sent over their families and effects to the Seminoles, who had fled to the east bank, and then prepared to meet the enemy.

Bowlegs had lost no time in retreating into the swamp. While some of the men ferried the remaining women, children, and belongings across the river to safety, the maroon warriors, joined by a few Seminoles, stayed behind on the west bank to cover the retreat. During the ensuing battle, the American troops caught the blacks at every conceivable disadvantage. Dazzled by the sunset, overmatched by the superior American rifles, and outnumbered by three or four to one, the two hundred to three hundred Africans covered the retreat for several precious minutes. Becoming overwhelmed, they realized that the time had come to make their own escape. Jackson's men killed nine maroons and two Indians and forced two other maroons to surrender during the action, but the rest managed to swim to safety on the opposite shore. Their resistance had fulfilled its primary purpose—the women and children had escaped into the swamp. They also had suffered few losses and had given up only two prisoners. In what turned out to be a taste of things to come, moreover, it was the blacks who did most of the fighting in what is considered to be the main battle of the First Seminole War.

The Creeks later killed three maroon warriors and captured five black and nine Indian women and children some six miles into the swamp, but they attempted no further pursuit as the fugitives had broken up into small parties that never could be hunted down. The military then summarily executed Ambrister and Arbuthnot on April 29. Before he left the Suwannee, Jackson ordered his men to sack and burn the maroon and Indian villages, bringing to an end what he later termed "this Savage and Negro War."[27] The American invasion had exposed Spain's inability

to resist any serious demand by the United States for the annexation of
Florida. As a result, on February 19, 1819, a treaty provided for its
transfer for a fee of five million dollars, and the United States formally
and finally annexed the province in July 1821.

The information arising out of the events leading up to the First
Seminole War and including the campaign itself provides the only
substantial body of documentation yet discovered on the history of the
Seminole maroons prior to the American annexation. It emerges that
Africans and Indians were joined in a close military alliance in opposition
to American expansionism. The two groups needed each other—the
blacks to preserve their freedom, and the Seminoles their land. Joint
military ventures tended to be well organized and usually were successful.
The maroons and Indians fought in separate companies under their own
leaders but cooperated well. The alliance appears to have been at its
strongest when assailed from without, and this would become a recurrent
theme in the history of Seminole-black relations. So too would the
separation that clearly was inherent in the relationship at a very early
stage. The many references to "Negro towns" bear ample testimony to
this. When not under threat, the maroons and Seminoles preferred to
live apart.

The change of flags brought an increase in information on Seminole-
black relations as American travelers and government officials began to
document their observations. In the early 1820s, reports came in that
the Seminoles had adopted a form of black slavery. They had captured
some Africans from southern plantations while their leaders, noting the
prestige attached by whites to ownership, had purchased others. But the
Seminoles had little practical use for African bondsmen. They were not
concerned with capitalist notions and hence the labor-saving potential
of enslaved blacks. The Seminoles also considered managing slaves
beneath the dignity of the warrior and alien to their culture. Thus, they
attached new connotations to servitude, determined by their continuing
need for a military alliance with the blacks, their retention of native beliefs
and practices, and the influence the Spanish had exerted upon them. As
part of the arrangement, the blacks moved off by themselves, cleared the
land, and established maroon communities.

From statements made by a number of observers during the 1820s
and 1830s, a composite picture emerged of the status of Africans within
preremoval Seminole society. The Seminoles certainly did not establish
a clear-cut master-slave relationship. These blacks were under no super-

vision and generally no obligation to their owner except for the giving
of a small annual tribute. In 1822, in the first known description of the
system operating among the Seminoles, William Hayne Simmons stated
that the blacks, "[Never] furnished the Indians with any surplus produce,
for the purposes of trade; but barely made them sufficient provisions for
necessary consumption."[28]

The blacks' tribute resembled a feudal tithe and was similar to the
payment made by the residents of Seminole towns to the micco. Seminole agent Wiley Thompson described the typical African contribution
in 1835: "[The] slave supplies his owner annually, from the product of
his little field, with corn in proportion to the amount of the crop; and in
no instance that has come to my knowledge, exceeding ten bushels; the
residue is considered the property of the slave." Major General George
McCall set a somewhat higher figure on the amount blacks donated in
this description of the Seminole maroons: "They are chiefly runaway
slaves from Georgia, who have put themselves under the protection of
Micanopy, or some other chief, whom they call master; and to whom,
for this consideration, they render a tribute of one-third of the produce
of the land, and one-third of the horses, cattle and fowls they may raise.
Otherwise they are free to go and come at pleasure."[29] Historian Kenneth
Wiggins Porter coined a neat phrase to describe the relationship when
he referred to it as "primitive democratic feudalism." But General Gaines
was the most precise in his summation that the maroons were the
Seminoles' "vassals and allies."[30]

The Seminoles also allowed Africans to live apart in settlements headed
by their own principal men and enjoy most of the products of their labor.
Observers again agreed on this point. Simmons wrote, "The Negroes
dwell in towns apart from the Indians, and they are the finest looking
people I have ever seen," and Wiley Thompson stated thirteen years later,
"They live in villages separate, and, in many cases, remote from their
owners, [enjoying] equal liberty with their owners . . .." Finally, John
Lee Williams observed in 1837, "The Seminole negroes, for the most
part, live separately from their masters, and manage their stocks and crops
as they please, giving such a share of the produce to their masters as they
like."[31] This term, *Seminole Negroes,* would become prominent in the
writings of white observers during the mid- to late 1830s and contribute
to outside perceptions that the maroons constituted a separate group.
The name helped to distinguish the maroons both from the Seminole

Indians and from other blacks. By that time, the group clearly had self perceptions as a corporate body, also.

The maroons prospered under these favorable conditions, as witnessed by the amount of crops, stock, and produce found in the black town at Alachua in 1813. Simmons reported that like the Indians, the blacks practiced a system of communal agriculture, their fields being set apart from those of the Seminoles. Communal landholding also had African precedents, and similar practices have been found among blacks in the Sea Islands of Georgia and South Carolina. A number of the Seminole maroons became quite wealthy. Wiley Thompson stated, "Many of these slaves had stocks of horses, cows and hogs with which the Indian owner never assumes the right to intermeddle." McCall completed the picture: "We found these negroes in possession of large fields of the finest land, producing large crops of corn, beans, melons, pumpkins, and other esculent vegetables. [I] saw, while riding along the borders of the ponds, fine rice growing; and in the village large corn-cribs were filled, while the houses were larger and more comfortable than those of the Indians themselves." The Seminoles permitted Africans to own not only property but also guns for use in defence and for hunting. They also could move around at will. There can be little doubt that the Seminole maroons were able to control most aspects of their existence.[32]

Africans were of great value to the Seminoles in both military and political terms. Formidable and uncompromising warriors, they would defend their freedom to the last. They also knew the ways of whites and were useful in the formulation of military tactics and during negotiations. As Florida came under the American flag, the Seminoles utilized maroons more and more as interpreters and intermediaries. By 1822, for example, the Spanish black Juan had emerged as a principal interpreter among the Seminoles, the Indians placing "the utmost confidence in him, when making use of his services, in their dealings with the whites." In such ways, Africans attained positions of power within the Seminole con-federation.[33]

An affection grew between the two that was reflected in the Seminoles' typical unwillingness to sell their blacks to whites or other Indians. Simmons observed, "Though hunger and want be stronger than even the *sacra fames auri*, the greatest pressure of these evils, never occasions them to impose onerous labours on the Negroes, or to dispose of them, though tempted by high offers, if the latter are unwilling to be sold." Again, this was supported by other observers, Thompson adding, "[An]

Indian would almost as soon sell his child as his slave, except when under
the influence of intoxicating liquors. The almost affection of the Indian
for his slave, the slave's fear of being placed in a worse condition, and
the influence which the negroes have over the Indians, have all been
made to subserve the views of the government." Woodburne Potter
wrote in 1836:

> [These] Indians have always evinced great reluctance to parting with
> slaves: Indeed, the Indian loves his negro as much as one of his own
> children, and the sternest necessity alone would drive him to the
> parting. [The] negro is also much more provident and ambitious
> than his master, and the peculiar localities of the country eminently
> facilitate him in furnishing the Indian with rum and tobacco, which
> gives him a controlling influence over the latter.

Williams went still further, suggesting, "There exists a law among the
Seminoles, forbidding individuals from selling their negroes to white
people; and any attempt to evade that law, has always raised great
commotions among them."[34]

These maroons lived in much the same way as the Seminoles. They
resided in cabins of palmetto planks lashed to upright posts and thatched
with leaves. They also dressed like southeastern Indians, on special
occasions wearing moccasins, leggings, a girted hunting shirt of bright
colors, a turban topped with plumes, and a series of polished metal
crescents hung from the neck. In addition, the economic arrangements
of the black and Indian towns were similar, being based upon communal
agriculture and hunting, the only significant difference being that the
Africans apparently were the more successful farmers and owned more
property than the Seminoles. Being able to work the land as a group for
the common good and keep the fruits of their labor differentiated the
maroons from other blacks, and contributed to their sense of identity as
a people.

But Africans were never fully functioning members of Seminole
society. Only a few seem to have been included in Indian clans or towns,
the mainstays of Seminole social organization. These two affiliations
determined or limited most facets of a Seminole's existence, including
family relations, marital partners, political allegiance, leadership
prospects, rights of inheritance, and social activities. To be excluded from
these meant being considered an outsider. Evidence suggests that the
Seminoles restricted adoption into their towns, or bands, to a small elite

group of maroon leaders. They did adopt some blacks into their clans, as they had earlier with enslaved Indians, but such occurrences appear to have been exceptional. Br'er Rabbit made only infrequent visits to the square ground.[35]

The maroons' kinship system was not based upon the matrilineal clan and thus differed fundamentally from that of the Seminoles. But, as Bateman has argued,[36] the maroons shared with the Seminoles a significant domestic organizational pattern. A number of prominent maroon leaders were polygynous, fathering children by different women, who were maintained in separate households. This practice can be traced among the Seminole maroons in the Indian Territory after the Civil War, but it probably dates back to pre-removal times. Polygyny was the prerogative of maroon leaders in many other areas, including Jamaica, French Guiana, Surinam, and Brazil, and was reported among the Black Caribs from as early as the late eighteenth century.[37] The practice had African precedents, but also seems to have developed independently within Seminole society and other southeastern Indian communities. Polygyny among the Seminole maroons almost invariably involved endogamous unions, contributing substantially to the complexity of kinship ties that bound the group together.

Intermarriage between Africans and Seminoles certainly took place, but not to the extent that has been claimed by some historians. Because of the matrilineal descent system, if an Indian man married a black woman who was not a clan or band member, his offspring effectively would be born outside Seminole society. Nor did adoption into clans or towns necessarily accompany intermarriage, particularly if the black participant were female. A small number of leading African males, however, seem to have been adopted into Indian clans and towns, Abraham, leader of the Alachua maroons, and John Kibbetts, who would become one of the principal maroons in Coahuila and Texas, being good examples. For these black men, adoption may have been a reward for services rendered.[38]

Though they were close allies, Africans and Seminoles preferred to remain separate, settling apart and maintaining their own economic and social arrangements. The black towns fitted easily into the confederation but, with few exceptions, the Indians did not consider Africans to be Seminoles. This would become much more obvious after removal. The Seminoles had modified their native version of slavery with elements of the Spanish system, the whole subject to military expediency, in order to accommodate Africans within their society. As a result, the Seminole black villages continued to constitute maroon communities on the Florida frontier.

While certain aspects of the maroons' and Seminoles' daily lives were similar, others were not. The differences formed the bases of the maroons' ethnicity and defined them as a people. There is no stronger marker of ethnic identity than linguistic distinctiveness. The maroons' first language was what linguist Ian F. Hancock has termed *Afro-Seminole*, a creole related to Gullah, its lexicon containing mainly English-sounding words but also including some African, Spanish, and Muskogee expressions.[39] The Seminoles' native tongue remained either Hitchiti or Muskogee. Though a number of blacks learned to communicate freely with Indians and assumed important roles within the confederation as interpreters, the languages spoken in the maroon and Seminole communities would have been very different.

Likewise, the maroons' religious beliefs and ceremonies differed from those of the Seminoles, incorporating African, southern plantation, Spanish, and Indian elements. Many of the maroons had been exposed to Christianity earlier. Southern planters had attempted to convert enslaved Africans to Baptism, and the Spanish in Florida had tried to add blacks to their Catholic congregations. Evidence suggests that the maroons added African and Indian elements to these Christian practices: dancing at Christmas; possibly drinking tea, a variant of the black drink, during communion services; pursuing "ring-shouts" and communal call-and-response forms of worship in public structures; and believing in the vision-conversion experience. Their marriage ceremony was a survival of the "jumping the broom" ritual practiced on southern plantations, and their funerals, featuring wakes and burials, also included elements from their diverse cultural past.[40] While the maroons' religion may have been a syncretic conglomerate of various faiths and practices, it nevertheless would have differed considerably from traditional Seminole belief patterns and ceremonies.

The maroons' naming practices were yet another manifestation of the cultural differences between themselves and the Seminoles. The use of West African day names, such as Cudjo and Cuffy or their English translations Monday and Friday, and the month names July and August, was linked with leadership and distinction.[41] The maroons also continued to utilize famous biblical and historical names, such as Sampson, Elijah, Isaac, Caesar, Pompey, and Titus, the practice dating back to their plantation experience when enslaved blacks were forced to drop their African names and adopt those chosen by their white owners. Other names, such as Carolina, or Slavery reflected the individual's or an ancestor's earlier place of residence or status. Surnames such as Bowlegs, Factor, Bruner, and Payne, meanwhile, derived from current or former Indian owners. Occasional use of busk names by but a few members of the black elite suggests only minimal Seminole transmission in this area, and the naming practices of the maroons reflected most dramatically their unique historical experience and cultural heritage.

Travelers and observers tended to stress the similarities between the maroons and Seminoles and draw comparisons with the situation in the white South. In the process, they overlooked or played down the differences between the two groups. Whenever possible, in fact, the blacks and Indians kept to themselves, interacting substantially only during military campaigns and even then fighting in separate units under their own leaders. Though he was referring to the immediate post-removal period and his words clearly embodied white Victorian sensibilities, the contemporary Joshua Giddings came closest to defining the underlying dynamic shaping the relationship:

> [Most] of the descendants of the pioneers who fled from South Carolina and Georgia maintained their identity of character, living by themselves and maintaining the purity of the African race. [They] settled in separate villages: and the Seminole Indians appeared generally to coincide with the Exiles in the propriety of each maintaining their distinctive character.[42]

Despite the proximity of their settlements and the strength of their military alliance, many facets of the lifestyles of residents of maroon and Seminole communities would have been quite different.

The maroons' ethnogenesis and cultural development places them within the frame of reference of what have been termed *neoteric societies,* explanations of which stress the multiple heritages of groups formed as a result of frontier expansion and clashes between Old and New World powers. Nancie González defines a neoteric group as "a type of society which, springing from the ashes of warfare, forced migration or other calamity, survived by patching together bits and pieces from its cultural heritage while at the same time borrowing and inventing freely and rapidly in order to cope with new completely different circumstances."[43] Such groups tended to welcome and even encourage rapid change to

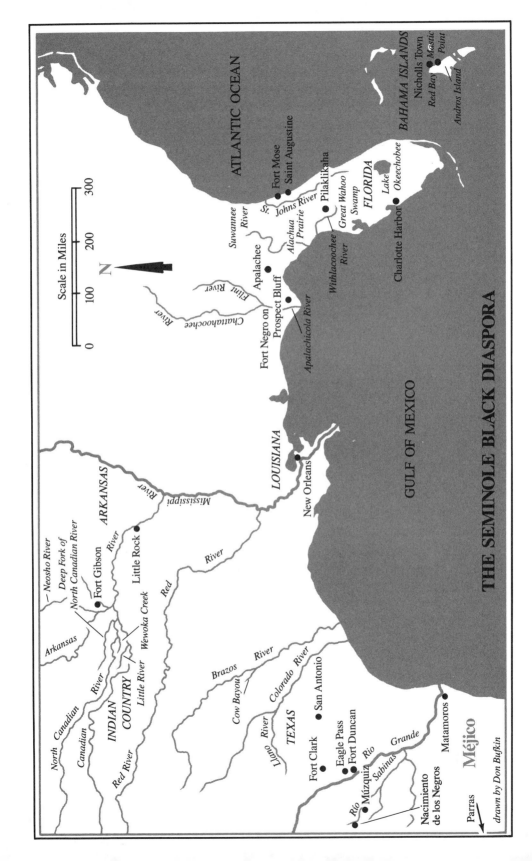

THE SEMINOLE BLACK DIASPORA

drawn by Don Bufkin

survive and prosper. Indeed, they might even be considered as having been created by the circumstances to which they adapted. By comparing and contrasting the ethnohistories of neoteric societies, proponents argue, significant insights can be gained into the larger historical and cultural processes contributing to the formation and development of new ethnic identities.

This approach seems useful in studying the history of the Seminole maroons, who sought to survive, adapt to life on the southeastern frontier, and maintain corporateness by fusing elements from their African past and slavery days with American Indian and European cultural forms. The model also facilitates placement of the group's experience within a larger, hemispheric context. Neoteric societies include communities established throughout the Americas by such groups as the Jamaican Maroons, the Ndjukas and Saramaka "Bush Negroes" of Surinam, and the Border Maroons of Haiti. Moreover, they include communities formed as a result of interactions between Africans and Indians, such as the Garífuna of Central America and the Miskitos of Nicaragua and Honduras. Though they constituted a distinct and unique people, the Seminole maroons shared a great deal in common with similar groups elsewhere. As with other neoteric societies, they incorporated adaptations of the most useful elements of their past and present experiences into a complex cultural whole.

After the 1818 Battle of Suwannee, the blacks and Seminoles found themselves homeless and displaced. The two again established communities approximate to each other. In 1821, Captain John Bell produced a list of thirty-five Seminole towns that included four African communities. Two of the black settlements were named after women, one being Mulatto Girl's town, south of Cuscowilla Lake; and the other Bucker Woman's town, near Long Swamp, east of Big Hammock. These towns probably were named after the owners of the inhabitants, Bucker clearly being a corruption of the African expression *Buckra,* a term meaning master or person of predominantly white rather than Negro blood, typically used by southern blacks in a disparaging way. After removal, it would emerge that, through matrilineal inheritance of property, Seminole women had come to own many of the maroons. The two other African towns listed by Bell were "Payne's negro settlements in Alachua; these are slaves belonging to the Seminoles, in all about three hundred"; and a village of Micanopy's blacks at Pilaklikaha, about 120 miles south of Alachua.[44] Pilaklikaha may have been named after *pakalala,* a challenge stance in the Kongo.[45] Certainly, the settlement had a strong African flavor, two of the three principal men being July and August, the third being Abraham.[46] Once again, the maroons and Seminoles had chosen to settle apart and live in separate villages.

Other Seminole blacks chose to quit the Florida peninsula altogether rather than fall prey to white slave hunters. Following the destruction of the Alachua towns, groups of fugitives made their way south to Cape Florida. There, those who could afford to bargained with captains of wreckers for passage to Andros Island in the Bahamas, the nearest substantial territory of their former ally Britain. Others made the crossing in Seminole dugout canoes fitted with sails and paddles. They established a settlement in the north of the island and called it Nicholls town after the British officer who built the Negro Fort at Prospect Bluff. Scipio Bowlegs was one of its early leaders. The Seminole blacks built other maroon communities at Mastic Point and Red Bay on the northeast coast. Little is known of these people's history, which well may survive only in oral tradition. Clearly, however, they had escaped the oppressor and found freedom across another border, over the ocean.[47]

During the 1820s, relations between Africans and Seminoles in Florida came under increasing strain. Some of the Indians may have held blacks responsible for the campaigns comprising the First Seminole War. Without the presence of large numbers of runaways among the Semi-noles, Jackson probably would not have invaded Florida. This may have weakened the alliance. Some Seminoles clearly became more receptive than they had been to overtures to trade Africans for profit as Indian owners disposed of thirty of the sixty-six blacks whose sales were recorded in St. Augustine in 1821.[48] Next, under the terms of the Treaty of Moultrie Creek, September 18, 1823, the Seminoles agreed to prevent further runaways from entering their settlements and to return those already living among them. Six of the most influential leaders signed the unfavorable treaty because of bribes and promises that they could remain on their extensive tracts of land north of Tampa. One of the signatories was Mulatto King, who had thirty men in his village on the Apalachicola.[49] Consequent to the annexation of Florida by the United States, the activities of slave hunters and speculators increased in the area. Many whites tried to secure the return of their slave property, while others sought to capture Africans for sale. The maroons might have suspected some of the Seminoles of being in cahoots with the slave catchers, and the signing of the treaty would have strengthened their fears.

Under the terms of the 1823 treaty, the Seminoles agreed to remove from their fertile lands in northern Florida to the interior country below Tampa. Most of the prospective five-million-acre reservation was swampland, inundated and impossible to cultivate. Over the next few years, many Africans and Seminoles became semitransient, surviving by stealing cattle from settlers to the north. Others did not acknowledge the treaty and stayed where they were. Their proximity to white settlements facilitated the work of slave catchers, who subsequently captured a number of blacks. The 1820s were a difficult period for the maroons and Seminoles, and their relationship suffered accordingly. Though the alliance soon would be revived as a matter of necessity, American military officials would come to expose and exploit its inherent weaknesses during the course of the forthcoming Second Seminole War.

The maroons and Indians soon would become involved in a massive conflict with the United States over the proposed removal of the Seminoles to the Indian Territory. The Indian Removal Act was passed on May 28, 1830. Anxious to appease Florida settlers complaining of African and Indian depredations, and southern planters concerned over the loss of runaways, the Jackson administration sought an immediate removal treaty with the Seminoles. Already suffering considerable hardship from the devastating effects of the drought of 1831, the Seminoles seemed ready to listen to offers of a tract of their own in the West, far away from white encroachment.

The principal men signed a provisional removal treaty on May 9, 1832, at Payne's Landing. The treaty stipulated that removal was conditional upon tribal approval of a selected site. The Seminoles sent a delegation of seven to explore the proposed area in the Indian Territory, accompanied by the African interpreters Abraham and Cudjo. The delegates signed an agreement on March 28, 1833, at Fort Gibson in the name of all the Seminoles, saying that they were satisfied with the land and willing to remove. Under the terms of the two treaties, the Seminoles agreed to settle among the slaveholding Creeks in the West and become a constituent part of that tribe. This stipulation subsequently would become a bone of contention and complicate both Seminole relations with the maroons and the groups' joint resettlement in the Indian Territory for more than two decades. Under another treaty, the Seminoles on the Apalachicola also agreed to remove, but the bands further east repudiated the Treaty of Fort Gibson. Nevertheless, United States officials ordered the Seminoles to prepare to remove west within the three years provided by the treaty.[50]

Africans would play a crucial role in fostering and strengthening Seminole opposition to removal. Whites attempted to seize the blacks among the Apalachicolas before they could be taken from Florida. The Seminoles also began to fear that if they removed to the West, the neighboring Creeks would steal their blacks. The maroons were afraid of being returned to their former owners or reenslaved under the Creeks, and exerted considerable pressure on the Seminoles to oppose emigration. In January 1834, Seminole agent Thompson expressed his belief that one of the major causes of Seminole hostility to removal was "the influence which it is said the negroes, the very slaves in the nation, have over the Indians." Governor William Duval of Florida concurred, noting, "The slaves belonging to the Indians have a controlling influence over their masters, and are utterly opposed to any change of residence." In March 1835, General Richard Call made the following recommendation to Jackson: "The negroes have a great influence among the Indians [and] are violently opposed to leaving the country. If the Indians are permitted to convert them into specie, one great obstacle in the way of removal may be overcome." The opposition of the maroons unquestionably paved the way for the onset of the Second Seminole War.[51]

When Wiley Thompson called them together on October 21, 1834, the Seminole leaders challenged the validity of both the treaties of Payne's Landing and of Fort Gibson, charging the government with trickery. Relations deteriorated rapidly during 1835. Agitation from white settlers to seize the maroons increased during the spring. Thompson then imprisoned Osceola in an attempt to force him to agree to the terms stipulated at Payne's Landing. African and Indian depredations escalated, culminating in King Philip's raids on the Saint Johns River plantations the two days after Christmas. The following day, December 28, 1835, the Second Seminole War began officially. At Fort King, Arpeka (Sam Jones) assassinated agent Thompson. Meanwhile, fifty miles away, north of the Withlacoochee River near the Great Wahoo Swamp, the black guide Louis Pachecho led a relief column under Major Francis Dade into an ambush of Africans and Seminoles. The allies annihilated the infantry unit, killing Dade and ninety-five of his command, the maroons returning later to mutilate the bodies of the victims.

The "Dade Massacre," as it subsequently came to be known, merely marked the beginning of massive casualties on both sides.[52]

The Second Seminole War cost the United States over twenty million dollars and the lives of fifteen hundred members of its armed forces, as well as uncounted fatalities among white settlers and militiamen, before it ended in August 1842. Seminole resistance to removal would not have been so widespread and sustained had it not been for African involvement. Upon assuming command of the United States forces in Florida in early December 1836, General Thomas S. Jesup noted, "This, you may be assured is a negro and not an Indian war; and if it be not speedily put down, the south will feel the effects of it before the end of next season."[53] The following spring, he stated, "Throughout my operations I found the negroes the most active and determined warriors; and during the conference with the Indian chiefs I ascertained that they exercised an almost controlling influence over them."[54]

Black participation in the Second Seminole War has been covered well by Porter.[55] The maroons assumed significant roles as warriors, spies, guides, interpreters and intermediaries. They also took part in all the major engagements of the war, the Withlacoochee campaign in March 1836, the Battle of Wahoo Swamp in November of that same year, John Caesar's raid outside St. Augustine in January 1837, and the Battle of Lake Okeechobee the following December. Should they lose the war, the maroons knew they could expect reenslavement, the breakup of their families, and loss of belongings. Consequently, they were every bit as firm in their resistance as the Indians. It is no exaggeration to state that the most expensive "Indian" war in the history of the United States was every bit as much about Africans as Seminoles.

Recruited by the maroons, refugees from Florida plantations as well as other blacks captured by the Seminoles joined the allies. Giddings estimated that by 1836, fully fourteen hundred Africans were associated with the Seminoles.[56] Though this figure is far too high, the military eventually sent nearly five hundred of the maroons west, while many others either were killed during the war or were returned to their former owners.

General Jesup instigated the policy of removing Africans to the West with the Seminoles as a matter of military expediency in an effort to conclude the war as quickly as possible. Expediency of this type would become a recurring theme in the army's relations with the Seminole maroons. Though it often appeared that the military was supporting their cause, such actions stemmed almost invariably from a desire to avoid conflict and, if possible, export the problem elsewhere. The army would take subsequent actions of this type after removal in the Indian Territory and later in Texas.

Jesup's first move came on March 6, 1837, at Camp Dade, when he concluded a treaty with representatives of Principal Chief Micanopy and Alligator, including the black interpreter John Cavallo or, as he was called more commonly at that time, Gopher John. Cavallo headed the Oklawaha maroons. Later, he would assume prominence in the Indian Territory and eventually lead emigrant Seminole blacks to Mexico, where he would become known as Juan Caballo or John Horse.[57] Under the terms of the Camp Dade accord, the Seminoles agreed to cease hostilities, make their way to Tampa by April 10, and board transports for the West. They surrendered hostages to assure compliance. Through the bargaining of Abraham, the agreement included important provisions concerning the maroons: "Major General Jesup, in behalf of the United States agrees that the Seminoles and their allies who come in, and emigrate to the West, shall be secure in their lives and property; that their negroes, their bona fide property, shall accompany them to the West . . .." The Seminoles thus had received assurances that their blacks would be allowed to accompany them to the Indian Territory and would remain their property after removal.[58]

At first, Jesup intended to carry out his side of the agreement. On March 26 he reasoned, "The negroes rule the Indians and it is important that they should feel themselves secure; if they should become alarmed and hold out, the war will be renewed."[59] But most of the Seminole maroons still were legally the slaves of white planters. Under pressure from Florida slaveholders, Jesup made the mistake of entering into an agreement with Coi Harjo and other Seminole leaders to surrender the blacks taken during the war. The maroons banded together in opposition and were supported by some of the more militant Seminoles. When several Florida planters arrived at the emigration camp to search for runaways, the blacks and many of the Indians fled. On June 2, moreover, Osceola, Wild Cat, and John Horse seized and carried off the Seminole hostages surrendered under the terms of the truce.[60]

The United States commander realized his mistake immediately and reintroduced the old "divide and rule policy" to separate the races. This strategy would prove to be largely successful and cause a rift between the Seminoles and maroons that would widen during the immediate postremoval period. In direct contradiction to his earlier treaty with the Seminoles, Jesup began to offer freedom to the blacks if they would separate from the Indians and surrender. He even proposed to reverse Jackson's removal program by allowing the Seminoles to remain in Florida:

> The two races, the Negro and the Indian, are rapidly approximating; they are identified in interests and feelings. [Should] the Indians remain in this territory, the negroes among them will form a rallying point for runaway negroes from adjacent states; and if they remove, the fastnesses of the country would be immediately occupied by negroes. I am very sure they could be confined to a small district near Florida Point and would accept peace and the small district referred to as the condition for the surrender of all runaway negroes.[61]

The question then remained of what to do with the Seminole blacks.

Jesup did not propose to allow the dissemination among southern plantations of maroons, trained in the use of arms and accustomed to freedom, who could take the lead in slave insurrections. To prevent this occurrence, Jesup engaged the United States government in slave trading ventures during September 1836. For the benefit of "the public," he purchased from the Creeks ninety captured Seminole blacks to prevent their being sold to unscrupulous slave dealers from Georgia. This one action created a myriad of problems after removal as the original owners pressed claims for their property. Not wishing to allow the maroons to remain among the Seminoles, be sold, or be returned to southern plantations, Jesup initially favored their expulsion from the United States, recommending Africa.[62] Quickly realizing the impracticality of this suggestion, however, he returned to his earlier position by proposing to send the blacks to the Indian Territory with the Seminoles as part of the removal program. In the belief that the more militant maroons would not surrender until they were assured of their freedom and that the Seminoles would hold out for as long as the blacks, Jesup sought a new treaty in early 1838 that would solve both problems.

In early February, from Fort Jupiter, Jesup appealed through African emissaries to the leading maroons, August, July, and John Horse, "[To] whom, and to their people, I promised freedom and protection on their separating from the Indians and surrendering." At a stroke, Jesup had granted freedom to the Seminole blacks, perhaps four-fifths of whom were either runaways or their descendants and still legally slaves. The Seminoles also claimed many of the maroons as their property. In view of Jesup's refusal to return them to southern plantations, "[It] was stipulated that they should be sent to the West as part of the Seminole nation." Black emancipation and removal suddenly had become the policy of the United States army.[63]

To give his new removal policy legal justification, Jesup resorted to the fiction that all the maroons were legitimate Seminole property. As a result, he dispatched to the West all the blacks who appeared at the emigration camps. With the onset of this policy, the Second Seminole War effectively came to an end for the maroons. Most of those remaining in the field took the opportunity to sue for peace under Jesup's promise of liberty and removal. During the campaign of September 1837 to March 1838, around two hundred fifty Africans either had surrendered or been captured. Under the counsel of Abraham, Alligator surrendered with John Horse and eighty-eight of his band, including twenty-seven blacks.[64] His capitulation led to the surrender of three hundred sixty more Africans and Indians in April. Those recent runaways or captured blacks who had managed to hold out until 1838 the United States government deemed free, and they boarded transports for the West alongside Seminole maroons of longer standing.

After 1838, having attained such favorable terms for themselves, Africans took on a new role as government agents who induced militant Seminoles to surrender and remove west. Black guides, interpreters, and negotiators, such as Sandy Perryman and Sampson, became indispensable in establishing contact with the remaining Seminole leaders. Most important of all was John Horse, who returned to Florida from the Indian Territory and often played a significant role in negotiating between United States officials and Seminole leaders remaining in the field. In 1842, General William Worth, the last of the American commanders in the Second Seminole War, estimated that there were only 301 Seminoles left in Florida. Realizing the futility of trying to force these resourceful Indians to remove, Worth met their leaders in council at Cedar Keys on August 14 and informed them that they could remain in Florida on a swampland reservation deep in the southern section of the peninsula.[65] Black removal ultimately had superceded Seminole removal on the American list of priorities.

By the time they prepared to leave Florida for the Indian Territory, the Seminole maroons had emerged as a separate and distinct people.

Whites had named them "Seminole Negroes" and had recognized them as an independent group during the Second Seminole War. We do not know how the maroons referred to themselves at this point. I would argue, however, that from an early stage in their development they would have felt a self-awareness and would have shared ideas about themselves as a people; that by the time of removal this had developed into a historical consciousness; that they had engaged in common pursuits, established an economic and social system and built communities based on group goals, collective action, and strong kinship ties; that they possessed a unique history and culture. In Robert K. Thomas's terms, they shared a common origin—a sense of "peoplehood"—and possessed an acute sense of both the significance of membership and the boundaries dividing them from others.[66] This is what gave the group cohesiveness, strength, and identity.

Weaknesses had begun to appear in the alliance between Africans and Seminoles in the 1820s, and these were exposed more fully in removal negotiations during the Second Seminole War. Although they had joined in fierce resistance to American expansionism, the Seminoles and maroons had done so for different reasons. The Seminoles wished to retain their land and slave property and maintain an identity separate from that of the Creeks. The maroons, however, were fighting for their freedom. Jesup's removal policies succeeded in dividing the races and drove a deep wedge between Africans and Seminoles that would lead to a host of difficulties. He had assured the Indians that they would be secure in their slave property, but the blacks had surrendered at different times and under differing circumstances. Hence, some were classified as slaves while others were deemed to be free. This would lead to massive and all-encompassing problems once the maroons and Seminoles reached the Indian Territory. A precedent had been set, and later attempts by United States officials at classifying the Seminole blacks in both the Indian Territory and Texas would prove similarly destructive.

One factor stands out clearly from the removal negotiations: the maroons had chosen promises of freedom and removal over further resistance and had separated from the Indians in order to secure that goal. No matter how mild the system of slavery practiced by the Seminoles, freedom was infinitely preferable. Above all, emancipation furthered the goal of self-determination. The American commander chose to deal with the maroons as an independent group, and the maroons in turn elected to pursue their own best interests unilaterally.

Later in the war, Africans had aided the removal program by bringing in Indians. This led to the belief among many Seminoles that the blacks had procured a good deal for themselves at the Indians' expense. The maroons, meanwhile, treasured their newly-won liberty, and later, many of the more militant would be prepared to go to extraordinary lengths to preserve it. The issue of the blacks' position in the Indian Territory would be complicated still further by conflicting claims to ownership by whites and other Indians, and the uncertain stance adopted by the United States government in determining their status. The whole made for a host of complex problems that faced the new arrivals in the West—problems that ultimately would lead to unforeseen and truly remarkable developments.

2

Emigrants from Indian Territory

The 1832 Treaty of Payne's Landing and the 1833 Treaty of Fort Gibson had stipulated that the Seminoles would settle among the Creeks in the West and become a constituent part of that tribe. Under the terms of the Fort Gibson treaty, the Seminoles had been granted a piece of land lying between the Canadian and North Fork rivers, to the western extremities of Little River. When Opothleyahola and his Upper Creek Tuckabatchee band emigrated west in 1837, however, they settled in the eastern part of this tract. Fear of, and opposition to, Creek domination of their tribal affairs had been a major cause of Seminole resistance to removal. Indeed, the two had been armed antagonists during the late conflict. Principal Chief Micanopy and the more conciliatory Seminoles chose to swallow their pride and settle on their assigned lands, taking their blacks with them. But those Seminoles who had held out longest in Florida or were most vehement in their opposition to change refused to remove to the Creek country or become a part of that tribe and settled instead on Cherokee lands around Fort Gibson.[1]

The reasons for their refusal were straightforward. Unification with the Creeks threatened the very lifestyle and mores of the Seminole traditionalists. As was the case among the Cherokees, Chickasaws, and Choctaws, intermarried whites and their acculturated mixed-blood offspring had come to dominate the leadership of the Lower Creek towns. This wealthy, elite group of plantocrats had acquired substantial holdings in slave property and utilized institutionalized bondage. In the West, the Lower and Upper Creeks united under a general tribal council. Roley McIntosh, the wealthy and acculturated head of the Lower towns, became principal chief of the entire nation, and his party came to dominate the Creek government. It was clear to the Seminole traditionalists that if a union of the tribes were to come about, the more numerous Creeks would insist upon Seminole assimilation. The subjugation of Seminole interests and the resultant loss of a separate identity then would become inevitable.

Creek individuals also laid claim to some of the maroons, and many Seminoles feared that their blacks would be seized. Seminoles traditionally associated slaveholding with prestige and leadership. Following the upheavals of removal, leaders were anxious to retain Africans within their parties to prevent a decline in their power base. The fear that Creeks would rob them of their blacks was the reason most often cited as the main source of their opposition to unification with the larger group. The maroons also opposed the proposed union strongly. The Creeks had adopted institutionalized bondage defined by harsh slave codes. Under a leadership dominated by acculturated mixed-blood Lower Creeks, the maroons could expect to be subjected to a rigid form of slavery, and sale. Between 1841 and 1845, therefore, they revived and strengthened their alliance with the Seminoles settled around Fort Gibson, based on their joint opposition to Creek domination.[2]

The architects of the alliance, John Horse and Wild Cat, had become close friends in Florida. They had been comrades at the Tampa Bay emigration camp after the capitulation at Fort Dade in 1837, and later they had cooperated in carrying off the hostages after Jesup had violated the treaty. Their relationship had been strengthened by their shared experience of capture, their subsequent imprisonment at and escape from Fort Marion, and their dual command during the Battle of Okeechobee in December 1837.[3] After removal, John Horse and Wild Cat became the leaders of their respective parties. Horse headed the maroons and Wild Cat, who had succeeded to the leadership of his band, became spokesman for those Seminoles most vehemently opposed to unification with the Creeks. The two ultimately would be responsible for forging the alliance that led to their supporters' emigration to the Mexican border country.

Wild Cat had continued the struggle in Florida until March 1841 and was the last important Indian leader to surrender in the Second Seminole War. When he removed to the Indian Territory in November, Wild Cat refused to settle among the Creeks and would remain as a squatter on Cherokee land for more than three years. By early 1842, more than fifteen hundred Seminoles, well over a third of the tribe, were encamped around Fort Gibson under Wild Cat, Alligator, and other leaders. Lacking building and farming equipment, these Seminoles could not construct homes or cultivate the land and were destitute, but they adamantly refused to remove to their assigned lands. The main reason for this reluctance remained the fear that the maroons would be claimed by Creeks. Unwilling to take any course but their own, these Seminoles stayed firm in their resolve not to locate among the Creeks, become subject to their control, or risk the loss of their blacks.[4]

John Horse had been the last maroon leader to surrender in Florida. After his capitulation with Alligator in April 1838, he was shipped immediately to the West. He suggested that the government send delegations of prominent leaders from the Indian Territory to persuade those Seminoles still in the field to surrender, and he returned to Florida himself in 1839. He became well known as a guide and interpreter, and participated in bringing in 535 Indians remaining in the field during the last two years of the war.[5]

John Horse left Florida for good in the summer of 1842. On July 22, he sailed out of New Orleans in a party of 102 Seminole captives on the steamboat *Swan* under the charge of Lieutenant Edward Canby. On August 5, because of low water in the Arkansas River, they landed at La Fourche Bar, six miles below Little Rock. Emigration officials were eager to remove new arrivals immediately to the Creek country south of the Arkansas to avoid adding to the numbers of those already settled on Cherokee lands, but Canby was unable to negotiate a draft to conduct the party farther. The remarkable John Horse had owned a great deal of property in Florida, including some ninety head of cattle. Apparently he had managed to dispose of it successfully, for he was able to provide a loan of fifteen hundred dollars for transportation. On August 12, Canby secured wagons and teams, and the party set out. The immigrants finally arrived at the Creek council grounds on September 6, where they were received by agent John McKee.

John Horse made his home on the Deep Fork of the North Canadian and helped to establish a Seminole maroon community at that location. Upon the death of his Indian owner in Florida, Horse had become the property of the Seminole chiefs. In February 1843, for his service in providing funds for the Canby party, the Seminoles declared him to be free. As a free black, John Horse was in great danger of being kidnapped by Creeks or whites and returned to slavery. Consequently, he spent much of his time around Fort Gibson serving as an interpreter and intermediary for those Seminoles residing in the Cherokee country. From this position, John was able to advance the views of the maroons and sustain Wild Cat and his followers in their opposition to the Creeks.[6]

There had been no change in the situation of the Seminoles encamped around Fort Gibson by early 1844, and Wild Cat complained that his followers were shelterless, destitute, and utterly dependent upon the Cherokees for support. During the spring, moreover, the Creeks instigated a kidnapping campaign to capture Seminole blacks. In one such incident, Siah Hardridge stole Dembo, who was owned by Sally Factor, a Creek woman who lived with the Seminoles. Wild Cat tried to enlist the aid of the military at Fort Gibson in recovering Dembo, stating that the Seminoles were outraged over the incident and feared an outbreak of hostilities with the Creeks if kidnappers like Hardridge went unpunished. Dembo later would quit the Indian Territory and become one of the leading Seminole maroons in Coahuila and Texas.[7]

Wild Cat determined upon more decisive action to try to end the dispute. Spurred on by John Horse, he organized and financed a delegation to Washington in April that included Alligator, Tiger Tail, and Tustenuggee, other leaders of Seminole bands still residing in the Cherokee country. Horse acted as interpreter and represented the views of the maroons. Micanopy and other Seminole leaders protested against Wild Cat's unauthorized initiative, but the delegates claimed to speak for the whole tribe in seeking fulfillment of treaty obligations.[8] In Washington, Wild Cat and Alligator informed Jesup that their strongest objection to settling in the Creek country resulted from the belief that "they would take by force our Negro property from us, as many bad men among them were setting up unjust claims to many of our Blacks on which account we still remain in the Cherokee Nation." The threat of loss of slave property remained the main source of Seminole opposition to unification with the Creeks.[9]

The Washington delegation came to represent the pinnacle of Seminole-black cooperation after removal prior to the events of 1849. Relations deteriorated rapidly after the delegates' return in July. John Horse had been back at Fort Gibson only a few days when a "Seminole, in the immediate vicinity of this Post, fired at him with a rifle, and killed the horse upon which he was riding. His friends on the 'Deep Fork' where he resides, have sent him word to remain here; that, if he goes home, he will certainly be killed." [10]

Lieutenant Colonel Richard Mason, the commander at Fort Gibson, believed the attack on John Horse resulted from his services as guide and interpreter to the American troops during the latter stages of the Second Seminole War. Cherokee agent Pierce Butler, however, reported that since John had returned he had become "obnoxious to many of the Seminoles, particularly his former owners who in consequence of some offensive language shot his horse under him and would have taken his life if not prevented." Jesup believed the Seminoles to be hostile to Horse and other leading African interpreters because they suspected them of having deceived the Indians during treaty negotiations and of being responsible for the failure of United States officials to fulfill certain promises. Each of these assessments had some validity.[11]

John Horse no longer could reside among the Seminoles and feel safe. Mason told him to remain at Fort Gibson where he and his family would be given rations until Washington furnished further instructions. Horse already had acquired over fifty head of stock, a wagon, tools, and farming implements on the Deep Fork. On August 2, Secretary of War William Wilkins instructed General Mathew Arbuckle to hold the Seminole chiefs responsible for Horse's life, family, and property. Later that month, the Seminoles sent an apology disapproving of the actions of this "one man" and offering reimbursment for the horse. No funds were available, however, and John never received payment.[12] Although he had made his home on the Deep Fork, John Horse had chosen to spend much of his time at Fort Gibson, the focal point of Indian affairs in the territory. From July 1844 until January 1849, however, he would be forced to reside at the post under the protection of the military. During and after 1845, both there and in Washington, John Horse would develop an independent and unilateral course of action for his supporters.

Wild Cat and Alligator also were greeted by troubles upon their return to the Indian Territory. As they entered the Cherokee country, they found their people encamped on the prairies around Fort Gibson, starving. The Arkansas and Grand Rivers had risen and driven them from their homes in the bottoms, destroying both the crop in the ground and the corn they had stored in cribs. Two hundred ninety-five Seminoles were utterly destitute, "subsisting on berries and what they could obtain by begging." American officials were quick to realize that Wild Cat's followers likely would be more amenable to a settlement with the Creeks if sufficient inducements were offered at this time.[13]

The United States commissioners entered into negotiations with the Creeks and Seminoles the following winter to try to settle the differences between them. The question of the Seminole blacks dominated the debate. Wild Cat and other Seminole headmen submitted a memorial on December 28 expressing their sincere hope that the Creeks would not interfere with "this species of property in our possession." The most vehement at first determined not to submit to Creek laws on any terms, but they eventually capitulated, and Wild Cat became a signatory to the tripartite treaty of January 4, 1845, between the United States, the Creeks, and the Seminoles. The destitution of his followers and increased incentives were the deciding factors that persuaded Wild Cat to sign.[14] The United States agreed to increase the Seminole annuity and pay the difference in goods, furnish the tribe with agricultural equipment over the next five years, issue the Seminoles rations during their removal to the Creek country, and subsist them for six months after their relocation.

Under the terms of the treaty, the Seminoles agreed to settle in bands or as a whole in any part of the Creek country. They would make their own town regulations subject to the general control of the Creek council, to which they could send representatives. There was to be no distinction between the two in any respect, save that neither could interfere with the pecuniary affairs of the other. The treaty thus mandated the union of the tribes.[15] During the spring, most of the remaining Seminoles removed to the Creek country. They established twenty-five towns some miles distant from each other and planted their fields on bottom lands, the majority settling some eight miles north of Little River. By the fall, the Seminoles had completed their relocation.[16]

The treaty proved to be disastrous for both the Seminoles and the maroons. As Wild Cat had feared, the Seminoles paid a high price for the clause allowing them to retain their social organization. They had only minority representation in the Creek council, and their interests would be subjugated to those of the larger group. Even their property was not secure. The treaty did not address the questions of title to, and control over, the Seminole blacks. Article 3 referred to contested cases between the tribes as a whole, but individual Creeks still could present fraudulent claims. The conflict over the maroons had been the main cause of Seminole opposition to the Creeks and would remain a major source of difficulty after 1845. The destitution of his followers had forced Wild Cat to agree to the treaty, but he soon must have regretted his decision and remained opposed to Creek authority. Deeply dissatisfied with his new home and position, Wild Cat began to seek a viable and attractive Seminole alternative to unification with the Creeks on unequal terms.

From around October 15, 1844, to April 15, 1845, different bands of Seminoles called upon John Horse to interpret, sometimes sending for him a dozen times a day. He was particularly active from the signing of the treaty until the main body of Seminoles relocated on February 9. For sixty days, from February until early April, Horse drove his wagon pulled by three yoke of oxen in the train that removed the Seminoles and their belongings from their camps near Fort Gibson to the Little River. But his position among the Seminoles remained precarious. During the removal, Indians made a second attempt on his life, and Thomas Judge, subagent to the Seminoles, believed that the assailants would try again. Once more, Horse was forced to take refuge at Fort Gibson under the protection of the military.[17]

By mid-April, John Horse faced a desperate situation. No longer could he live safely among his people, and his former allies had agreed to a treaty that gave the Creeks dominance over the Seminoles. Free blacks such as he could be reenslaved through questionable or fraudulent claims, or kidnapping. Blacks owned by Seminoles faced similar dangers and stood to be subjected to a much harsher system of servitude. With unification, Creek slave codes could be applied to the Seminole maroons. These laws, formulated as part of the Creek constitution of 1825, affected free as well as enslaved blacks. Suddenly, the Seminole maroons faced inequality before the law, its most immediate effect being confiscation of their personal property. Later additions to these laws forbade blacks to live in separate towns or to bear arms. Under Creek slave codes, which with every revision resembled more closely those operating in the South, the maroons could expect loss of privilege and property and the breakup of their families and townships.[18]

Apparently deserted by Wild Cat, John Horse determined to act independently. In April he visited Washington with Mason "with the view of obtaining permission of the Government to return and settle in Florida."[19] In late May Horse applied once more for compensation for his loss of property the previous summer: "I hereby authorize and request Mr. Judge Seminole agent to pay to my wife *Susan* such sum of money as the Seminole council may allow to me from their annuities as compensation for a horse shot under me by one of their people in 1844."[20] The use of "their people" is indicative of the polarization of the maroons and Seminoles that was taking place after the tripartite treaty. John Horse would spend the next year in Washington promoting the exclusive interests of *his* people.

After the treaty of 1845, the maroons removed to the Creek country and in their customary fashion, established communities separate from the Indians. They settled mostly on Wewoka Creek and its tributaries to the north of the Seminole towns. The Creeks then began to present claims and assert jurisdiction over them. In Washington, meanwhile, John Horse successfully solicited the aid of Quartermaster General Jesup. On July 17, Jesup visited Fort Gibson to direct the construction of new stone buildings. He sent word to the maroons, many of whom the Seminoles still claimed to own, that they were free under the promises he had made in Florida and should meet him at the post. The blacks arrived after Jesup had returned to Washington, but he left behind a list of those he considered free. During the summer, many of the men, some with their families, left their homes and sought refuge under the protection of the military at Fort Gibson. In 1845 and 1846, some sixty or seventy of them helped build the old commissary building and other structures at the fort, some of which still can be seen today.[21]

John Horse continued to press the cause of the maroons in Washington, and on April 8, 1846, Jesup informed Arbuckle, "The case of the Seminole Negroes is now before the President." Jesup requested that Arbuckle prevent any interference with the blacks at Fort Gibson until the president determined whether they were to remain in the Creek country or be allowed to remove elsewhere. John Horse had achieved as much as he could have hoped for in the capital. During his year there he had been responsible for Jesup's intervention, the protection of the maroons by the military at Fort Gibson, and the referral of the case to the president.[22]

Recalling his previous return to the Indian Territory, John Horse had Jesup prepare a statement that he had not interfered in Indian affairs but had concerned himself only with those of the maroons, and, further, that he had acted only in the capacity of interpreter to Wild Cat's delegation during his previous visit. Nevertheless, Horse found more problems awaiting him upon his return. Wild Cat's "brother" had stolen a horse from Horse's wife Susan during his absence. Horse dared not try to retrieve the animal as he feared for his life among the Seminoles. The Indians also began to kill his livestock on the Deep Fork. He presented claims for his losses, but they never were paid. Around this time, the mixed-blood Seminole owner of his sister Juana sold two of her children to the Creek Siah Hardridge, and a long battle over their custody began.

By now, John Horse and his followers at Fort Gibson were alienated completely from the main body of Seminoles.[23]

The maroons on the military reserve remained under the protection of the army and awaited the decision of the president amid Seminole claims and kidnappers' raids. They would not venture outside the fort for provisions, fearing attack or abduction. Consequently, when their work on construction projects terminated in late 1846, they had no means of support, and Colonel Gustavus Loomis, the post commander, had to issue them rations to prevent their starvation. The following summer, the Creeks threatened to seize and reenslave all the maroons on the reserve, thereby forcing the United States officials to make an immediate decision in the case. As the threat of Creek aggression increased and kidnapping ventures continued, more Seminole blacks called at Fort Gibson for "free papers" and protection during the fall of 1847. Slave raids by Creeks and Seminoles escalated during the spring and summer of 1848, but the maroons at the post remained firm in their resolve to maintain their freedom and independence at any cost.[24]

In the midst of these slave-hunting campaigns, John Horse again sought permission to remove his supporters from the Indian Territory. In early December 1847, he and Tony Barnet, another leading African, informed Loomis that they were satisfied they never would be allowed to enjoy their freedom among the Seminoles in the Creek country. The maroons were "willing and desirous to emigrate to any place where they can be free and unmolested." Loomis suggested the government transport them to Africa, "[Where] they can be free and this they desire: or to any place separate from the Indians." Arbuckle seized upon the idea and recommended that measures be adopted immediately "for the removal of these unfortunate people from the vicinity of the Indian country [to] Liberia." He suggested they be sent to New Orleans and from there to Africa. If it were deemed inadvisable to remove them at public expense, the Colonization Society might be persuaded to take charge at New Orleans. Arbuckle's superiors chose not to implement his recommendations, but it is significant that the maroons were prepared to go almost anywhere to retain their freedom.[25]

Loomis praised the blacks living at Fort Gibson. They attended Sunday school and during the summer of 1847, had raised large quantities of corn and rice. In April 1848, however, the Creek delegation in Washington stated that the Seminole maroons had become a "positive nuisance":

As things now exist they are apparently subject to no control, they violate the laws of the United States and the laws of the Creek Nation with perfect impunity. They are idle and worthless constantly engaged in bringing whisky into the nation stealing and rioting, and offering inducements to the slaves belonging to the various surrounding tribes of Indians to run away and when they are detected in crime, they at once take protection on the Government reservation where they are sustained by the commanding officer at the Post.

The Creeks demanded the "removal of these Negroes from their country" or their placement "under the control of their laws." Whether they were hard-working Sunday school attenders or bootleggers, or simply a mixture of the two, the blacks on the reserve clearly continued to live apart from the Indians, follow independent lifestyles and courses of action, and view themselves as a separate and distinct social group. In fact, they had established a maroon settlement approximate to their new ally and former adversary at a distance from their former ally and new adversary.[26]

On June 10, John Horse sent a list of the Seminole maroons' complaints to Jesup: "We have great many enemies, great many who think only of doing us injuries—many who fabricate false claims and who for a few goods or a little whisky make false titles to our great annoyance. [We] are much annoyed, our people carried away, and our horses an object for many bad persons—so much so that we are now reduced to great poverty." From his strategic position as interpreter to the Seminoles at Fort Gibson, Horse had heard that the maroons probably would be returned to their former masters. To cover himself against this eventuality, he sought to establish his free status "on another title" by reverting to the 1843 decision of the Seminole council under which he had been emancipated. Later, he would attempt to purchase his wife and children from their legal owner. Horse's assumptions proved to be correct and his preparation timely. Before the end of the month, the decision he had anticipated was handed down.[27]

On June 28, Attorney General John Mason delivered the opinion that would decide the fate of the Seminole maroons. Jesup had based the authority for his emancipation proclamation on the convention of war that held that captured movable property was at the disposal of the captor. To Mason, however, the legal principles were clear: regarded as persons, enslaved Africans had no power to enter contracts and therefore could not be a party to any treaty or convention; regarded as property, when captured from an enemy in war, they were to be treated as any other movable belongings and not subject to the law of prize. Whether the maroons were prisoners of war or booty, the executive department of the government, under whose authority they were captured, would decide their disposition. On consideration of public policy or for other reasons satisfactory to the executive, therefore, these blacks could be restored to their owners and their antebellum status reestablished.

Mason explained that he could find no precedent for the qualified freedom Jesup had promised the Seminole maroons. The government had no right to incorporate freed blacks with the Seminoles without their consent given by treaty. Hence, there was no authority for such a promise. Creek opposition to such a settlement of maroons in their country also showed the impracticality of such an arrangement. Mason concluded, therefore, "My opinion is, that the Military authorities should be instructed to restore the Negroes to the condition in which they were with the Seminoles, prior to the date of Major General Jesup's letter of the 8th of April 1846." President Polk approved Mason's opinion on July 8.[28]

Quickly, military officers set in motion the process of restoring the maroons to their former condition. During the first week of August, Arbuckle received instructions to deliver the blacks to the Seminole chiefs who then would return them to their proper owners. He should report to the war department those who apparently were not owned by Seminoles, along with any claimants. Also, the post commander at Fort Gibson should not issue rations to the maroons except to prevent them from starving. John Horse still was trying to establish his free status, as American officials were having problems tracing his emancipation papers. He asked Wild Cat, therefore, to make a statement that the Seminoles had granted him his freedom, and Wild Cat complied on August 28. Realizing that the maroons could expect no further aid from the United States government, John Horse established his own liberty and then sought to strengthen his association with Wild Cat in order to pursue the larger goal of freedom for all of his people.[29]

The removal of the Seminole blacks to the Creek country was delayed for several months. A raid by Creeks on a maroon settlement in September and the continuing plots of slave speculators persuaded Arbuckle to keep at Fort Gibson all the blacks reported free on Jesup's list. Arbuckle also decided to bring in other blacks who were not on Jesup's list or living on the reserve and who were not claimed by Seminoles, until the matter was decided. A summer drought had hit hard the maroons living at Fort Gibson, reducing their harvest severely. By the late fall, their provisions had run out, and they were destitute. In mid-November, the military felt it necessary to issue rations to almost all of them. The Seminole chiefs decided to receive the maroons at Fort Gibson on December 22. Then, they would take them to the Seminole settlements and return them to their owners. Due to bad weather, however, the military did not hand over the blacks to the Seminoles until the new year.[30]

From the time of the 1845 treaty to the restoration of the maroons to the Seminoles, Wild Cat had become ever more disaffected with Creek attempts to dominate Seminole affairs and had pursued an increasingly independent course of action. Upon removing to their assigned lands, the Seminoles had experienced more poverty, drought, starvation, and dependency on agency officials. The Creek country was almost devoid of game and much colder than Florida; hence, it was harder for the Seminoles to support themselves. Wild Cat quickly became disillusioned with his new home in the West and began to explore alternatives.[31]

His diplomatic maneuvers began as early as May 1845 when he attended the Grand Council on the Deep Fork as the "Counsellor and Organ" of Micanopy. Representatives of twelve tribes attended the Council, and Wild Cat became acquainted with plains Indian delegates, including those of the Kickapoos, Quapaws, and Caddos. Throughout, the Seminole delegation sat behind that of the Creeks. The proud Wild Cat likely would have felt insulted and humiliated by this display of Seminole subordination and determined that, from then on, his future relations with the plains tribes would be conducted on a more independent level.[32]

In the winter of 1845–46, Wild Cat took the opportunity to explore the Southwest and develop relations with the tribes of the southern plains when he joined the Butler-Lewis peace commission to the Comanches. The party crossed the Red River, explored the Cow Creek region of the Middle Brazos, parleyed with Kickapoos, Caddos, Lipan Apaches, and Tonkawas, and concluded a peace treaty with the Comanches. Wild Cat enjoyed his position of Seminole representative and began to explore trade links with these tribes. Upon his return to the Indian Territory, he found his people once more in a state of destitution. This prompted him to organize two hunting, exploring, and trading expeditions in the spring and summer of 1846 in which he met again with representatives of tribes from the southern plains.[33] During the year, he had developed his role as diplomat and had become familiar with the southwestern territory. The notion of a traditionalist confederation, based on the Florida model and linked by trade, to be composed of Seminoles, maroons, plains Indians, and other splinter groups and refugees, probably began to take firm shape in Wild Cat's mind.

Throughout 1847 Wild Cat continued to complain about the way the government had treated the Seminoles since their removal, and by early 1848, he was advancing the idea of a confederation based in the Creek country. A band of Kickapoos that had settled on the Canadian near the Seminole agency furnished him support. During January and February, Seminole and Kickapoo envoys visited the Texas tribes promoting the scheme. The Texas Indian agent reported that these envoys had threatened or otherwise sought to induce every tribe within his jurisdiction to remove to the Indian Territory. This kept the Texas Indians in a constant state of fear and excitement. Agency and military officials became anxious and remained on alert. Wild Cat planned to use this situation to his advantage at a later date.[34]

John Horse and Wild Cat soon would renew their alliance. During the winter of 1848–1849, two events took place that would have a dramatic effect on the history of Seminole-black relations and lead ultimately to the joint emigration of the followers of these two leaders to Mexico. On or before December 22, 1848, Micanopy died, and on January 2, 1849, the Seminoles received the blacks at Fort Gibson.

Jim Jumper of the pro-Creek faction succeeded his uncle Micanopy, signaling the beginning of a regime that promised to be destructive to both the traditionalists and the maroons. Wild Cat probably had hoped for the principal chieftainship and felt thwarted. Jumper's selection may have been influenced by Seminole subagent Marcellus Duval, who had a personal interest in the blacks, but traditional Seminole behavior explains the choice sufficiently. Whatever the reason, the deeply disaffected Wild Cat now would resist Creek laws, especially those affecting the maroons. He also realized his best alternative would be to establish his frontier confederation outside the Indian Territory, on the new Mexican border.[35]

The transfer of the maroons took place only after the Seminole leaders had given certain assurances. When news of the decision first had reached Fort Gibson, the commanding officer had notified all persons concerned that sales made prior to the transfer would not be recognized. Notwithstanding, Creek, Cherokee, and white speculators purchased about one-third of the maroons from Seminoles who frequently had no shadow of a claim. Some Seminole slave owners, becoming influenced by their more acculturated neighbors, viewed Africans more and more as property and sold them for as little as a bottle of whisky. The chiefs had promised a further third of the blacks to William J. Duval, brother of the subagent, for his services as attorney in bringing about their return to the Seminoles. The maroons on the reserve had heard that two-thirds of their number had been sold or promised to whites or slaveholding Indians of other tribes, and that they would be distributed among the claimants as soon as they left Fort Gibson. After being promised their freedom, they declared that they would die where they were rather than submit to such a fate.[36]

Arbuckle was apprehensive that many of the blacks would make their escape and that others would oppose the transfer by force of arms. The Seminoles agreed, therefore, that the maroons "would be permitted to live in 'towns', as they had formerly done, and that they should not be sold, or otherwise disposed of, to either white men or Indians, but be kept in the Seminole country."[37] The chiefs told the blacks that they would not distribute them to the various claimants, but would allow them to remain among the Seminoles, who would treat them kindly. The maroons stated that they would be satisfied to live near the Indians as they had before. As a result, the military turned over to the Seminoles nearly 260 of them as slaves. More than half of the blacks were living on the reserve, the remainder mostly on the Deep Fork or Little River. The list also included fourteen free blacks, headed by John Horse.[38] On January 3, the post commander reported, "No difficulty has arisen in the performance of this duty, either from the Indians, negroes or claimants, nor do I anticipate any. As soon as the weather permits, I shall send the negroes to the Indian country."[39] The transfer went smoothly, but speculators were waiting in the wings.

Owing to the severity of the winter, the maroons did not remove from Fort Gibson to the Seminole country until the early spring of 1849. The military advised them to be prepared to defend themselves against slave hunters during the journey, but they determined to protect themselves against all speculators who came among them to execute claims. The Seminoles specified an area where the blacks should locate, some fifteen miles from the agency. Upon reaching the Seminole country, however, the most militant began to defy the authority of the Indians. John Horse led his followers to Wewoka Creek, around thirty miles from the agency, where they established a maroon community some distance from the Seminoles and cultivated the bottom lands. The black town of Wewoka was situated just north of the present-day settlement of the same name.[40]

Those maroons who had continued to reside among the Seminoles also defied the orders of Chief Jim Jumper. Most did not relocate to their designated site, but settled instead at Wewoka or remained on the Deep Fork. Seminole leaders deemed it advisable not to interfere with the blacks until they had determined the outcome of the various claims, but at that time they planned to return them to their rightful owners.[41] The maroons settled into their new towns and armed themselves heavily for protection:

> They retained their arms, and lived under no restraint whatever from their owners; in fact they seemed to be regarded by the Chiefs as common property, and the negroes considered themselves free, and merely under the guardianship of those Indians who claimed them as property in Florida before the emigration west.[42]

John Horse's position in the Seminole country was still precarious. On April 8, he had the military at Fort Gibson issue a document allowing him "to pass and repass from the Seminole country, his place of residence to this post or to any other portion of the Indian Country where his necessary business might take him." John had ensured his mobility and planned to use it to further his interests and those of his supporters.[43]

The maroons had stated their willingness to live among the Seminoles as before, but events had taken place since removal that made such an occurrence unlikely. The Seminoles now found themselves subject to Creek law, which had no provision for the qualified slavery they had practiced in Florida or its resultant social arrangements: separate and independent settlements of armed blacks. The new Seminole leadership, moreover, sought to change the nature of the group's relations with Africans, bringing them more into line with the Lower Creek model. Many of the maroons, meanwhile, had grown increasingly independent and insubordinate under Jesup's promise of freedom during their three-and-a-half-year residence at Fort Gibson. By now, the more militant no longer were prepared to offer the same deference to the Seminoles that they had shown in Florida; and under no circumstances would they submit to Creek slave codes.

Difficulties arose in June when two Seminoles arrived in Wewoka, purportedly to capture one Walking Joe for horse theft. When the Indians tried to take him, Walking Joe drew a knife, but they succeeded in disarming and apprehending him. Before they could leave, however, all the men of the town arrived armed with guns and knives. They threatened the two Indians, and set Walking Joe free. The maroons then sent Cuffy to the Seminoles with the message that the Indians were not to come to Wewoka to take anyone without first consulting the town leaders. Asked to explain the incident, John Horse blamed the "young and unmanageable negroes."[44] In reality, however, the maroons were prepared to defend their liberty and settlements to the death, if necessary.

In early July, the Seminole leaders determined who had owned each of the blacks before the military had given them protection, and the present owners who derived right and title through tribal law. The Jumper faction wished to comply with Creek codes by disarming the blacks, breaking up their townships, and distributing them throughout the country to their respective owners. The maroons refused to be separated or allow their settlements to be broken up, however, and told the Seminoles that the army would support them. They were described as well armed, rebellious, and living mostly in one town, and therefore able to offer strong resistance should the Indians attempt to enforce the law. The maroons also refused steadfastly to recognize the right of their owners to dispose of them as they wished.[45]

Reluctant to confront the maroons, the Seminoles sought the aid of Marcellus Duval. Duval hoped to witness the safe transference of the blacks to their owners, for the Seminoles had promised about ninety of them to his brother. Duval wrote twice to Arbuckle requesting that the military disarm the maroons to facilitate the transfer, but the general made excuses and declined. It became obvious that for selfish reasons, the army supported the cause of the Seminole blacks, knowing that to disarm them would only facilitate the activities of speculators and cause even more trouble.[46] John Drennen, superintendent of Indian affairs for the western territory, however, supported Duval and made requisition for troops "to protect the Indian and quell domestic strife."[47]

The future seemed bleak indeed for the Seminole maroons. After removal, they had found themselves on the wrong side of a border. On the other side, by now beyond the Rio Grande, lay the prospect of liberty.

Their efforts at reestablishing communities and their former relationship with the Seminoles had failed in the face of white and Indian slave claims. Following Attorney General Mason's decision and the blacks' relocation in the Seminole country, the army was powerless to offer them effective aid and could not maintain for long its policy of noninterference in the face of growing pressure from the Indian office. The Seminole subagent had a vested interest in seeing the maroons disarmed and returned to slavery, and he now had support from the powerful superintendent of the western territory. The blacks could expect no help from the supporters of Jim Jumper, and the Creeks were threatening to enforce their slave codes themselves if the Seminoles could not or would not. Faced with an impending crisis and in dire need of allies, John Horse's followers turned once more to Wild Cat.

With the Jumper party firmly in control of Seminole affairs, Wild Cat determined to obstruct all operation of the Creek laws as they affected his people:

> He was strongly influenced by Gopher John and others of the chief negroes, to resist any interference in reference to the condition of the negroes, and was urged by them to resist all influence of the Creeks over the Seminoles. [The] negro chiefs have exercised a controlling influence over the Seminoles, and have induced them to resist the government and laws of the Creek nation.[48]

On September 8, Wild Cat and a group of his followers called on Arbuckle. They stated that the Seminoles had no complaints against the blacks turned over to them and refuted Duval's charges that the blacks were disorderly, rebellious, and insubordinate. The blacks had settled in three towns sufficiently convenient to the Seminoles and the Indians wished them to retain their arms for hunting purposes, as they were poor. Wild Cat expressed the hope that the blacks would be allowed to remain where they were without being disturbed further.

Although they claimed that Jim Jumper had sent them, Wild Cat and his supporters undoubtedly acted on their own initiative and in no way represented the views of the principal chief or his party. The delegates stated that Jumper possessed no blacks of his own but had promised one-third of those returned to the Seminoles to William J. Duval without even conferring with their owners. Recently, moreover, Marcellus Duval had told the chiefs that one-third was not enough and had threatened to withhold the annuity if they did not give up more. He had arranged a council under the Creek leader Jim Boy for September 3 near the maroon settlements, the object being to disarm the militants. Wild Cat claimed that the Seminoles were opposed to such an action, however, and had boycotted the council. Accepting Wild Cat's account as an accurate indication of Seminole sentiments on the subject, Arbuckle deemed it advisable to delay military intervention until he received further instructions. Wild Cat's initiative demonstrated most clearly the widening breach that was taking place among the Seminoles. Increasingly influenced by the maroons, the traditionalists were in open opposition to the Duval-instigated policies of the Seminole leadership.[49]

At the time of his visit to Arbuckle, Wild Cat was putting the final touches to his plan to remove from the Indian Territory and establish a confederation on the Mexican border. As early as 1843, an emissary of the Mexican government had visited the Creeks in the Indian Territory. As a squatter among the Cherokees, Wild Cat would have been interested in offers of land to those who would oppose Texas. During his exploring, hunting, trading, and diplomatic trips to the southern plains, Wild Cat had become familiar with the southwest territories as far as the Rio Grande and with plains Indian relations with Mexico. In 1849, moreover, Creek agent James Logan reported that Wild Cat had acquired and thus "owned" a Mexican boy kidnapped earlier by Comanches.[50]

Doubtless, Wild Cat was also aware of Mexican colonization schemes. In December 1846, Mexico passed a law providing for the establishment of "military colonies, composed of Mexicans or aliens, or both, along the coasts and frontiers as the government shall designate, especially to restrain the incursions of savages."[51] Little was achieved, however, until after the Treaty of Guadalupe Hidalgo, which brought the Mexican War to a close. Under the eleventh article of this treaty, the United States accepted responsibility for controlling the Indians who traditionally plundered the settlements of northern Mexico and then resided on the American side of the border. Due largely to an insufficient cavalry force on the Mexican frontier, however, the United States proved incapable of coping with this problem.[52]

On July 19, 1848, less than six months after Guadalupe Hidalgo, the Mexican minister of war and marine decreed that the new boundary required urgent attention, "Both to preserve our territorial integrity and to defend the frontier states from the frequent and cruel incursions of the savages." The following day, President José Herrera encapsulated the decree in a bill entitled "Military Colonies: A Project for Their

Establishment on the Eastern and Western Frontiers of the Republic," which became the guideline for directing Mexican colonization.

The government left the organization of the colonies largely to the discretion of the inhabitants and included many other liberal benefits. The most immediately attractive were contained in Article 17, "Upon the establishment of a colony, the government will advance to the colonists a six-months supply of provisions, to be charged to the public treasury, and tools, plows, oxen, horses, and whatever is needed to build houses for the colony."[53] This would have appealed to Wild Cat as a means of putting an end to the destitution of his supporters and establishing a solid base for the confederation. For the Seminole maroons, however, the biggest incentive by far was that Mexico had outlawed slavery twenty years earlier and now offered them freedom.

Wild Cat maintained his contacts with the southern plains tribes and further promoted the confederation during 1849. On March 6, for example, he met with a band of Southern Comanches at the Seminole agency. During this same period, he recieved from Duval a document allowing him "to pass uninterrupted through the Texas Settlements on a hunting expedition and to visit General Worth." Wild Cat would have used this privilege to put the final touches to his plans for resettling outside the Indian Territory. A spark was all that was needed to put his scheme into action.[54]

During the summer of 1849, some of the blacks left the Seminole country again to take up residence at Fort Gibson, much to the dissatisfaction of the Creeks. Undoubtedly, there was collusion between these Seminole maroons and free blacks of the Creek and Cherokee nations who resided in the vicinity. In October, further kidnapping raids occurred around the post.[55] The situation was becoming intolerable. Earlier, the Creeks had sought the aid of the government to enforce their laws and reduce the Seminole maroons to a position of subordination, but after Wild Cat had persuaded Arbuckle to delay military intervention, they had determined to act independently and unilaterally. A Creek onslaught, which would spell disaster for the maroons, appeared imminent. Working in close association with Wild Cat, John Horse and his supporters prepared to leave the Indian Territory for Mexico.

In early October, a Seminole delegation headed by Duval and Halleck Tustenuggee assembled at the North Fork with the intention of traveling to Florida to persuade Billy Bowlegs and his followers to remove to the Indian Territory. Foreseeing the new Creek initiative, Wild Cat sent a proposition to Duval that he wished to have communicated to the president: he proposed to remove all the Seminoles to Mexico. That was the first time Wild Cat had mentioned settling across the border. He stated that the Seminoles wished to do so because they were tired of living among the Creeks, and the new country would suit them better. He claimed that he could persuade Bowlegs and the remaining Seminoles and blacks in Florida to remove to Mexico, whereas they never would relocate willingly among the Creeks. Duval believed, however, that Wild Cat had told delegates secretly to advise Bowlegs to remain in Florida until he could persuade the government to allow them to remove with him to Mexico. The members referred to were probably Jim Bowlegs, Tom, and Toney, three Africans who were to accompany the delegation as interpreters. Billy Bowlegs had owned Jim Bowlegs in Florida. Jim Bowlegs had served as his owner's interpreter and adviser and likely would exert great influence over the principal chief. Jim Bowlegs had become a leading Seminole maroon after removal and would head a later migration to Mexico.[56]

Wild Cat took the opportunity to put his plan into action when the delegation left North Fork Town for Florida on October 16. Capitalizing on Duval's absence, Wild Cat mobilized his forces. He told his Seminole supporters that Mexico suited their every need and informed the maroons that the plains tribes had agreed to let them pass unharmed if they followed him. In the face of more raids by slavers, the maroons hurriedly gathered together their belongings, and one night around November 10, the allies, numbering around two hundred, hastily quitted the Seminole country. Some of the maroon men, apparently, had to depart so quickly that they left behind their wives and children.

The emigrant Indians and blacks were represented in approximately equal numbers and included some twenty-five Seminole families, almost exclusively of Wild Cat's band, a few dissatisfied traditionalist Creeks, twenty Seminole maroon families, and several families of Creek and Cherokee blacks. It was believed that these Creek and Cherokee blacks were to learn the route and then return to the Indian Territory to act as guides for others wishing to join Wild Cat and John Horse across the Rio Grande. Despairing of ever finding peace and happiness on the American side of the border, the Seminole maroons prepared to open in Mexico another chapter in their search for freedom.[57]

The emigrants crossed the Red River and made their way south through Texas. They may have ridden along the route taken by Pierce's

1845 treaty expedition party, or they could have followed other hunting trails. The Indians under Wild Cat led the way, and the maroons under John Horse brought up the rear. A young black girl, Kitty Johnson, shared a horse with Wild Cat's son Billy, and the two friends rode at the head of the train. John Philip, or Picayune John, named after Wild Cat's late father King Philip, served as the Seminole leader's orderly and took care of his horse.[58]

The allies traveled slowly, hunting and fishing as they went. At streams they made rafts of logs tied together with ropes, and the women and children boarded with their belongings. The young men then swam to the other side and pulled the rafts across. At the end of May 1850 Duval reported that Wild Cat had located for the summer on Cow Bayou, which runs into the Brazos just south of the present-day city of Waco, to enable the blacks to raise a crop. In fact, the emigrants had traveled farther to the southwest, John Rollins, the Indian agent for Texas, reporting that he had met Wild Cat and his party on the Llano. The Indians and maroons had encamped there and planted small patches of corn, which they intended harvesting before proceeding farther.[59]

At their meeting, Wild Cat informed Rollins that he intended to visit Mexico and agree to campaign against the incursions of border tribes, provided the Mexican authorities offered him suitable lands in exchange. If he were able to negotiate an agreement, Wild Cat would return to the Indian Territory next winter and remove all of the remaining Seminoles and maroons across the Rio Grande. While his supporters raised a crop on the Llano, Wild Cat explored the region and visited Indian bands in the area to promote his Mexican colony. The excitement and intrigue surrounding Wild Cat's activities gave rise to many exaggerated reports. According to the *San Antonio Western Texas,* for example, there were seven hundred to eight hundred Seminoles, Lipans, Wacos, and Tonkawas camped on the Llano in June under Wild Cat's command. Despite all his efforts with the tribes of the southern plains and border-lands, however, Wild Cat succeeded in persuading only a band of around one hundred Southern Kickapoos to join his enterprise.[60]

In June, Wild Cat crossed over to Mexico. The Mexican authorities were immediately receptive to his petition for land. The immigration of Native Americans and Africans into northern Mexico, particularly Coahuila, had precedents. In 1835, a move to resettle the Texas Cherokees across the Rio Grande was frustrated by the events leading up to the Texas rebellion of the following year. Following the abolition of legal servitude in the republic in 1829, it was recommended two years later that fugitive blacks be placed on the frontier to protect the borderlands against Anglo-American filibusters. And in 1834, Benjamin Lundy, the northern abolitionist, received promises that he could colonize formerly enslaved blacks in Tamaulipas. Mexican officials would have been influenced further by widespread depredations that Coahuila had experienced since the Treaty of Guadalupe Hidalgo. Bands of Indians had ravaged several towns, killing and plundering. Financial shortages and poor management had hindered the establishment of the colonies so that by 1850, only nine of the eighteen planned for the frontier had been settled even partially. The borderlands were in a state of chaos, and the Mexican government desperately was seeking an influx of settlers into the region.[61]

Wild Cat thus was able to negotiate a quick, favorable agreement for his supporters. On June 27, as leader of the Seminoles and representative of the maroons and Kickapoos, he signed an agreement with Antonio María Jaúrequi, inspector general of the eastern military colonies, in San Fernando de Rosas, present-day Zaragoza. The followers of Wild Cat were assigned "16 sitios de ganado mayor," about seventy thousand acres, in Coahuila; half at the headwaters of the Río San Antonio some fifty miles southwest of present-day Ciudad Acuña, and half at the headwaters of the Río San Rodrigo.

Jaúrequi named Wild Cat head of the combined tribes. The immigrants would be considered Mexican citizens and should obey the laws and authorities of the republic. They were to help prevent further incursions by raiding bands of Comanches and Lipan and Mescalero Apaches, but should maintain good relations with citizens of the United States. An important additional clause facilitated initial attempts by the Seminoles and maroons to revive the economic and social arrangements they had practiced in Florida: "Although the Kickapoos, Seminoles, Mascogan Negroes, and other Indians who may come to Mexico must subject themselves to the laws of the country, it is not demanded of them to change their habits and customs." The Mexican authorities agreed to furnish the immigrants with a small food subsidy and tools to clear the land and build dwellings. Having concluded his mission successfully, Wild Cat returned to Texas to instruct his supporters to prepare to emigrate.[62]

In early July, perhaps due to the activities of slavers in the area, the maroons and Seminoles hurriedly abandoned their crops on the Llano and set out for Mexico. At Las Moras Springs, later the site of Fort Clark, the emigrants came across the encampment of a military train bound for El Paso under the command of Major John T. Sprague. The emigrants displayed a white flag and were allowed to enter the camp. Sprague issued Wild Cat and his party a pass allowing them to proceed to Eagle Pass.[63] From Fort Duncan, Cora Montgomery, a local resident and journalist, observed the emigrants' arrival at the border and furnished this colorful description:

> [Emerging] from the broken ground in a direction that we knew was untraversed by any but the wild and hostile Indians, came forth a long procession of horsemen. The sun flashed back from a mixed array of arms and barbaric gear, but as this unexpected army, which seemed to have dropped upon us from the skies, drew nearer it grew less formidable in apparent numbers, and opened upon us a more pacific aspect. Some reasonably well-mounted Indians circled round a dark nucleus of female riders, who seemed objects of special care. But the long straggling rear-guard was worth seeing. It threw Falstaff's ragged regiment altogether in the shade. Such an array of all manners and sizes of animals, mounted by all ages, sexes and sizes of negroes, piled up to a most bewildering height, on and among such a promiscuous assemblage of blankets, babies, cooking utensils, and savage traps, in general, never were or could be held together on horseback by any beings on earth but themselves and their red brothers. The party began to break away and vanish into the little ravines that dip down to the river edge, and we understood by these signs they were encamping among us.

Wild Cat, who clearly was enjoying his new role, later called on the Montgomery household. He came attended by several of his Seminole supporters and was "marshalled with all ceremony" by John Horse, who acted as interpreter.[64]

Eagle Pass was the border crossing used most by runaways fleeing to Mexico. Slave catchers, dealers, and kidnappers tended to congregate there in the hope of finding fugitives, and the town had become a hive of slaving activity. The emigrant Seminole maroons obviously would wish to cross over into Mexico as soon as possible. A few days after their arrival at the border, Wild Cat, John Horse, and Chief Papicua of the Kickapoos appeared before Colonel Juan Manuel Maldonado, inspector of the Colonia Militar de Guerrero a few miles south of Piedras Negras, to request lands, tools, and livestock; and on July 26, Maldonado granted their petition provisionally.[65]

When the three returned to Eagle Pass, the commanding officer at Fort Duncan refused Wild Cat permission to proceed to Mexico. Sensing an impending attack by slave hunters, however, the maroons and Indians stole across the Rio Grande in the dead of night at Lehman's Ranch, north of Eagle Pass across from El Moral.[66] The dramatic crossing was made on a log raft propelled and steered by long oars. In a maneuver reminiscent of the 1818 Battle of Suwannee, some of the men ferried over the women and children first while others stood guard. In 1930, Becky Simmons, a maroon member of the party, recalled the scene vividly: "Chulluns about to cry out cause dey is sleepy and de oluns scared dat dey is going to start aballin' out before we can git ober." They managed to reach the far bank; then the oarsmen returned quickly for the remaining men and ferried them across. The crossing was completed without discovery, and the Seminole maroons landed safely on free Mexican soil. Once again, however, the cost of their liberty was exile.[67]

Thus, in July 1850, 309 Seminoles, blacks, and Kickapoos entered Mexico as immigrants. They settled temporarily some distance from each other, the Seminoles at San Fernando de Rosas (now Zaragoza); the maroons at El Moral near Monclova Viejo about twenty miles above Piedras Negras; and the Kickapoos at Tuillo, near the Colonia Militar de Guerrero. Interesting insights into the nature of relations between the maroons and Seminoles were furnished at that time. Presumably under advisement from the Seminoles or the blacks themselves, the Mexicans gave the maroons their own name, *Mascogos,* and a tract of land at a distance from the Indians. From the very start, the Mexicans treated the blacks as a separate social unit or "tribe," as independent of the Seminoles as were the Kickapoos.[68]

As they prepared to settle in Mexico, the maroons and Seminoles were joined in an unstable alliance based more on mutual need than identity of interest. The immigrants had united in opposition to the Creeks and the Jumper party, but this stemmed from different motives. Wild Cat believed that unification with the more numerous and acculturated Creeks was detrimental to Seminole interests. Creek predominance over Seminole affairs also jeopardized his status as a slaveholder, both by fraudulent claims to his blacks and by kidnapping campaigns. On more than one occasion during the 1840s, Wild Cat had expressed this fear as the major source of his opposition to the Creeks. Duval's meddling in Seminole affairs simply threatened to aid and abet those activities.

John Horse also had been opposed to the Creeks and the Jumper leadership, but for different reasons. Whereas Wild Cat had been concerned with the Seminoles' loss of status and uncertain political future, John Horse had stood to lose his freedom and perhaps his life. Under the Creeks, John had experienced assassination attempts, the loss of his home, the destruction of his property, and the breakup of his family. Most of the other emigrant blacks had experienced similar problems and were the ones most likely to lose their freedom, families, or property. This was true for John Kibbetts, Dembo and Hardy Factor, Sampson July, and most of the leading maroons who had left for Mexico. The new Seminole leadership had made it clear that it intended to conform to Creek standards by exerting greater control over the African population. The blacks thus had faced the prospect of living under harsh codes, reenslavement, and the threat of sale. Their culture and traditions, indeed their very existence as a group, had been put in jeopardy. By 1849, these people had needed to leave the Indian Territory to protect their lives and loved ones. The immediacy and desperation of the maroons' situation was removed from that of their Seminole allies: whereas Wild Cat elected to seek a better life outside the Creek country, John Horse had no choice.

The blacks and Indians also had different goals for their new community. The maroons sought to live in peace, build homes in remote areas, raise families, and work the land, free from disturbance. The Seminoles sought independence, but they also looked to expand their interests. Wild Cat would head the confederation, and the Indians would assume positions of ultimate control. Adhering to the ideal of restoring traditional social arrangements in the new community, the Seminoles would expect the same deference from the maroons that they had received in Florida. Here lay a source of future conflict. The borderlands military colony also offered Wild Cat the opportunity to assume a position of strength and increase his own importance. He would enjoy promoting Seminole interests through politicking with the tribes of the southern plains and constituting a threat to the frontier. John Horse, on the other hand, wished to remove his supporters from the center of attention. During the 1840s, he had asked that they be sent to Africa, Florida, or any place they would be left alone. Horse followed Wild Cat to Mexico not for power or military glory but because that country offered the best hope for freedom—for a more insular and secure lifestyle.

But the immigrants did need each other. Wild Cat had become the undisputed champion of the maroons' cause among the Seminoles after removal, and the blacks held a great deal of affection for the colorful Indian leader. They also were quick to realize how useful he could be to them once they had settled in Mexico. Wild Cat had a reputation that had spread far and wide, and he was on good terms with many of the tribes of the southern plains. He was familiar, also, with the border country. Wild Cat could prove invaluable as a guide, military commander, strategist, and diplomat. In addition, his Seminole supporters were excellent hunters and warriors and would give solidity to the new community.

The maroons were of even more potential use to the Seminoles, and Wild Cat greatly appreciated their value. They could play a vital role as agriculturists, interpreters, intermediaries, and advisers, much as they had in Florida. The blacks were tried and trusted warriors and had proved that they would defend their freedom to the last. A large number of African attendants also would underscore Wild Cat's leadership status and importance. He hoped that these emigrants would act as a lure and expected that runaways from Texas plantations and the Indian Territory as well as Indian slaveholders wishing to rejoin their blacks on the Rio Grande would supplement the colony. Wild Cat painted a picture of a Florida-style confederation. The Indians perceived the maroons to be valuable neighbors who would strengthen the new community both quantitatively and qualitatively and help ensure its survival.

Nevertheless, an underlying conflict remained within the alliance. The postremoval experiences of the maroons and Seminoles had been very different. Prolonged periods of separation and the development of independent black initiatives had added strain to their relations. The two had little mutual interest and few joint objectives. The alliance relied heavily upon the charismatic Wild Cat, but even his strong personality was no substitute for a singularity of motivation and purpose. Once the maroons and Seminoles had removed themselves from the proximity of their common enemies, it remained to be seen whether their fragile alliance could withstand the hardships of life in Mexico.

3

Los Mascogos

The spring and summer of 1850 were troubled times for those Seminole blacks left behind in the Indian Territory. The Florida delegation returned in April, and the Seminoles asked Marcellus Duval to recover the runaways who had ridden off with John Horse to the border. Duval's personal interest prompted him to request the commissioner of Indian affairs to issue orders for their arrest. He reasoned that if they were allowed to remain outside the United States, the maroons' settlement would attract other runaways and renegade Indians. Duval also believed that a large number of blacks from the Seminole and Creek nations intended to leave for Mexico in the fall.[1]

Jim Bowlegs had assumed the leadership of the Seminole maroons remaining in the Indian Territory. He had served as interpreter for the Florida delegation and probably had tried to influence his owner Billy Bowlegs and Bowlegs's band to emigrate to Mexico. In April 1850, Billy Bowlegs wrote to the Seminole leaders in the Indian Territory, placing Jim Bowlegs in charge of his fifty blacks in his absence.[2] Jim Bowlegs was talented and intelligent, he had acquired property and a considerable personal following, and he was the interpreter and adviser of a principal chief. He thus acquired considerable influence among the maroons and was a natural successor to John Horse.

In early June 1850, Creek slave hunters entered the Seminole country and took three blacks, including Jim Bowlegs. General William Belknap rescued them, and Roley McIntosh protested against their being protected by the military once again. McIntosh told Belknap that Creek law prohibited Bowlegs from owning arms and horses, but really, the Creeks were more anxious to remove this new threat to their authority. As had John Horse earlier, Jim Bowlegs felt threatened, and his situation in the Indian Territory was becoming similarly intolerable.[3]

Matters came to a head on June 24, when a party of armed Creeks, Cherokees, and whites arrived in the vicinity of Wewoka to take forcible possession of a number of maroons they claimed they owned. Many of the Seminoles determined to assist the blacks in defending themselves. Duval arrived the next day and prevented a clash by ordering the party to return to the Creek country above the North Fork. Leaders of the Jumper party met later with the group's leaders and agreed to assist the Creeks by delivering a number of the maroons. Together, they took about 180 and held them at the Seminole agency. Many later were retained to prevent their giving information and assistance to those attempting to escape to Mexico.[4]

The cooperation of Jumper's supporters in aiding the Creek slaving party proved to be the last straw for Jim Bowlegs and his supporters. Immediately following the seizure, Jim Bowlegs forsook the protection of Fort Gibson and gathered his followers for an attempt to join Wild Cat and John Horse in Mexico. By early July, some 180 armed maroons under his command were en route for Coahuila, bidding defiance to any who should confront them. The blacks split into parties of between forty and eighty and made their way across the southern plains towards the border.[5]

Shortly after he had concluded the agreement with the Mexican authorities and had seen his supporters settled on their designated lands, Wild Cat returned to Texas. On September 1, he informed Texas Indian Agent John Rollins that he was returning to the Indian Territory to remove all the remaining Seminoles to Coahuila.[6] During his sojourn through Texas, Wild Cat spread word of the land grant and the establishment of the military colony. The fugitives crossing the plains seem to have heard this news and to have decided to await his return from the Indian Territory before entering Mexico.

Comanches attacked several of the Seminole black parties while they were traveling through Texas, capturing and torturing some individuals and killing others. The Indians took prisoner at least one group, that under the command of Jim Bowlegs himself, to sell the maroons into slavery. Another entire party was put to death, the only exceptions being two girls whom the Comanches sold to a Delaware trader. The Indians had conducted experiments on the girls to see if their flesh were black beneath the skin and to discover if they experienced the same sensations of pain as the Comanches themselves. Captain Randolph B. Marcy saw the girls later and described them as shockingly scarred and mutilated.

Marcy asked the Comanches why they were so hostile to Africans. They told him it was because blacks were enslaved by whites and they felt sorry for them. Marcy speculated, however, that the Comanches' real motive was fear that the maroons would increase Wild Cat's force and interfere with their raiding activities along the Rio Grande. Comanches also were reported to have killed Shawnees and Delawares who, they suspected, would join the borderlands confederation.[7]

Wild Cat arrived in the Seminole country on September 18, accompanied only by a woman and a young man. He expressed the wish to remove all the Seminoles to Mexico and called a council for September 27 to discuss his plans. According to Duval, at the ensuing meeting, Wild Cat tried all means of persuasion to induce the Seminoles to emigrate. He told the slaveholders that their runaways were living in Mexico and that if they followed him they could control them again. He also stated that he had made arrangements for the government to disburse the Seminole annuity on the Rio Grande. Duval, however, informed owners that Mexico had abolished slavery and that they would have no authority over their blacks there. The subagent also told them that Wild Cat's statements concerning the annuity were false and that he himself was opposed to their removal. For the most part, the Seminoles seemed unimpressed by Wild Cat's enterprise.[8]

In contrast, the blacks were attracted strongly by the idea of the Mexican colony, and Wild Cat's return caused great disruption among the Creeks, who feared losing their slave property. In late September they adopted measures to foil Wild Cat's plans, and Duval feared a clash might ensue. The Creeks sent three hundred men into the Seminole country with instructions to prevent any blacks from leaving and to detain Wild Cat until the object of his mission could be ascertained. The Creek party, after learning that a number of blacks were preparing to leave, halted at Wewoka but then returned home for unknown reasons.[9]

Duval informed Wild Cat that Roley McIntosh had ordered his arrest for conspiring to entice away enslaved blacks and create disorder, and had sent out mounted law enforcement officers, the Creek lighthorse, to apprehend him. According to the subagent, Wild Cat responded by challenging the Lower Creeks to meet with him and his Texas Indian supporters south of the Canadian outside Creek and Seminole limits. Thus, in early October, under the threat of arrest, Wild Cat left the Seminole country for the last time. He took with him some thirty to forty Seminole families, numbering in all around one hundred, together with a few blacks.[10]

The Creek lighthorse pursued Wild Cat and his followers across the Canadian, but near Camp Arbuckle, they came upon the band of Comanches that had captured Jim Bowlegs's party as it was crossing the Texas plains. The lighthorse paid the Comanches a ransom for the captives and set off back to the Seminole country. Along the way, the maroons attempted to escape, provoking a bloody battle and casualties on both sides. Doctor Rodney Glisan attested to the fact that the prisoners had fought valiantly but largely in vain when he remarked upon the number of wounded among the sixty captives who passed by his camp in late October en route to the Seminole country. Jim Bowlegs and a few others, however, escaped from their Creek captors and made their way to Mexico.[11]

On his return journey through Texas, Wild Cat visited the Caddos, Wacos, and Comanches in an attempt to persuade them to join him in Mexico. He told them he intended to unite the tribes of the southern plains and border country in a war against the whites, but none was impressed sufficiently to join his enterprise. His only success came with the Southern Kickapoos. Despite the opposition of Chiefs Pecan and Pacanah, Wild Cat persuaded some two hundred young men from the Canadian and Wild Horse Creek bands to join him by assuring them that the Mexican government would pay them well for their services and by promising them all the money and booty taken from the Comanches. Thereupon, Wild Cat rejoined his followers across the Rio Grande.[12]

Despite the frustrations of his trip, Wild Cat had persuaded around a hundred Seminoles, a few blacks, and two hundred Kickapoos to join his confederation. Another fifty to a hundred maroons, who had left the Indian Territory with Jim Bowlegs in July and had escaped the ravages of the Comanches, also managed to reunite with their kinsmen in Mexico. Once established in Coahuila, the colonists would come into contact with other groups of Indians and Africans who would become part of the Seminole and maroon communities through settlement, military campaigns, or intermarriage.

A group of more than twenty Creek maroons, mostly of the Wilson and Warrior families, and a family of Biloxi Indians, had preceded the followers of Wild Cat and John Horse as immigrants. The blacks seem to have been owned formerly by Pink Hawkins, a Creek who had moved to Texas in the mid-1830s. One theory has it that they had escaped from his plantation near Nacogdoches during the war with Mexico and had made their way across the Rio Grande. They became associated with the Creek blacks in John Horse's band, were reinforced by further defections from the Indian Territory, and came to constitute a significant faction within the maroon community. The immigrants also encountered a Biloxi family named Neco residing in Mexico. In March 1839, a skirmish had taken place between Texas Rangers and a refugee band of Mexicans, runaways, and Biloxis at Mill Creek, Texas, after which the survivors had fled across the Rio Grande. The sisters María and Laura Neco married blacks, and this small Biloxi remnant became interwoven into the maroon community. A family named Shields, free mulatto settlers from South Carolina, intermarried later with the Mascogos and increased still further the numerical strength of the group.[13]

Wild Cat and John Horse thus found themselves surrounded by a diverse group of supporters that included Seminole Indians; Kickapoos; Seminole, Creek, and Cherokee blacks; intermarried Biloxis; and free mulattoes from the South. Mexican *mestizos,* Indians, and blacks; and Texas runaways would add to the population during the 1850s. The large borderlands confederation that Wild Cat had envisaged failed to materialize, however, and the number of his supporters actually peaked in late 1850 at around two hundred Seminoles, more than two hundred maroons, and over three hundred Kickapoos. For the Seminoles, this early disappointment marred their new beginning and would prove difficult to overcome. For John Horse and his followers, however, the future seemed bright indeed. Again, these maroons had crossed a border to secure their liberty. Gone were the supporters of Jim Jumper, the Lower Creek slaveholders, and the white kidnappers. In their place lay the promise of freedom and the chance to build a home of their own.

The Mascogos soon were to learn that they had not heard the last of the scheming Marcellus Duval. Shortly after Wild Cat had left the Indian Territory for the last time, Duval began appealing to Texas officials to assist him in capturing the runaways. On October 20 and 21, he wrote to Governor Peter Bell asking him to arrest those blacks who recently had escaped from the Seminole country as they journeyed through Texas towards Mexico. The Indian owners were prepared to pay the legal reward for their apprehension and had authorized the agent to offer fifty dollars for each one returned to them. As there were so many runaways and most were women and children, speculators or a company of Texas Rangers would find it profitable to assist in their capture, and Duval had given instructions that this reward be advertised in hand bills and the Texas press. The enterprise was of vital concern to Texas, he wrote, for if they should reach Mexico, these maroons would attract other runaways and engage in border raids with Wild Cat.

Duval asked to be informed should the blacks be apprehended as he planned to seek permission from their Indian owners to have them sold in Texas. The agent's own monetary interest best explains his concern. His brother William had died leaving him some twenty blacks who had run off with Wild Cat. Duval had heard that twelve of these were on the Texas side of the Rio Grande, and he offered a reward of fifty dollars per head for their capture. As his duties prevented him from visiting Texas personally, he would send a list of their names with his agent George Aird.[14]

Duval also had asked General George Brooke, commanding the Department of Texas at San Antonio, to arrest any maroons found by the military. Governor Bell believed the best interests of Texas would be served by complying with this request and asked Brooke to send out a force to capture the fugitives. He also informed Duval that many speculators in the area were interested in helping to recapture the runaways. On November 12, however, Brooke replied to Bell's request and put a stop to any further speculation that the military would assist Duval in apprehending the Seminole blacks.[15]

Brooke argued that it was difficult to determine whether the maroons were owned by Seminoles living in Coahuila or were runaways from the Indian Territory. Duval had not provided names, and the rights of ownership had not been determined. There was no proof that Wild Cat had carried off these blacks or even advised them to leave their owners. Under the circumstances, the owners were responsible for retrieving their property. To employ the military in such a venture would be unprecedented. Brooke did direct the commanding officer at Fort Duncan to detain all blacks trying to cross over into Mexico until they could prove positively that they were free. He also told Texas Indian Agent Rollins to instruct the Comanches to prevent more blacks from passing through their country. Rollins should promise the Indians a considerable reward for each runaway delivered at Fredericksburg and warn them that they could expect trouble if they failed to comply. Brooke effectively had taken preventive action only after the main body of emigrant Seminole maroons had entered Mexico. At least for the moment, Duval's designs had been thwarted.

While Wild Cat was away in Texas and the Indian Territory, the Seminole, maroon, and Kickapoo men twice joined with Mexican troops to repel Indian raiders. The colonists fought well, and the raiders were defeated with heavy losses. As a reward for their fidelity and bravery, on October 16, President Herrera granted the immigrants' petition for land under the same conditions as in the original agreement.

On November 18 at El Moral, Colonel Maldonado explained the terms of the new grant, which lay at the headwaters of the San Rodrigo and San Antonio rivers. The three leaders, Wild Cat, John Horse, and Papicua, accepted the terms and took the oath of fidelity the following day. They received gratuities from the inspector, who promised them the lands they had solicited. On February 4, 1851, the Mexican authorities appointed Wild Cat colonel, and *alcalde* of the new colony. The Indians raised objections to their original grant, and officials gave them lands near the military colonies of Monclova Viejo and Guerrero in early March. The Seminoles settled at La Navaja, and the Kickapoos at Guerrero. The maroons remained at El Moral, some distance from the Seminoles.[16]

Wild Cat soon appeared dissatisfied with the new Seminole land grant at La Navaja and anxious for another move. Following Duval's reports, the war department became concerned about Wild Cat's motives in removing to Mexico and sent out Colonels Samuel Cooper and Robert Temple to investigate. On March 22, Mexican officials had ordered Wild Cat with one hundred Seminoles and Mascogos and seventy Mexican colonists to counter Indian raiders entering Mexico via Francia.[17] When the allies had completed this mission, Cooper and Temple interviewed the Seminole leader at Eagle Pass.

Wild Cat told the commissioners that the Creeks had come upon his land, taken his blacks, and tried to provoke him. He had left the Indian Territory to avoid war and look for a new home. Since his departure, the Creeks had stolen all his remaining blacks and other property. Wild Cat stated that he was living in a tent in Mexico and only planned to stay there temporarily. He wished to exchange the Seminoles' tract of land in the Indian Territory for one in Texas, to which all of his people later would remove. The officers advised him to return to Coahuila and remain there unless granted permission to do otherwise. Wild Cat recrossed the Rio Grande to fulfill his obligations to the Mexican government, but remained unsettled.[18]

Continued depredations by Indian raiders led the Mexican frontier states to return to the traditional scalp bounty. The colonists could earn $250 for a live warrior or $200 for his scalp, and $150 for a live woman or a live child under the age of fourteen. During 1851, Coahuila suffered ninety-four incursions by more than three thousand Comanches and Lipans resulting in sixty-three deaths, many wounded and captured, and heavy livestock losses. To try to curtail these raids, officials ordered 113 Seminoles, Mascogos and Kickapoos, together with 280 Mexican colonists, to commence a hunt for hostile Indians on June 13. The route was to follow the Texas, Chihuahua, and Durango borders of Coahuila to Laguna de Jaco and Laguna Tiahualila.

Nocosa Emathla and Manuel Flores led the Seminoles, and *El Capitán* Juan Caballo, or John Horse, led the Mascogos, both groups being under the general command of *Colonel Gato del Monte,* or Wild Cat. The maroons dressed like the Seminoles in brightly colored turbans, shirts, and leggings, and wore bracelets and bangles. They were armed heavily and rode in their own companies as during the Seminole Wars. For almost seven weeks the Mascogos helped comb the region. The allies saw action against Comanches and Lipans and recovered over one hundred head of livestock. They divided the plunder, but on the return journey, the Kickapoos defected and crossed the border into Texas driving before them all the captured livestock, including that of the blacks and Seminoles. These Kickapoos also were thought to be in league with slave hunters at Eagle Pass who had designs upon the maroons.

At the end of the campaign, the Seminoles and Mascogos received enthusiastic praise from the Mexicans for their patriotism, resolution, and zeal. But the expedition proved costly to the colonists. The Seminoles and maroons had lost not only their captured livestock but also many former allies. The Kickapoos' abandonment of the enterprise also led to further defections. In the fall, the Southern Kickapoo leaders Pecan and Pacanah rode to Mexico from their camps in the Indian Territory and persuaded almost the entire Kickapoo faction to return with them. By the end of the year, Chief Papicua and twenty of his followers were the only Kickapoo supporters of Wild Cat's enterprise remaining in Mexico. They were reported to be living near Morelos and engaging in agricultural pursuits.[19]

Shortly after returning from the campaign, Wild Cat called at Fort Duncan with his customary colorful entourage. This time, a servant and two interpreters attended the Seminole leader. According to Cora

Montgomery, one of the interpreters was a Moor, who had been tricked into boarding a Spanish trader and carried off to slavery in Cuba, where he had learned Spanish. He had escaped to Florida and had become an interpreter to the Seminoles. The other interpreter was John Horse. Horse was languid, probably because of the rigors and disappointments of the recent expedition. Wild Cat's energy and ambition burned as fiercely as ever, however. He now wished to become a United States soldier and win renown as the foremost Indian leader by quieting the refractory border tribes.[20]

The schemes of Texas slave hunters proved a far greater threat to the Mascogos than Indian raids. Mexico attracted large numbers of runaways and presented a serious problem for slaveholders. Since 1850, United States officials had been attempting to negotiate an extradition treaty that would include such runaways, but the Mexican government would not consider such a stipulation. The Seminole maroon settlement in Coahuila was anathema to the slaveholding interests of Texas, and the Texas press was critical of the land grant to John Horse as slave owners feared that their blacks would attempt to join him.

Occasionally in the past, small armed parties of slaveholders had pursued runaways across the border without permission. In the fall of 1851, however, a group of Texans made a more organized effort to break up the maroon community, recover runaways, and halt the flow of fugitives across the Rio Grande. After receiving assurances that the revolutionary leader would enact a slave rendition law once in power, a large group of Texans threw their support behind the filibustering campaign of José María Jesús Carvajal. Carvajal intended to separate the northern states from the rest of Mexico and create an independent republic to be called Sierra Madre. In mid-September, he crossed the Rio Grande, quickly took Camargo, and advanced on Matamoros where he was joined by three hundred to four hundred discharged Texas Rangers under John S. "Rip" Ford. The insurgents laid siege to the town for nine days but then were compelled to retire. The Mexican authorities sent forty Seminoles and twenty Mascogos under the general command of Wild Cat to help resist the invaders, and they encountered the enemy at Cerralvo. At the ensuing battle in late November, the Seminoles and blacks fought bravely, inflicting heavy losses and forcing Carvajal to retreat to Texas.[21]

While Carvajal was invading Mexico, Texas slave hunters launched a concurrent attack on the Seminole maroon settlement. Having failed to engage the support of the military for his schemes, Duval was ready to try a new strategy to recover the fugitives. In April, the Seminoles had asked him to proceed to San Antonio with a view to recovering their runaways. Being unable to travel to Texas himself because of his duties as subagent, Duval employed self-styled "Captain" Warren Adams, the famous runaway catcher, as the Seminoles' agent and then again asked Governor Bell for assistance. As many recent Texas runaways had made their way to Eagle Pass, Bell complied. The day before the Carvajal invasion, Bell issued an official request to citizens of Texas to aid Adams in recovering and apprehending the Seminole maroons. Adams treated this document as *carte blanche* to recover them in any way he could and quickly gathered together a group of speculators to attack their settlement while so many of the men were engaged elsewhere in repelling Carvajal.[22]

In early November, the commander at Fort Duncan crossed over to Piedras Negras to advise the Mexican authorities that he had heard of the approach of a group of more than one hundred American adventurers from Béjar (or San Antonio) who intended to cause trouble on the border and that Adams "the negro hunter" was at Leona with seventeen men. A week later, Colonel Emilio Langberg, inspector of the military colonies, reported that filibusters, intending to attack and capture the Mascogos, were across the Rio Grande from La Navaja. Immediately, the Mexican authorities assembled 150 volunteers, who marched to La Sauceda in the jurisdiction of Villa de Nava and fought off the slave hunters. Hearing of this, the Adams party turned southwest from Nava, captured a black family living at Múzquiz, and then retreated to Texas. It had been a close call, but the Seminole maroons again had escaped unharmed.[23]

Mexican officials saw that they could not allow the Mascogos to remain so close to the Texas border. The maroon settlement always would be surrounded by intrigue and would remain a target for slave hunters and filibusters. In view of American suspicions of Wild Cat's intentions, moreover, the proximity of the colony to the border threatened to undermine the treaty of Guadalupe Hidalgo and endanger relations between Mexico and the United States. Also, the Seminoles found the land at La Navaja too dry for agriculture and asked to be relocated. As a result, in late 1851, Mexican officials agreed to the removal of the maroons and Seminoles farther into the interior to the Santa Rosa Mountains, northwest of the town of Santa Rosa, or present Múzquiz.

The government promised them a land grant at the Hacienda de Nacimiento at the headwaters of the Río San Juan Sabinas on a tract recently relinquished by the Sánchez Navarro family. The residents of Múzquiz furnished the settlers with agricultural equipment and seed and, early the next year, the Mascogos and Indians moved up to Nacimiento and planted a crop. Thus began the Seminole maroon community of Nacimiento de los Negros, Coahuila, which still exists today.[24]

Prominent family names among the Mascogos were Factor, Payne, Bowlegs, Philips, Fay, Perryman, Daniels, Wilson, Bruner, and July. The Factors had been owned by Nelly and Sally Factor, descendants of a prominent Creek known as the Black Factor, who had settled in Florida and become associated with the Seminoles. The Paynes had belonged to Payne, principal chief of the Seminoles from around 1784 to 1812. His brother Bowlegs and the latter's descendants Billy Bowlegs and Harriet Bowlegs inherited many of Payne's blacks and gave them their name. The Philipses and Fays (from Felipe) were associated in Florida with Wild Cat's father King Philip, leader of the Saint Johns River Seminoles. The Perryman, Daniels, Wilson, and Bruner families had been owned by prominent Creek families of the same name, and the July family was descended from an African owned by Nelly Factor. July had become a leading maroon in Florida. The army had employed him as a guide and interpreter during the Second Seminole War, and Seminoles had murdered him for his defection.

John Horse, John Kibbetts, Cuffy, three Factors—Hardy, Thomas, and Dembo, Sampson July, and Jim Bowlegs headed the early Seminole maroon community in Coahuila. John Horse remained the undisputed head of the Mascogos, and the Mexican authorities referred to him as *Capitán* of the group. John Kibbetts, formerly owned by the Seminole Kubichee, was his military second-in-command, and Hardy Factor, his counselor. The maroons recognized Cuffy, who had played a leading role in the Walking Joe incident at Wewoka in June 1849, as leader in the absence of John Horse. Horse's leading advisers were Thomas and Dembo Factor and Sampson July, the uncles and brother respectively of his wife Susan, and Jim Bowlegs, his successor as leader of the Seminole blacks in the Indian Territory. Prominent women in the maroon community at Nacimiento were Susan and Juana, the wife and sister of John Horse; Nancy Kibbetts, the wife of John Kibbetts; and Nancy Kibbetts's daughter Kitty Johnson.

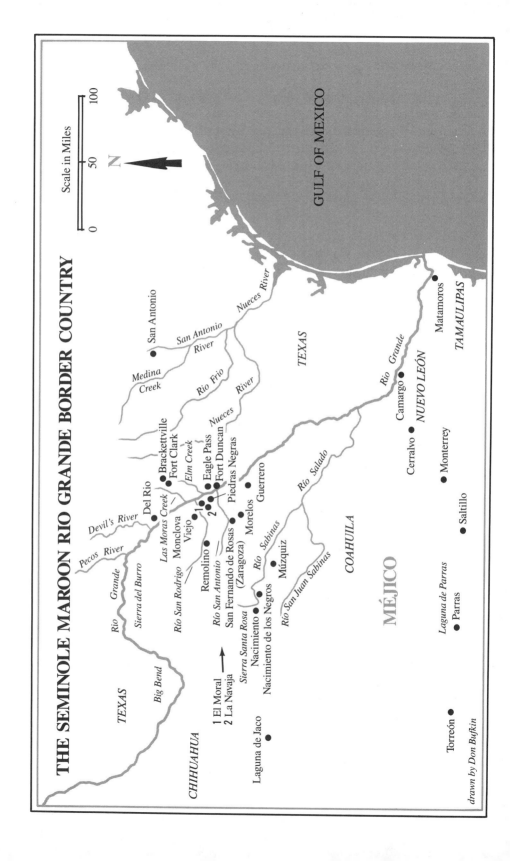

THE SEMINOLE MAROON RIO GRANDE BORDER COUNTRY

Scale in Miles

100

50

0

N

GULF OF MEXICO

TAMAULIPAS

Matamoros

NUEVO LEÓN

Rio Grande

Camargo

Cerralvo

Monterrey

Saltillo

TEXAS

San Antonio

San Antonio River

Medina Creek

Río Frío

Nueces River

Nueces River

Brackettville

Fort Clark

Elm Creek

Eagle Pass

Fort Duncan

Piedras Negras

Guerrero

Río Salado

Río Sabinas

Morelos

Del Rio

Las Moras Creek

Monclova Viejo

1

2

Remolino

San Fernando de Rosas (Zaragoza)

Múzquiz

Río San Juan Sabinas

COAHUILA

Devil's River

Pecos River

Río Grande

Sierra del Burro

Río San Rodrigo

Río San Antonio

Sierra Santa Rosa

Nacimiento

Nacimiento de los Negros

MÉJICO

Laguna de Parras

Parras

TEXAS

Big Bend

CHIHUAHUA

Laguna de Jaco

1 El Moral
2 La Navaja

Torreón

drawn by Don Bufkin

Border tribes continued to devastate the Mexican interior. Early in 1852, for example, Indian raiders twice stole or killed livestock belonging to the Mascogos and Seminoles at Nacimiento. Again, Mexican officials sought assistance to help curb these incursions. Several parties of maroons under John Horse and Seminoles under Parsakee subsequently took part in a campaign against Comanches that extended as far as the Laguna de Jaco in Chihuahua. During the expedition, the Mascogos and Seminoles took many Comanche scalps. Between January 6 and May 15, for example, they presented seventy-four scalps and prisoners, for which the state of Chihuahua paid eighteen thousand dollars. The maroon campaigners returned to Nacimiento in June to find that their kinsmen had established a thriving settlement based on agriculture and hunting.[25]

As the Seminoles and Mascogos were pleased with their new location at Nacimiento, Wild Cat chose not to accompany the campaign but to travel instead to Mexico City with the Kickapoo Chief Papicua to confirm the grant. On July 26, 1852, the two leaders signed a treaty whereby the Mexican government awarded the Seminoles, maroons, and Kickapoos four *sitios de ganado mayor*, or approximately 26.5 square miles of land, at the *hacienda de Nacimiento*, and an equal amount in Durango which they never utilized, in recompense for their efforts against Indian raiders. In return, the immigrants would settle in villages and be prepared to muster two hundred warriors on demand, although it seems unlikely that they ever would have been able to raise such a number. The Mexicans signed over the lands in perpetuity provided the colonists continued to oppose depredating bands. The casting of a bronze medal in relief on which appeared the seal of Mexico, the peace-pipe of the Seminoles, and two clasped hands symbolizing peace and harmony confirmed the treaty. A second peace medal, proclaiming *"Mexico* [sic] *a los Seminoles,"* now in the collection of the Thomas Gilcrease Institute in Tulsa, also may have been cast at this time. The governor of Coahuila ratified the agreement in August, and Wild Cat returned to Nacimiento the following month.[26]

As the few remaining Kickapoos in Mexico were living at Morelos, the Seminoles and Mascogos alone utilized the Nacimiento land grant. The Seminoles settled at the headwaters of the Sabinas, and the maroons moved off to establish their own community near the hill of Buenavista, about four miles from the Indians. Here they built cabins, planted gardens and crops, hunted and fished, and raised livestock.[27]

Once again, the maroons lived apart from the Seminoles, tended to their own fields and herds, bore arms, and during campaigns, organized into their own companies under black officers. Yet, though the maroons were now legally free, evidence appears to suggest that there was an initial restoration within the colony of the earlier relationship they had shared with the Seminoles. Ahalakochee, a grandson of Wild Cat, recalled later that the Mascogos worked the land and carried out "the instructions of those whose bondsmen they were," a notion attested to by Cora Montgomery.[28] The Seminoles apparently continued to look to the maroons for agricultural support. Several of the leading Mascogos also were employed as Spanish interpreters, while others remained counselors and advisers. Early Seminole-black relations at Nacimiento thus seem to have resembled somewhat those that had existed between the two groups in Florida prior to the 1823 Treaty of Moultrie Creek.

The Mascogos had relocated well inside the Mexican interior, but this served neither to allay the fears of United States officials nor to put a stop to the efforts of slave hunters. In mid-November, Lieutenant Duff Green, commanding an escort party attached to the United States Boundary Survey Commission, came upon the settlers at Nacimiento. Green was stopped by black sentries outside their settlement, and he remarked later upon the distance between the maroon and the Seminole villages. After an interview with Wild Cat, Green concluded that the colony was "very injurious to the slave interests of Texas, as runaways will always find a safe home."[29]

Warren Adams, meanwhile, had failed to recover any of the maroons, and in the fall, Duval traveled to San Antonio to ask him to step up his efforts. The Seminole owners had issued bills of sale for all their blacks to enable Duval to make quick and easy transfers. Again, Duval was unsuccessful in his mission and started back to the Seminole country, but at Austin he received news of charges being made against him because of his slaving activities. Before he could return to the Indian Territory, he was discharged from office as Seminole subagent for having been absent from his post too often and too long. As he no longer would be able to use his official position to further his slaving interests, Duval's dismissal had removed a great source of danger to the maroons.[30]

Late in 1852, Adams, at last, enjoyed some success—albeit of a limited nature. John Horse was extremely unpopular with Texas settlers on the border, being regarded as impudent, troublesome, and boastful of having killed many whites in Florida. To the great delight of local residents and the border press, John earlier had been expelled from Fort Duncan while laying claim to a horse that had been taken from him and sold. Then, while attending a dance in Piedras Negras, he became involved in a brawl and was shot and wounded by a Texan. Adams rushed across the border with some professional slave hunters, captured John, and took him back to Eagle Pass in handcuffs.

Some two days later, Wild Cat crossed over from Mexico, prepared to pay a high price for the release of his friend and counselor, the acknowledged and trusted leader of his maroon supporters. He agreed to pay Adams five hundred dollars and deliver up young runaways who recently had escaped from their owners if Adams would free John. That same day, Wild Cat crossed back to Mexico and returned with the five hundred dollars in twenty-dollar gold pieces. The coins were stained with blood, which the post surgeon at Fort Duncan declared was human. Adams took heed and allowed John Horse to return to Nacimiento with Wild Cat, but the Seminole leader did not deliver up any of the young runaways.[31]

In return for the land grant, the Mexican authorities expected the Seminoles and Mascogos to engage in campaigns to remove the threat of Indian raids in the borderlands. They were to repel and pursue raiders, undertake regular and lengthy expeditions to seek out and attack such bands, and be ready for service at the state or national level in times of emergency. Their compensation would be livestock and pillage, and they would be paid at the same rate as national troops when mustered into service. Occasionally, the Mexicans furnished the men with rations and supplied their families with money or food in their absence. They also promised bonuses of money and goods from time to time. In spite of these incentives, however, the maroons became less and less interested in the prospect of military campaigns.

Developments soon were to take place that would give rise to tension between the Mascogos and the Seminoles. In June 1853, Cuffy appeared before the *Comandante de Monclova Viejo* and accused Wild Cat of engaging in slave trafficking. The previous year, he said, Wild Cat had persuaded Cuffy to accompany him across the Rio Grande as his interpreter. When the two reached Texas, Wild Cat sold Cuffy to an American for eighty pesos. Cuffy was taken off to Béjar, where he spotted another maroon sold by Wild Cat. Soon after, Cuffy was able to make his escape and rejoin his family at Nacimiento.[32] The notion that Wild Cat was willing to part with his black allies for profit at times

is supported by other evidence. Kitty Johnson's daughters Molly Perryman and Penny Factor later told the story that, while the Seminoles
and maroons were traveling through Texas, Wild Cat had gotten drunk
in Fredericksburg and had tried to sell Kitty and Picayune John to a
bartender, the two being saved only by John Horse's quickness of wit.
It even has been suggested that on at least one occasion, Wild Cat played
the "Skin Game," selling Rosa Fay's mother Clara for a barrel of whiskey
in Eagle Pass and then stealing her back.[33]

A second factor worked to increase still further the friction between
the Seminoles and Mascogos. From the start, the maroons had taken
better to the *hacienda de Nacimiento* than had their Seminole allies and
they had become involved heavily in agricultural and domestic pursuits.
The Mascogos became disinclined to leave their families and possessions
poorly defended while undertaking arduous and dangerous expeditions
against Indian raiders. The Seminoles engaged in several expeditions
during these two years while the maroons continued to work the land at
Nacimiento. Only when their own interests were directly at stake or they
were mustered into service during times of emergency did the Mascogos
agree to engage in such campaigns.

Early in 1853, the Seminoles undertook an expedition into the Laguna
de Jaco without the maroons and received praise from Mexican observers
for their zeal and perseverance. Again, in August, a small party of
Seminoles and Múzquiz residents repelled and pursued Indian raiders
with no help from the Mascogos. Finally, in the spring of 1854, two
parties of Seminoles under Wild Cat and Coyote engaged in a campaign
into Chihuahua against Mescaleros and Comanches without maroon
support. The Mascogos, as yet, still answered the call to arms when so
ordered by the government. During August and September 1854,
Mexican officials mustered the maroons and Seminoles into service three
times: twice to counter anticipated filibuster invasions and once to
oppose hostile Indians.[34] It was becoming increasingly clear, however,
that the two groups were developing different interests and priorities.
Cracks were beginning to appear in the Seminole-black alliance.

In 1854, Texans accused the Seminoles and Mascogos of committing
depredations. These actions probably came about partly in retaliation
for the Texans' support of Carvajal and the humiliation experienced by
John Horse at the hands of Warren Adams with the resultant loss of five
hundred dollars, and partly because the Seminoles and maroons needed
good horses to defend their settlements and fulfill their obligations to

the Mexican government. In February, raiders from Mexico drove across the border a herd of some thirty horses and mules belonging to residents of Eagle Pass. Citizens of Texas implicated Wild Cat's band immediately as an African had been spotted with the rustlers. They provided further evidence in the shape of a Seminole moccasin, which had been found at the point where the raiders recrossed the Rio Grande. One of the owners of the herd trailed Wild Cat's party to San Fernando where he requested the alcalde to recover the livestock for him. Wild Cat was called before the authorities where he boasted of his deeds and declared that he could not return the animals as half belonged to General Cordona, the governor of Coahuila, he and the general being partners in the enterprise. The alcalde appeared to be satisfied and allowed the Seminoles and Mascogos to retain their prize.[35]

These accusations focused attention on Wild Cat and his supporters. A resident of Múzquiz described the maroons as "well armed and good fighters" and concluded that the colony could resist an attack by five hundred men.[36] Colonel Joseph Plympton furnished a description of Seminole-black relations that closely matched earlier reports from Florida: "The Seminole Indians have with them between 50 and 60 negroes, who are on terms of perfect equality with them, and entitled to as many privileges as though they were Indians. They are armed, and almost invariably accompany them in their depredating excursions." The Seminoles and Mascogos would put two companies into the field, "One company, composed entirely of Indians, is commanded by Wild Cat; the other, made up of negroes only [is] under the command of a negro known as Gopher John." Separation and cooperation continued to be the watchwords for the maroons and Seminoles during their first few years in Coahuila.

Plympton estimated the total number of Mascogos and Seminoles at Nacimiento to be 318, of which 183 were warriors. No official census of the colony was taken at that time, but Plympton apparently miscalculated both the total population and its makeup. There were never as many as 130 Seminole warriors in Mexico, and the Seminole population did not increase substantially after 1850. The number of men the Indians could muster probably was nearer to the "about 50" estimated by T. B. Holabird, perhaps totaling sixty or sixty-five.[37] Moreover, the maroon population was growing and by 1854 would have outnumbered that of the Seminoles. Evidence suggests that the Mascogos could put at least eighty men into the field if necessary. More than two hundred

Seminole maroons already were resident in Coahuila by late 1850, and their numbers increased substantially in succeeding years through new recruits from Texas. These runaways continued to be a great cause of concern to slaveholders and would be the reason for further filibustering activities.

Earlier, Carvajal, Ford, and Adams had attempted unsuccessfully to break up the Nacimiento colony in order to capture blacks. After 1852, Ford became the undisputed leader of the movement to return runaways living in Mexico to their Texas owners. During the mid-1850s, Texans became incensed by reports of losses in slave property. Frederick Olmsted, who was traveling in Mexico at that time, reported that at least forty runaways had passed through Piedras Negras in one three-month period and that a great many more had crossed the Rio Grande farther to the south.[38] In June 1855, moreover, Ford estimated there to be some four thousand fugitive blacks in northern Mexico, at a combined value of more than 3,200,000 dollars. Following these disclosures, slaveholders assembled in public meetings in West Texas to formulate measures to restrain their blacks and capture runaways, even if it meant crossing over into Mexico.[39]

Before resorting to force, the Texans sought a peaceful solution to the problem. In late August 1855, residents of San Antonio wrote to Langberg to inquire under what conditions he would deliver up runaways who had taken refuge in Mexico. The letter ended, however, with a covert threat of unilateral action if agreement could not be reached. Langberg gave a favorable reply, suggesting a reciprocal agreement for the rendition of runaways living in Mexico and peons who had escaped to Texas. He then relayed the request to General Santiago Vidaurri, the new revolutionary governor of Nuevo León y Coahuila. Vidaurri crushed the hopes of the Texas slaveholders and took away any possibility of a peaceful solution, however, by vetoing Langberg's suggestion on September 11. He insisted that any such arrangement should be handled by the respective state governments and not by private individuals. Should the Texans choose to invade Mexico to recover runaways, Langberg should use whatever force was necessary to drive them back.

Meanwhile, during the summer, Governor Elisha M. Pease authorized Texas Ranger Captain James Hughes Callahan to raise a mounted company to patrol and protect the area around San Antonio against Indian raids. The company was mustered into service in July for three

months, during which time the interested slaveholders apparently
secured Callahan's support for their mission by promising him a percentage of the blacks captured. William R. Henry, another adventurer and
speculator, joined Callahan, and the company patrolled the frontier until
it engaged some Seminoles and Mascogos about thirty miles from
Bandera northwest of San Antonio. By late September, Callahan's force
was encamped four miles north of Eagle Pass prepared to cross over into
Mexico to break up the Seminole maroon community and return the
Texas runaways to their owners.[40]

Under the pretext of pursuing Lipans and other hostile Indian bands,
Callahan's expeditionary force crossed the Rio Grande some three miles
below Fort Duncan on the night of October 1. The filibusters numbered
111 men divided into three companies. Once in Mexico, Callahan
planned to draw off the Seminole and maroon men, leaving Henry to
seize the black women and children at Nacimiento. The Seminoles and
Mascogos ambushed and defeated Henry's party, however, before con-
fronting Callahan. Callahan's men made for what they believed to be
Wild Cat's headquarters at San Fernando, but on October 3, Seminoles
and maroons led them into an ambush at Escondido Creek. During the
ensuing battle, the Texans suffered four killed and seven wounded, and
Callahan was forced to retreat to Piedras Negras, which he took the
following day.

A force of some seven hundred armed Mexicans, Seminoles, and
Mascogos arrived outside the town on October 5. The Rio Grande was
swollen, and Callahan could not withdraw to Texas, so the commanding
officer at Fort Duncan gave a show of force to prevent the filibusters
from being harmed. The next day, Callahan's brief excursion ended
when he set fire to the town and escaped across the river under the smoke
screen and the cover of the guns at Fort Duncan.[41] Callahan's hasty
withdrawal may not have been so well planned, however. The Seminole
maroons retained a tradition that their forebears chased the Texans from
Piedras Negras by shooting fire arrows into the buildings and burning
down the town around them.[42]

Much speculation has arisen over the motives behind the Callahan
expedition. The filibusters claimed that their purpose was to pursue
hostile Indians, but the weight of evidence supports the notion that their
main intention was to break up the Seminole maroon settlement and
return fugitive blacks to their Texan owners. The comments of contemporaries clearly implicate Callahan in slaving activities. Frederick

Olmsted wrote that Callahan's party was really on a reconnaissance to recover runaways and Jesse Sumpter believed that, "Callahan, being the owner of most of the Seminole Negroes (those Seminoles were all runaway slaves), determined to raise a party, go into Mexico and take them out by force," the inference here being that Texas slaveholders had promised Callahan a percentage of all the maroons he captured.[43]

Other contemporary evidence supports this view. On October 10, General Persifor Smith reported that a party was preparing to cross over into Mexico to capture Texas runaways.[44] The following day, Smith informed Pease that he did not believe Callahan's expedition had been in pursuit of hostile Indians: "I am advised that the burning of the town and the designs on the Seminole settlement have exasperated to the highest degree both that band of Indians and the Mexicans. [I] have no doubt plans of revenge will be formed and executed on the peaceful inhabitants of our frontier. [We] may look for an inroad from the Seminole to murder and scalp—not merely to steal."[45]

Callahan himself admitted some connection with the Texas slaveholders in a letter of October 13 to Pease. He had met with Colonel Bennett Riddells, a representative of the Bastrop slaveholders, at San Antonio. Riddells had conferred previously with Vidaurri about the recovery of runaways and had received assurances of success. Callahan claimed to have been told that he would experience no difficulty in crossing the Rio Grande and that Riddells would procure the necessary authority.[46]

The Mexican border commissioners, who reviewed the affair later, certainly were not impressed by Callahan's explanation: "The pretext was the pursuit of the tribe of Lipan Indians of whom the Texans complained. [It] is probable, nevertheless, that one of the incentives was the capture of fugitive slaves, a great number of which had taken refuge on the frontier of Coahuila."[47] The direction the invasion took suggests that the Americans intended to attack the Mascogos at Nacimiento. The maroons themselves believed that the invaders posed a direct threat to their community and for years passed down a tradition of the time the filibusters came to steal their children. The Mascogos responded promptly to the invasion, helping to defeat Henry and force Callahan to retreat to Texas.[48]

The affair heightened diplomatic tension between the two nations. James Gadsden, the United States minister to Mexico, responded aggressively to Mexican complaints of the invasion and the burning of

Piedras Negras by recounting the reasons for the filibustering expedition. Another grievance cited was that Mexico had invited a lawless band of Seminoles to settle within its boundaries who since had committed depredations on the frontier of Texas. The Mexicans also had interfered with the institution of slavery by protecting runaways. The presence of the Seminole and maroon settlements on the border continued to threaten the interests of Texas and put added strain on the treaty of Guadalupe Hidalgo.[49]

Though he had suffered a humiliating defeat, Callahan became involved in organizing a second, more extensive foray into Mexico. Again under the pretext of pursuing hostile Indians, Callahan joined with other influential Texans in inviting the people of Texas to join a campaign into the Mexican interior and request that the United States government provide arms. Langberg became aware of the threatened invasion and sent seven Mascogos under John Kibbetts and a party of Seminoles under Wild Cat and Coyote to Nava to oppose the American volunteers. Several other maroons refused to comply, however, and openly defied the Mexican authorities for the first time. Some excused their nonattendance by citing the needs of farming, while others simply would not leave their families.

The failure of more of the Mascogos to respond to Langberg's orders brought criticism from the *State Gazette,* and the authorities threatened six families with expulsion. Callahan's projected second invasion failed to materialize, and the Seminole and maroon warriors were not needed. The circumstances surrounding the first expedition became public, and the uncooperative posture assumed by United States government officials put an end to any further attempts. The independent and insubordinate attitude adopted by the maroons in the face of threatened invasion, however, would play a crucial role in determining their future relations with the Seminoles.[50]

In spite of this disobedience on the part of the Mascogos, the Mexican authorities at Múzquiz gave a glowing report on the Seminoles and maroons at the end of 1855. The military colonists had given no cause for complaint and were "industrious, warlike, and desirous of education and religious instruction for their families."[51] In late 1855 and early 1856, Governor Santiago Vidaurri appointed for the Seminoles and Mascogos salaried instructors in agriculture, reading, writing, and religion. A chapel and a school for the children were established during the spring.

An order of 1853 that children should be baptized began to be enforced around this time. Apparently, it also affected adult maroons. From late 1856 on, John Horse is sometimes referred to as "Capitán Juan de Dios Vidaurri (alias Caballo)," the name probably deriving from his being baptized Catholic and adopting as his godfather the Mascogos' instructor in religion and agriculture, Juan Nepomuceno Vidaurri. The Seminoles and maroons continued to progress and impressed the Mexican authorities. Governor Vidaurri even provided them with an armorer, Pedro Sains, a Mexican black, receiving the first appointment. In early 1856, officials reported the colonists to be living in wooden houses, dedicated to agriculture, implacable in their enmity to hostile Indians, and engaging in regular campaigns against such bands.[52]

Vidaurri soon would instigate a series of expeditions designed to remove the threat of Lipan and Tonkawa depredations from Coahuila. During March 1856, twelve Mascogos, forty Seminoles, and more than one hundred Mexicans scoured the country for ten days but returned without success.[53] The disproportionate number of maroons to Seminoles was typical of the colonists' involvement in the campaigns against Indian raiders. Although by now they outnumbered the Seminoles, the Mascogos put fewer warriors into the field and increasingly became disinclined to support such expeditions. This would be cited later by the Seminoles as a major grievance against the maroons.

The first serious outbreak of disagreement between the Mexican authorities, the Mascogos, and the Seminoles took place during April and May of 1856. The recent runaways from Texas who had joined the maroons were charged with abandoning work and engaging in theft and other excesses. Vidaurri ordered their subordination to Wild Cat and instructed them to live honestly and industriously. The maroons, however, did not wish to subject themselves to Wild Cat, arguing that they always had recognized John Horse as their leader, and that in his absence they recognized Captain Cuffy. Vidaurri clarified his position on May 28. He approved of the Mascogos' selection of John Horse as "captain of that tribe," but insisted that Wild Cat retain overall leadership of the maroons and Seminoles. Vidaurri went on to stress the necessity of the Mascogos' obeying John Horse and awarded him a cart, plough, and oxen for subjecting his people to the Seminole leader.[54] By the summer of 1856, Wild Cat's charisma and strength of character and the respect and affection of John Horse for his old friend were all that held the alliance intact.

Seminoles also came to challenge Wild Cat's leadership. Coyote and a group of his supporters had begun to act independently, and in late April, Vidaurri felt forced to order that from then on Coyote be recognized as second-in-command of the Seminoles. During this period, Wild Cat was undergoing treatment in Monterrey for an illness. His enforced absence from the colony may have been decisive in bringing about this development. Whatever the cause, factionalism within the Indian leadership served only to weaken still further relations between the maroons and the Seminoles.[55]

The Mascogos were beginning to assert their position as an independent group. They had a history of opposition to imposed authority, and their numbers had been swelled by hardened frontier maroons and recent runaways so that now they were more numerous than the Seminoles. These latest recruits had no tradition of showing respect for, or deferring to, Indian leaders, and they were not prepared to accept Seminole authority. In the face of black insubordination and unilateral initiatives, the alliance began to deteriorate. No longer would the maroons subscribe to an association with the Seminoles on unequal terms. They had different interests and priorities and now were in a position to take control of their own destiny.

For the remainder of 1856, the Mascogos continued their policy of not cooperating with the Seminoles and Mexican officials when it came to engaging in expeditions. From May to October, the Seminoles took part in campaigns, scouring the country from San Vicente to the Big Bend for hostile bands, killing Comanches, Kiowas, and Tonkawas, and capturing horses and other spoils, for which actions they received praise and gifts from the authorities at Múzquiz. During this entire period, not one black accompanied the Seminoles on any of these campaigns. The contrast in attitude was most marked during late June and early July when the entire body of Seminole warriors engaged in an expedition, leaving their women and children without protection while all the maroon men remained behind with their families.[56]

Vidaurri ordered fourteen Mascogos and twenty Seminoles to join his army at Monterrey in late October in preparation for a rebellion against the central government, but the maroons refused to obey. John Horse and four other blacks, together with Coyote and a party of Seminoles, went to Monterrey to explain their position. The secretary of war ordered that the Mascogos be reproved for disobeying the public authorities, but decided that as they claimed they did not wish to become involved with the internal political turmoils of Mexico, they should be used instead against hostile Indians. Once again, however, it was Seminoles rather than maroons who responded. Coyote sought out Indian raiders around Parras, while John Horse returned home to Nacimiento.[57]

In the winter of 1856, smallpox hit the Seminoles and Mascogos. The Seminole warriors who recently had returned from campaigns and were encamped at Alto, near Múzquiz, were the first victims. The disease then spread quickly to Nacimiento. Juan Long, a resident of Múzquiz and cousin of Vidaurri, established a vaccination program in the Seminole and maroon villages, but in late January 1857, the terrified Indians fled into the hills in search of safety. By mid-March Long had the disease under control, and the Seminoles returned to Nacimiento, but by then it had taken a heavy toll on the Indians. Twenty-eight women and twenty-five men, including nineteen warriors, had perished, and Wild Cat and Coyote were among the victims. The Mascogos suffered fewer losses than the Seminoles. The presiding physician believed this to be attributable to a healthier diet and stricter adherence to curative methods.[58]

The death of Wild Cat proved crucial in further alienating the maroons from the Seminoles. Though they had helped undermine his leadership during 1856, the Mascogos had continued tacitly to accept Wild Cat's position as joint head of the combined groups. Lion succeeded Wild Cat as leader of the Seminoles, but the maroons would not accept his overall sovereignty. To the Mascogos, the situation had changed dramatically. As Joseph Philips recalled later, "After Wild Cat dies, then John Horse took the command as chief." From this point on, the maroons looked exclusively to their own leaders and paid no further allegiance to the Seminoles.[59]

During 1857, Vidaurri attempted to remove the remaining Florida Seminoles and maroons to Mexico. The governor was quick to appreciate the value of the colonists as a buffer against hostile Indians. In September, he signed a contract with Edward Luis Bernard of Corpus Christi in which he agreed to pay for the sea transportation of five hundred Seminole warriors and their families from Florida to Mexico. Vidaurri also agreed to furnish the immigrants with arable land provided they helped defend Coahuila, particularly against depredating Indians. The scheme failed to materialize, however, as Bernard learned at New Orleans that he would not be allowed to enter into such a treaty with the Florida Seminoles. There would be no further attempts to remove the remaining Indians and blacks in Florida to Mexico.[60]

The Mascogos took part in only one brief campaign in 1857. During the spring, maroons under John Horse and Seminoles under Juan Flores engaged in a retaliatory expedition against Indian raiders that resulted in the capture of seven horses. In July, Long reported that the Seminoles were valued opponents of the Lipans and Mescaleros. He began to pay them for scalps and advised Vidaurri to organize a company of Seminoles and Mascogos to pursue such raiders. Once again, however, it was the Seminoles alone who engaged in three actions against Lipans and one against Comanches during July and August. Finally, in December, the Seminoles and Mexicans took part in a successful campaign against Lipans and Tonkawas, after which complaints arose that the maroons did not participate or cooperate.[61]

The dispute between the Mascogos, the Seminoles, and the Mexican authorities soon came to a head. The conflict had deep roots and had continued to gather momentum since the first outbreak in April 1856, provoking intense feelings on all sides. Mexicans and Seminoles accused the recent runaways of abandoning work and of theft and other excesses, and charged the Mascogos as a whole with giving only grudging support to campaigns. The maroons, for their part, wished to be governed by their own leaders. In July 1857, the Seminole leader Felipe had brought up a new source of contention when he complained of abuses by the Mascogos in their use of water for irrigation. Finally, in December, serious complaints had arisen over the maroons' lack of cooperation during the recent expedition.

In August 1858, Lion, together with his second-in-command Nocosa Emathla, and Juan Flores, appeared before Vidaurri at Monterrey with a list of complaints. The maroons owned more horses and property than the Seminoles because they remained behind at Nacimiento while the Indians engaged in expeditions. Also, being superior in number, the Mascogos used more water than they were entitled to. Finally, the delegates tried to put an end to the maroons' independence by requesting that they subject themselves to the care and command of the Seminole chiefs, as they had under Wild Cat.

To add to the complaints, the alcalde of Múzquiz charged again that the more recent runaways did not respect private property and engaged in cattle-stealing. The Seminoles were discontented and unsettled and wished to move to Mazatlan, but if any group were to go it should be the maroons, who were not so helpful and were the target of Texas slave hunters. Vidaurri warned the Mascogos to respect property, avoid crime, devote themselves to labor and warfare against hostile bands, and separate themselves from the more reckless recent runaways. If they continued to cause trouble, the guilty would be sent to Monterrey and forced to labor on public works. Vidaurri also ordered that Mexican officers assume the command of the maroons and Seminoles during future expeditions, and appointed a justice of the peace to regulate their land and water rights.[62]

The continuing dispute emphasized the conflicting interests of the Mascogos and Seminoles. For most of their lives, the maroons had been a source of contention in wars and slave controversies. They had been hounded by United States troops and white and Creek slave hunters and kidnappers. In Coahuila, the Mascogos looked for freedom, security, and a place to build communities. They did not wish to take part in lengthy expeditions against hostile Indians or filibusters unless their interests were affected directly. As farmers and stock-raisers, naturally they objected to leaving their crops and livestock, and they had been given good reason in the past to fear for the families they would leave unprotected. The maroons were better agriculturists than the Seminoles and cleared more land. As their numbers and acreage increased so did their need for water. They acquired more property and improvements, and grew closer to the hacienda than the Indians. The Seminoles, on the other hand, preferred to engage in hunting or military expeditions than raise stock or work the land. At the height of their dispute with the Mascogos, many of the Seminoles were camped permanently outside Alto, merely awaiting the call to take part in campaigns.

When they had left the Indian Territory, the Seminoles and maroons had been joined in a weak alliance based primarily on their joint wish to live far away from their common enemies. With that exception, they had harbored different reasons for leaving, had sought different goals for their new community, and subsequently had established different life-styles. In Mexico, the maroons again had found liberty across a border. As in Florida, their alliance with the Seminoles was at its strongest when assailed by external forces. For a time, the two would unite to repel the enemy from without—the slave hunter, filibuster, or Indian raider. But their relationship was far weaker in Coahuila than it had been in Florida. The differing interests and lifestyles of the maroons and Indians, the growth of Seminole factionalism and the demise of Wild Cat, the continuing trend towards black independence and separatism, and the influence of new members of the community on initiatives all worked to undermine the alliance, and ultimately led to a breakdown in relations.

Africans and Seminoles would combine on one more expedition during the spring of 1858. In early March, Mescaleros stole thirty horses belonging to the Mascogos and six belonging to the Seminoles. Sufficiently incensed, the maroons sent twenty warriors in pursuit with an equal number of Seminoles. They encountered their foes on the banks of the Rio Grande and routed them, killing two of the Indians and recapturing their horses as well as additional livestock and plunder. With the exception of one other minor joint expedition in September, this campaign marked the end of military cooperation between the maroons and Seminoles in Mexico.[63]

During the fall of 1858, the Seminole leaders Long Tiger, Parsakee, and Young Coacoochee visited their kinsmen in the Indian Territory. They learned that the Seminoles there had entered into a treaty with the Creeks and the United States on August 7, 1856, that had resulted in the creation of a separate and independent Seminole Nation. The Seminoles had received their own tract of land to the west of, and adjoining, the Creek country and no longer were subject to the laws of the larger tribe. The Mexican Seminoles' main reason for remaining outside the Indian Territory thus had been removed. The following January, the delegates returned to Coahuila with the news and an invitation from the Seminole leadership to return with the rest of the band to the new nation.[64]

The idea appealed to the Seminoles remaining in Mexico. They had experienced hard times of late. In contrast to the Mascogos, many were poverty-stricken and starving. Much of the Seminoles' enthusiasm for the Mexican colony had died with Wild Cat, and many had taken to drink. The civil war then racking the country, constant disputes with the maroons, and jealousy of their neighbors' success only increased their dissatisfaction. Once the new treaty had removed the obstacle of the Creeks, the Seminoles welcomed the opportunity to return to their former home. In fact, the wheels had been set in motion as early as August 1858, when it was suggested that the Indian bureau allow the Seminoles to return to the Indian Territory and receive annuities. The commissioner had agreed, and in September the Secretary of the Interior had granted them permission to return to the United States.[65]

On February 17, 1859, Chief Lion, thirteen men, and thirty-seven women and children set out for the new Seminole Nation. The Mexican authorities regretted their loss on account of the good service they had rendered against hostile bands. An agent of the United States government met the Seminoles at Eagle Pass and escorted them through Texas to the Indian Territory. They were starving and in need of government rations.[66] Along the way, the train passed through the camp of Major Zenas Bliss who described the Seminoles as poorly mounted, "poverty stricken, sullen and generally played out."[67] This spectacle offered sad testimony to the demise of the Seminole community at Nacimiento. It also served to emphasize how much more successful the maroons had been in creating a new life for themselves in Coahuila.

With the departure of Lion's band, around one hundred Seminoles remained in Mexico. The Mascogos had no wish to return to the Indian Territory. A separate Seminole Nation meant little to them. Slavery still existed in the United States and among the Five Civilized Tribes, and the efforts of white slave hunters and kidnappers would continue to pose a threat. Also, Mexico suited the maroons at this time. They had their liberty and had become fairly prosperous. This was more than they could hope for if they went back to the Indian Territory.

Lion's departure weakened the Mexican colony and ushered in a new phase of filibustering activity. In March 1859, General David Twiggs learned that an expedition was being organized near San Antonio with the purpose of capturing runaways in Coahuila and selling them for profit, and he warned the alcalde of Piedras Negras that the filibusters intended to kidnap the maroons at Nacimiento. The invasion did not materialize, but its threat was sufficient to bring about the removal of the Mascogos further into the Mexican interior.[68]

On March 23, the state government of Nuevo León y Coahuila ordered that since they were the principal target of filibusters, the maroons should remove from the border to the Laguna de Parras, some three hundred miles to the south of Nacimiento in southwestern Coahuila, where they would be more secure. Here they would be supplied with land, water, and other assistance, and in return, the Mascogos again would help repel Indian raiders. The move would be in the best interests of all concerned, putting an end to speculation and the threat of invasion.[69] The loss of their Seminole companions-in-arms, continuing activity in slave trafficking, and the hostility of some of their Mexican neighbors led to the Mascogos' concurrence with the scheme.

The first group, numbering more than eighty, set out for Parras on May 21, transporting their possessions in carts supplied by the Mexicans. Most of the remaining Mascogos removed during the summer, leaving behind only a few of their number at Nacimiento.[70] These maroons now lived farther from the Seminoles than at any time since their relationship began in Florida. Further interaction between the two groups would be minimal, and their alliance drew to a close.

The Seminoles who had remained behind at Nacimiento were dissatisfied more than ever. With the departure of both Lion's band and the Mascogos, the Seminole colony at Nacimiento fell prey to incursions by Indian raiders. There had been disputes between maroons and Seminoles and between maroons and Mexicans, but after the Mascogos had removed, the local authorities turned on the Seminoles, accusing them of disobeying orders. Moreover, a fight for the leadership between Konip and new Principal Chief Nocosa Emathla racked the Seminole community. Clearly, changes had to come. By March 1861, twenty-two of the Seminoles had decided to leave Mexico. The hacienda, meanwhile, changed hands and the new owner, Dona Guadalupe Echaiz, declared that the Indian occupants either should remove or have their holdings reduced. This proved to be the final straw for the remaining Seminoles, and the entire party prepared to leave for their former homeland.[71]

On August 1, 1861, Seminole leaders in the Indian Territory concluded a treaty with Confederate Commissioner Albert Pike that effectively signaled the beginning of the tribe's involvement in the American Civil War. Principal Chief John Jumper sent emissaries to the Mexican Seminoles with orders to return to the Indian Territory and support the war effort. Consequently, on August 25, those remaining in Coahuila set out for the Seminole Nation. Confederate Captain Buck Barry furnished an escort and rations to the party en route to the Red River.[72] The Seminoles left behind them in Mexico the main body of maroons at Parras, together with a few more recent runaways at Nacimiento.

By this time, a large proportion of the total population of Seminole maroons was living in Mexico, the remainder having stayed behind in the Indian Territory. Most of the maroons in Coahuila would have no further contact with the Seminoles. From this point on, they would be destined to create their own exclusive and dramatic history as they continued to pursue that elusive notion of freedom on the border.

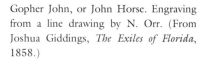

Gopher John, or John Horse. Engraving from a line drawing by N. Orr. (From Joshua Giddings, *The Exiles of Florida*, 1858.)

Wild Cat. Engraving from a line drawing by N. Orr. (From Joshua Giddings, *The Exiles of Florida*, 1858 .)

Seminole delegates in Washington, 1826. *From left:* Sarparkee Yohola, Fasatchee Emathla, Jumper [?], Abraham (leader of the Alachua maroons, who served as interpreter and counsellor to the Seminole chiefs), Billy Bowlegs, Chocote Tustenuggee. A drawing from a photograph made in New York and published in *The Illustrated London News,* May 21, 1853. (Courtesy of National Archives.)

White fears of African and Indian collusion were realized with the "Dade Massacre" and the onset of the Second Seminole War. This propagandistic wood engraving of 1836 was designed to gain early and strong support for the cause. (Courtesy of Library of Congress.)

92

This silver peace medal of the 1850s proclaims boldly, "Mexico [sic] a los Seminoles." The medal might have been given to Wild Cat by the Mexican government as evidence of the treaty signed on July 26, 1852, under the terms of which the Seminoles, Mascogos, and Kickapoos received land grants at Nacimiento, Coahuila. The medal would have been worn around the neck, and the reverse shows signs of wear. (Courtesy of Thomas Gilcrease Institute of American History and Art.)

Gravestone of Sergeant John Kibbitts (or Kibbetts), Seminole Indian Scouts Cemetery, Brackettville. Kibbetts headed the negotiations with United States military officials that led to the removal of most of the Mascogos from Coahuila to West Texas. The maroons claimed later that Kibbetts had in his possession a "treaty" stipulating that the military would remove the group to the Seminole Nation in Indian Territory, but he would allow nobody to see it. They stated that the document was destroyed in the fire that burned down Kibbetts's house after his death in September 1878. (Courtesy of Scott Braucher.)

(Above left) Lieutenant John Lapham Bullis. Bullis led the Seminole Negro Indian Scouts during the height of the Texas Indian Wars. Sergeant John Ward, Trumpeter Isaac Payne, and Private Pompey Factor won Medals of Honor for rescuing this white officer from almost certain death at the hands of Comanches in 1875. (Courtesy of Institute of Texan Cultures.)

(Above right) Colonel Ranald Slidell Mackenzie. Mackenzie had overall command of the scouts during the Remolino raid and the Palo Duro campaign. (Courtesy of National Archives.)

Medal of Honor winner Pompey Factor in old age. (Courtesy of William Loren Katz.)

Seminole Negro Indian Scouts, 1889. *From left:* Plenty Payne, Billy July, Ben July, Dembo Factor, Ben Wilson, John July, William Shields. The group in this photograph includes both active and retired scouts. Dembo Factor took part in the "Dade Massacre" and after removal was kidnapped by slavers in the Indian Territory. He escaped to Coahuila with John Horse and returned later to Texas and became a scout. By the time of this photograph, John Horse and John Kibbetts had died, and Factor had assumed the leadership of the Texas group. (Courtesy of Institute of Texan Cultures.)

The Scouts, *circa* 1890. (Courtesy of Museum of the Big Bend, Sul Ross State University.)

To all whom it may Concern.

Know ye, That _David Bowlegs_
a _First Sergeant_ of ~~Captain~~ _1st Lieut. John L. Bullis 24th Inf._
Company, (Detachment Regiment of _Seminole Negro Indian Scouts_
~~VOLUNTEERS~~ who was enrolled on the _twenty fifth_ day of _April_
one thousand eight hundred and _seventy nine_ to serve _One_ ~~year~~ ~~at~~
~~during the war,~~ is hereby **Discharged** from the service of the United States
this _First_ day of _May_ ,1880 , at _Fort Clark,_
Texas by reason of _Expiration of term of service_
(_No objection to his being re-enlisted is known to exist."_)
Said _David Bowlegs_ was born in _____
in the State of _Florida_ , is _forty six_ years of age,
five feet _eight_ inches high, _Black_ complexion _Black_ eyes,
Black hair, and by occupation, when enrolled, a _Scout_
Given at _Fort Clark Texas_ this _First_ day of
May 1880 .

[☞ *This sentence will be erased should there be anything
in the conduct or physical condition of the soldier
rendering him unfit for the Army.*

[A. G. O., No. 99.] _Character_ _Good_

D S Stanley
Colonel, 22d Infantry
Commanding ~~the Reg't~~ Post

John L. Bullis's
1st Lieut. 24th Infty, Comd'g Com Negro Indian Scouts

Army discharge papers of First Sergeant David Bowlegs, May 1, 1880. The following month, Bowlegs began to investigate the possibility of returning to the Indian Territory. In December 1882, he, his wife Fanny, and their nine children moved from Fort Clark to the Seminole Nation, providing a catalyst for other maroons wishing to immigrate. (Courtesy of Western History Collections, University of Oklahoma.)

96

Scouts Corporal Fay July *left* and Private William Shields *circa* 1895. (Courtesy of Institute of Texan Cultures.)

Joe Coon, son of John Horse. Coon might have accompanied Horse on his final journey from Nacimiento to Mexico City in 1882. (Courtesy of Whitehead Memorial Museum.)

John Jefferson, son of Joe Coon and grandson of John Horse, *circa* 1900. Jefferson is wearing the trumpeter's uniform of Troop D, Tenth Cavalry, and sports a marksman's medal. A descendant told the author that Jefferson fought in the Spanish-American War, served in World War I, chased Pancho Villa with Pershing, and had seven wives. He served with the scouts from 1905 until the unit disbanded in 1914. (Courtesy of Institute of Texan Cultures.)

In this extremely rare turn-of-the-century photograph, members of the maroon community at Fort Clark appear dressed for a special occasion. (Courtesy of Whitehead Memorial Museum.)

Sampson and Mary July *seated* with their son First Sergeant Ben July *left* at the Seminole maroon village on Las Moras Creek, *circa* 1900. (Courtesy of Museum of the Big Bend, Sul Ross State University.)

The Seminole Negro Indian Scouts in 1903 pattern dress uniform, *circa* 1905. *Front row, from left:* Thoma Daniels, George Kibbetts, John Jefferson, Sam Washington, Curley Jefferson, unidentified. *Back row:* at left Fa July, second right Willie Wilson, the remainder unidentified. (Courtesy of Seminole Indian Scout Cemetery Association.)

First Sergeant Charles Daniels with his wife Mary and daughter Tina, *circa* 1905. Daniels first enlisted with the scouts in 1871 and saw service during the most intense period of the Texas Indian wars. He retired in 1909, just five years before the unit disbanded. The stripes on his lower sleeves show the old scout's long history of enlistment. (Courtesy of Institute of Texan Cultures.)

Last mount of the Seminole Negro Indian Scouts, Fort Clark, 1914. (Courtesy of Institute of Texan Cultures.)

Blas Payne, grandson of Medal of Honor winner Trumpeter Isaac Payne, 1982. After the scouts disbanded, many of the men went to work as hands on local ranches and became well known and respected for their horsemanship and livestock skills. For most of his life, Blas Payne lived in the commanding officer's quarters at Camp Pena Colorado that his grandfather had helped build, and worked on the Combs Ranch east of Alpine. He was considered by many to be the finest cowboy ever to ride a horse in the Big Bend country. (Copyright *Houston Chronicle.*)

Chink houses of the maroons, Brackettville, 1917. (Courtesy of Seminole Indian Scout Cemetery Association.)

Mount Gilead Baptist Church, Brackettville, 1990. So central was this building to the community that the maroons moved it from their village at Fort Clark to Brackettville after the army expelled them from the reservation in 1914. In 1924, the group was reported to be practicing within these walls an exotic syncretic religion, incorporating African, Native American, Baptist, Presbyterian, and Roman Catholic elements. (Courtesy of Scott Braucher.)

St. John's Church, Brackettville, 1990. Factionalism at Mount Gilead apparently led to the creation of a new congregation and the building of this church a short distance away. (Courtesy of Scott Braucher.)

The Seminole Indian Scouts Cemetery, Brackettville, 1990. This photograph, taken from behind the headstones, shows the oldest graves, in the southern corner of the cemetery. Founded in 1872, close to the maroons' village on Las Moras Creek, the site remains a focus of group pride and community action. (Courtesy of Scott Braucher.)

Billy Joe Pierce, 1990. A descendant of Medal of Honor winner Sergeant John Ward, Pierce is the current president of the Seminole Indian Scout Cemetery Association and the owner of BJ's Bar, a social hub for the Brackettville group. (Courtesy of Scott Braucher.)

William "Dub" Warrior, great-grand-nephew of John Horse's son Joe Coon, 1988. Warrior has been a leading force in the community for many years, is a source of much information on the scouts, and actively keeps the military tradition alive. (Courtesy of William "Dub" Warrior.)

Miss Charles Emily Wilson, 1990. "Tribal historian" Miss Charles is one of the last of the "Seminoles" to have been born in the maroon village on the Fort Clark reservation. She is the granddaughter of Sampson July and the daughter of Rebecca Wilson, one of Kenneth Porter's principal informants in the 1940s. A former schoolteacher and an educator for more than forty years, Miss Charles continues to be a pillar of the community, passing on the traditions and helping to organize the annual Juneteenth and Seminole Day celebrations. (Courtesy of Scott Braucher.)

The group celebrates Juneteenth 1990 with a traditional American parade—floats and all—through the streets of Brackettville. (Courtesy of Scott Braucher.)

Juneteenth parade winner 1990, "Aloha" float. In a piece of pure Americana, Seminole maroon descendant Beverly Ward presents the trophy to Hispanic children dressed as Hawaiians during an African American emancipation celebration on the border. (Courtesy of Scott Braucher.)

Following the rigors of the Juneteenth parade, the descendants of the maroons take to the shade at the rear of the Seminole Indian Scout Cemetery Association building and enjoy Texas barbecue and good conversation. (Courtesy of Scott Braucher.)

4

The Seminole Negro Indian Scouts

By the fall of 1861, all of the Seminoles in Mexico had returned to the Indian Territory, and most of the 350 maroons were living at the Laguna de Parras in southwestern Coahuila.[1] The Mascogos camped at first at the Hacienda de Los Hornos, but soon afterwards they established their main settlement at the Hacienda El Burro about halfway between the lake and the city of Parras. Here, they settled in small family groups and tried again to farm and hunt, but they never would be allowed to live in peace at this location. During the next decade, the maroons would experience local conflicts and foreign wars, poverty, hunger, and displacement, prompting their continued search for a better alternative.

For several years, as members of the garrison at Parras, the Mascogos helped defend the devastated Laguna against Apache depredations and received the scalp bounty as compensation. Although they were adept Indian fighters, however, the constant raids depleted their numbers and disrupted their settlements continually. Thomas Factor was shot and killed, Friday Bowlegs lost his wife and several children, and Jack Bowlegs lost his entire family during attacks by Indian raiders on the maroons' village. The men of the Wilson and Grayson families mounted a successful retaliatory expedition, but again the Mascogos suffered heavy losses in their victory.[2]

The power struggle between Benito Juárez, leader of the Mexican Reform, and Santiago Vidaurri, governor of Nuevo León y Coahuila, also deeply affected the security and stability of the area. The residents of the Laguna remained in a constant state of unease because of the threat of revolution, military retaliation, and civil war.[3] But the French invasion of Mexico under the Emperor Maximilian and the subsequent occupation of Coahuila would prove to be the greatest source of disturbance to the Mascogos.

French troops under Brigadier General Armand Alexandre de Castagny entered Saltillo on August 20, 1864, and a few days later they pacified Parras. Soon afterwards, they destroyed the settlements around the Laguna and burned El Burro. The Mascogos retained a tradition that John Horse, his son Joe Coon, and David Bowlegs persuaded the invaders not to burn their dwellings. The French commanders then ordered the maroons to return to Nacimiento so as not to be confused with Mexicans, but John Horse remained at Parras with most of the group. It has been said that Horse joined the Mexican army against Maximilian's troops and that his exploits were so successful that he was commissioned colonel. John Horse did become known on the border as El Coronel Juan Caballo, but more likely, his office resulted from service against raiding Indians rather than French invaders. As a further reward, the Mexican government gave John Horse a silver-mounted saddle with a gold-plated pummel in the shape of a horse's head. He used that saddle when riding his favorite horse American.[4]

Evidently, the Mascogos were divided over whether they should oppose the French. By 1865, the threat of filibustering raids from Texas had been removed, and John Kibbetts and a large number of maroons felt it safe to return to Nacimiento. The Bruner families, meanwhile, chose to settle near the Gulf of Mexico at Matamoros, across from Brownsville. Elijah Daniels and a party of Creek blacks had left the Indian Territory after the main migrations and had joined the Mascogos in Mexico. After slavery was abolished in the United States, that group left Parras and returned to Texas, settling on Medina Creek in Uvalde County. The main body of Mascogos remained at the Laguna under John Horse until late 1870, however. Due to pressure from external forces, the maroons had split into factions, and the community had become fragmentary and dislocated.[5]

The Kibbetts group returned to Nacimiento to find that all of the Southern Kickapoos, with a population of around 950 divided into four bands, had removed from Kansas and settled there.[6] According to Chief Nokoaht, when the Kickapoos arrived they found around ten black families and some northern whites who had taken refuge there during the American Civil War. The blacks had established thriving farms in a valley alongside of the San Juan Sabinas and paid the Mexican government rent and taxes in produce and stock. They raised cattle, sheep, and horses, and grew corn, pumpkins, sugar cane, and sweet potatoes.[7] These families, which may have included both Mascogos and more recent immigrants, subsequently would become identified with the Kibbetts group.

Kibbetts's followers were concerned by the presence of the Southern Kickapoos at the hacienda. On October 8, 1864, Machemanet's band had asked permission to remain in the municipality of Múzquiz until they could solicit a permanent place of residence from the president of the republic. Their request was granted, and the entire tribe settled at Nacimiento the following spring. In October 1866, the Kickapoos and Potawatomies were granted two *sitios de ganado mayor*, or 8676 acres, which had been appropriated from the Sánchez Navarro estate and abandoned by the Seminoles and Mascogos in 1861. The maroons feared that their claim to the Nacimiento grant, which derived from their agreement with the Mexican authorities in 1852, had been overlooked, and they determined to reestablish and secure their title.

Once the French had evacuated Coahuila in late July 1866, John Horse turned his attention to gaining recognition from the Mexican government of the Mascogos' right to own land at the hacienda. This would furnish him the option of returning there with his followers from Parras. On February 20, 1867, therefore, John Horse and John Kibbetts requested land at Nacimiento equal to that which the Mexicans had granted the Kickapoos. The authorities approved the Mascogos' petition, and later that year, President Juárez confirmed the terms of the 1852 agreement.[8]

The maroons established a community on their old land grant some five miles south of the Kickapoo villages,[9] but remained unsettled and discontented. The threat of Indian raids remained continuous, and once again, the men were expected to engage in lengthy expeditions against hostile bands. The land at the hacienda, meanwhile, failed to yield the expected returns. The Mascogos accused the Mexicans of stealing their horses and robbing them, and John Horse was accused of leading raids into Texas to supplement the maroons' dwindling herds.[10] Though their liberty had been secured, it seemed that in Coahuila, the maroons never would be permitted to live in peace, or establish the thriving agrarian community of which they dreamed. As conflict and poverty came to dominate their existence, forcing them to live "in a state of semi-barbarism," they thought more and more of removing to a more settled and productive environment.[11]

By the late 1860s, American officials were suggesting that the Mascogos return to the United States as part of a policy aimed at relocating border Indian bands hostile to white settlers. The annual reports of the commissioner of Indian affairs for 1868 and 1869 recommended that the Mexican Kickapoos at Nacimiento be returned to the United States to put an end to their raids on settlements in Texas.[12] Commissioner Ely S. Parker explained later, however, that he had intended his recommendation to include the Seminole blacks, who could be resettled "among their people from whom they separated." Clearly, the commissioner envisaged at this stage that the government would relocate the maroons in the Indian Territory.[13]

Citizens of Texas were prepared to take the initiative, also, in putting a stop to the continuous raids by bands of Indians that had taken refuge in Mexico. Popular meetings resulted in the appointment of an investigative committee designed to bring the problem to the attention of the state and national governments. The committee chose one S. S. Brown to undertake a mission to Mexico to confer with Indian leaders and discover their disposition towards returning to the United States. If they displayed a willingness to return, Brown would act as mediator between the groups and the Mexican and American governments to ensure their removal.

On June 15, 1868, Brown obtained permission from Victoriano Cepada, governor of Coahuila, to proceed to Múzquiz and confer with the various leaders. Brown then wrote to M. Menchaca y Longoria, mayor of Múzquiz, that he hoped to meet with all the bands living in Coahuila that formerly had resided in the United States. He asked Menchaca to notify the various tribes, "Kickapoos—Seminole, Potawatomie, Lipan, Delaware, Mescalero, Muscayus [Mascogos] etc.," to send their headmen to confer with him on the subject of removal. As a result, public meetings were held at the courthouse in Múzquiz on July 23 and July 26.[14] Although these meetings failed to induce any of the groups to remove at this time, the Seminole maroons seriously began to consider returning across the border and were made aware that this would be welcomed. In the future, they would be more receptive to such overtures.

In 1869, another smallpox epidemic struck Nacimiento, quickly wreaking havoc upon the Kickapoo population and threatening to decimate the maroon community.[15] The Mascogos wished now more than ever to leave the hacienda. During the summer, John Kibbetts sent his son Bob on an investigative mission to the Seminole Nation in the Indian Territory. Major Zenas Bliss reported later, "The Indians there stated that they were anxious to have the Seminole negroes come over and join them."[16] During the Civil War there had been a revival of the alliance between the Seminole traditionalists and the blacks, and the tribal leadership at that time rested firmly in the grasp of the conservatives. This best explains the positive response to the Mascogos' petition.

Bob Kibbetts would have been impressed by the separate and thriving maroon communities that were arising in the Seminole Nation during Reconstruction and by the comparative ease of the freedmen's lot. Not only had slavery been abolished, but also the Seminoles were incorporating the blacks into the tribe with full citizenship rights. The Indians treated the freedmen equally before the law, allowed them to organize socially, economically, and politically, gave them an equal share in annuities and the tribal domain, and permitted them to send representatives to the tribal council. No doubt Kibbetts returned to Mexico with glowing reports and positive recommendations.

By 1870, as a result of a decade of continuous turmoil, the Seminole maroons living on the border of Texas and Mexico had split into four main groups. John Horse and the main body of 150 still were based at Parras; John Kibbetts and 100 others were residing at Nacimiento; several families had moved to Matamoros; and the Elijah Daniels band had settled in Texas. The disillusioned and impoverished Mascogos at Nacimiento were determined to rejoin their kinsmen in the Indian Territory, and the other groups soon would follow their lead.

In response to an invitation from Colonel Jacob De Gress, the commander at Fort Duncan, to discuss the possibility of the maroons' return to their former homeland, John Kibbetts crossed over to the post on March 17. Ever the innovative border diplomats, the maroons used this initiative to advantage in negotiating a favorable agreement for themselves with United States officials. Kibbetts requested permission for his group to remove to the Seminole Nation and asked for food and forage while in transit, adding that although they were poor, his people were willing to work. Clearly influenced by the earlier recommendations of the commissioners of Indian affairs, De Gress gave Kibbetts rations and feed and a document granting the Mascogos permission to cross the Rio Grande and camp on the military reservation while the Department of Texas considered their request. The department commander approved the De Gress initiative on March 25, setting in motion the process that would lead eventually to the return to Texas of most of the Seminole maroons living in Coahuila.[17]

John Kibbetts returned to Nacimiento to discuss the meeting with his
people and prepare for removal. Shortly afterwards, the department
instructed Captain Frank Perry, successor to De Gress as commander at
Fort Duncan, to receive the group. On May 15, Perry suggested that as
they were familiar with the river crossings used by the Kickapoos, the
maroons could be useful in helping to curtail Indian raids. Official
approval came quickly, and Perry received instructions to bring about
their removal and encourage them to remain at Fort Duncan. He should
issue them rations, consisting of fresh beef or salt meat, corn meal, hard
bread or flour, sugar, and coffee, and ascertain whether the men would
enlist in service against the Kickapoos and Lipans.[18]

Captain Perry had expected the main body of maroons to remove to
Texas by May 15.[19] By mid-June, however, they still had not arrived,
and Perry crossed over to Nacimiento to confer with John Kibbetts.
Their principal concern was that they would have to pay customs duties
on their stock as they were not United States citizens. Perry made an
agreement with the collector of revenues at Eagle Pass until the treasury
department could attend to the matter. The maroons wished to remove
to the military reservation at Fort Duncan and proceed in due course to
the Seminole Nation. They requested rations and permission to hunt
and work while at the post and expressed willingness to enlist as scouts
if they received the pay of regular troops. Perry was quick to add that
he believed them to be "well capable of performing the duties of
Scouts."[20]

Perry and Kibbetts finally arrived at an agreement that the Seminole
blacks later would term "the treaty." The maroons' understanding of
this was that if they moved to Texas and the men enrolled as scouts, the
United States authorities would pay their removal expenses and provide
them with money, rations, land, stock, and agricultural equipment until
they could return to the Indian Territory.[21] If it ever were put in writing,
however, that document failed to survive. Consequently, the authority
under which it was concluded and the details of its terms would prove
points of great contention in the future.[22]

As the Mascogos prepared to leave Nacimiento, Perry's initiative
received official approval. The secretary of war responded to his suggestion that the services of the blacks could be of use to the military by
authorizing the enlistment of the men as Indian scouts, providing only
that the number did not exceed the Department of Texas quota of two
hundred. On July 1, the maroons were invited to cross over to Fort

Duncan, and the Kibbetts group arrived at the post three days later. John Horse and his party remained for the moment at Parras, but it was their intention to remove to Texas as soon as was practicable.[23]

Major Bliss, who had succeeded Perry as post commander, received the maroons at Fort Duncan. During the course of several conversations with John Kibbetts, Bliss learned of the leader's wishes. Kibbetts wanted to return to the Seminole Nation or receive land in Texas which he could cultivate free from attack, and he sought permission to work and hunt in the vicinity of the fort. The maroons wished to settle on Elm Creek, situated on the military reservation some five miles above the post, where there was good arable land. They were "willing and anxious" to become scouts and asked only the same pay that the Tonkawa scouts received when actually employed in the field. Bliss believed that as they were good trailers and understood Indian behavior, the blacks would make excellent scouts. He asked for authorization to enlist twenty of the men, allow the maroons to cultivate as much ground as they wished on Elm Creek, and grant them permission to hunt and work around Fort Duncan.[24]

The Department of Texas authorized the enlistment of twenty of the maroons, or such number as Bliss found fit for service, as scouts for six months. The army would give them the same compensation as cavalry privates with the exception of John Kibbetts, who would receive the pay of sergeant.[25] Technically, the men would become Indian scouts, for that was the only option available to the department. No provision existed for enlisting a detachment of maroons into the ranks as scouts in any other way. This association caused confusion in the minds of United States officials unfamiliar with the situation and led to the popular misconception that the Seminole blacks were Indian. It also would confound simplistic efforts to classify the group, and cause serious problems for both the maroons and the government for the next two decades.

The military authorities allowed the maroons to settle on the reserve, cultivate the land, and tend to their livestock, the entire group being under the jurisdiction and protection of the commander at Fort Duncan. As a result, they were "treated and controlled at this Post, exactly as camp followers."[26] The group went into camp on Elm Creek, and while the women planted gardens and the old men and those unfit for service sought work in the surrounding settlements to support their families, Sergeant John Kibbetts and ten privates were mustered into service on

August 16, 1870, as a new military unit that came to be known as the Seminole Negro Indian Scouts.[27]

The military furnished the enlisted scouts with rations, arms, and ammunition. At first, they were expected to provide their own mounts, but later they came to rely heavily upon horses captured from Indians. They were not required to wear uniform and dressed in modified Indian fashion supplemented by clothing associated more with frontier whites, such as boots, hats, neckerchiefs, and jackets. On occasion, some even wore buffalo-horn war bonnets. Only later would they come to wear the uniform of army scouts.

Sergeant Kibbetts, who also had given his former Seminole busk name of Sittertastonacky (Chitto Tustenuggee), or Snake Warrior, when enrolling, assumed general command of the unit. Described by Bliss as "a very smart and reliable negro," Kibbetts was acknowledged as leader and obeyed implicitly by his men. His son Bob, who later received a promotion to corporal, assisted him.[28] John Kibbetts remained the leader of the scouts until his death in 1878. David Bowlegs succeeded him, followed by Sampson July, and eventually, Bob Kibbetts became sergeant and assumed that role. Although he came over to Fort Duncan in the winter of 1870 and remained in Texas for several years, John Horse never served with the scouts but acted instead as adviser to John Kibbetts.

Between 1870 and 1875, the offers of United States officials persuaded members of the other Seminole maroon groups living in Mexico and Texas to remove to Fort Duncan. Most of the Matamoros families and the Elijah Daniels band came in to the post in the summer and fall of 1871, and eighteen of their men joined the scouts the following spring. In response to promises that he would receive the same treatment as Kibbetts and have the duties paid on his property and stock, John Horse had crossed over to the military reservation in early December 1870, reporting that the rest of his band was on the road and would be arriving soon. Some of his followers removed to Duncan in late 1872 and early 1873, and a dozen or so joined the scouts. Others came over later in the winter of 1873 and still others during 1874 and 1875. Again, several enlisted along with some Texas freedmen, Mexican blacks, and Mexicans who either had married Seminole maroon women or otherwise become associated with the group. Later, former black cavalrymen and infantrymen, many with Native American connections; other American freedmen; and several Indians from border bands would serve with the scouts.²⁹ Most of the Mascogos at Parras, however, preferred to return to Nacimiento during the 1870s.³⁰

In early June 1872, Lieutenant Colonel Wesley Merritt, the commanding officer at nearby Fort Clark, requested permission to enlist as many as ten Seminole maroons as scouts at that post to combat depredating Indian bands. On June 17, Major Henry Merriam, in command at Fort Duncan, recommended increasing the number of scouts at his post from thirty to forty to meet the need for mounted men to police the border. The commander of the Department of Texas authorized their enlistment with a view to transferring twenty-five of the scouts immediately to serve at Fort Clark.

Members of the Daniels band told Merriam that they wished to remove to Fort Clark to be able to support themselves better. Soon afterward, the Bruner family joined the group, and the band could claim seventeen enlisted scouts, mostly from the Daniels, Bruner, Payne, and Wilson families. Additional band members suitable for service could be enlisted at Clark. The reduction in numbers at Duncan would be offset by more recruits from the Kibbetts group and later, from Mexico. The scouts within the Daniels band insisted upon being accompanied by their families, and that was authorized. Consequently, the entire party removed to Fort Clark by horse and wagon under military escort in early August 1872. The band built homes on the lush wooded banks of Las Moras Creek some three miles south of the fort, below the post garden. John Kibbetts and his supporters would remain at Fort Duncan another four years before they, too, transferred to Fort Clark and settled nearby.³¹

The Seminole maroons possessed qualities that made them extremely useful to the frontier army, and they were recruited heavily as scouts. They understood and spoke both English and Spanish and could converse in "Mexican," the *lingua franca* of the region. In addition, they had lived in the border country for more than twenty years and knew the terrain and the Indian bands that inhabited or frequented the area. The maroons were hardened and proven warriors, also, and experts in frontier combat.³²

Military officials put these skills to use straightaway. Between 1870 and 1872, they employed John Horse and John Kibbetts as mediators during negotiations with the Mexican Kickapoos over that tribe's proposed return to the Indian Territory. During the second week of February 1871, Horse accompanied a deputation of five Kickapoo men and six women that journeyed from Múzquiz to Fort Duncan to begin talks on the removal. Later, Kibbetts displayed his cognizance of Kick-apoo customs and behavior in sensing the Indians' hostility to the American proposal and might have saved the life of Major Bliss by advising him not to visit their camp.[33]

The maroons were skillful trackers and often could pick up a trail many weeks old. On one occasion on the Red River, a scout was able to inform his commanding officer that they were following a band of Kiowas consisting of one warrior, five women, several children, six horses, and four lodges. Though he had not seen his quarry, the scout was able to deduce further from clues left on the trail that the band had provisions of corn and buffalo meat, the warrior was sick, and one of the horses was half blind.[34] Regularly throughout the Texas Indian wars, the Seminole Negro Indian Scouts were described as faithful and loyal to their commanding officers, excellent horsemen, fine marksmen, fearless fighters, and highly effective in hand-to-hand combat.[35]

The scouts had great powers of endurance and were able to engage in many fatiguing campaigns without rest or food. At other times, they were able to get by on the barest minimum. Frederick Phelps, a contemporary officer, noted that they could go longer on half rations than any other body of men he had known, and if there were no other food available, they would resort to eating rattlesnake.[36] That the scouts were true survivors was displayed most dramatically during their greatest feat of endurance in early 1879. Thirty-nine of them took part in an expedition charged with apprehending Mescaleros who had absconded from their reservation at Fort Stanton, New Mexico. The United States troops chased the Indians across the desert in freezing weather for a month. By the end of February, they had been without water for several days and seemed about to perish. At the height of their distress, First Sergeant David Bowlegs managed to discover and unearth an underground desert spring and saved the expedition, the troops later naming the spot "Salvation Springs." The scouts trailed the Mescaleros all the way back to their reservation before returning to Texas. They finally rode into Fort Clark after eighty days in the field, having covered more than twelve hundred miles.[37]

Contemporaries lavished praise upon the scouts, and terms such as "extraordinary," "uncanny," and even "superhuman," have been used to describe their feats.[38] Their commanding officers led the acclaim. Zenas Bliss described them as "excellent hunters and trailers, and splendid fighters" and Lieutenant John Lapham Bullis reported them to be "fine trailers and good marksmen and [very] useful on this frontier."[39] An 1876 description termed them "the terror to marauding Indians,"[40] and a contemporary black trooper of the Ninth Cavalry later recounted that they came to be considered "the best body of scouts, trailers and Indian fighters ever engaged in the Government service along the border."[41] The scouts proved to be so successful that Colonel Loomis Langdon was led to declare in 1898 that they had fully "justified the action of the Government in availing itself of their services."[42]

The duties of the scouts between 1870 and 1872 mainly had involved patrolling West Texas for Indian raiders, and they had yet to engage in a serious skirmish. The commanding officer at Fort Duncan reported, nevertheless, that they already had proven to be very faithful and efficient trailers and guides.[43] On March 6, 1873, Lieutenant Bullis of the Twenty-Fourth Colored Infantry, who had considerable experience commanding black troops, received the command of the scouts.[44] Bullis's accession marked the beginning of a truly remarkable eight year period for the unit. Between March 1873 and June 1881, when Bullis relinquished the command, the Seminole Negro Indian Scouts engaged in twenty-six usually lengthy expeditions, twelve of them major, and though often heavily outnumbered by their adversaries, had not a single man killed or seriously wounded in action. Although they never numbered more than fifty, moreover, the scouts won an unprecedented four coveted Medals of Honor at the height of the Texas Indian wars. During this period, the Seminole maroons played a major role in helping to clear West Texas of Indian bands hostile to white settlement of the area.[45]

The scouts would engage in their first major expedition in May 1873 as part of Colonel Ranald Mackenzie's force that attacked the Mexican Kickapoos at Remolino. These Kickapoos had removed from Kansas and the Indian Territory to Coahuila during the 1860s. Texas militiamen had set upon them twice during the journey. Once settled across the border, the Kickapoos had retaliated with a continuous stream of raids into Texas. They had come to rely for their livelihood upon plunder from these raids, having found a ready market for stolen stock in Múzquiz and other surrounding towns. Between 1865 and 1868, Mexican Kickapoo raiders had killed sixty-two Texans and wounded many others. The upper Rio Grande area of Texas counted only one-tenth of the livestock in 1872 that it had held in 1865, and its flourishing horse-raising industry had been wiped out. By 1873, total regional losses to the raiders were estimated to be forty-eight million dollars.[46]

Eventually, United States government officials took action to put an end to these raids. On March 31, 1873, the Bureau of Indian Affairs appointed two commissioners, Henry Atkinson and Thomas Williams, to bring about the peaceful return of the Mexican Kickapoos to the United States. Even as Atkinson and Williams made their way to confer with Coahuilan officials, however, the Kickapoos committed further depredations in West Texas. In early April, a raiding party from Mexico stole a horse herd from the Delorus ranch just eight miles south of Fort Clark. On the 13th, officers at the post sent out fifteen Seminole Negro Indian Scouts to pick up the trail. Though they could not overtake the raiding party, the scouts found evidence implicating the Kickapoos. Soon after, at Howard's Wells in the Nueces valley, a band of Kickapoos, Lipans, and Mescaleros engaged in a raid in which an officer of the Ninth Cavalry was killed. In the light of these latest hostilities, United States military officials determined to use more direct means to put an end to the Mexican Kickapoo menace.[47]

Mackenzie's Fourth Cavalry was dispatched from Forts Richardson and Concho to meet the Kickapoo challenge.[48] In April, Secretary of War William Belknap and General Philip H. Sheridan, commander of the Military Division of the Missouri, instructed Mackenzie, "To control and hold down the situation, and to do it in your own way. [When] you begin, let it be a campaign of annihilation, obliteration and destruction." Having been given free rein, Mackenzie determined upon a surprise attack on the Mexican Kickapoo villages.[49]

Army officers appreciated the importance to the campaign of the Seminole Negro Indian Scouts, who had lived close by the Kickapoo villages in Coahuila and were familiar with both the area and their adversaries. The scouts, warming to the opportunity to gain recompense for the thirty head of horses the Kickapoos had stolen from them earlier in 1851, contacted their kinsmen at Nacimiento. The Mascogos, concerned about their land rights at the hacienda, apparently welcomed the chance to conspire against their neighbors, and during the course of the next month, furnished valuable information on the three Kickapoo, Lipan, and Mescalero villages situated just north of Nacimiento and west of Remolino, a Mexican town on the San Rodrigo River.[50]

Mackenzie completed his preparations for the expedition by mid-May. At eleven o'clock on the night of the 16th, the scouts reported that they had learned from Nacimiento that the Kickapoo warriors had ridden off to the west that morning on a hunting expedition, leaving the villages virtually unprotected. Mackenzie realized that his chance to strike had arrived and put his plan immediately into effect.[51]

The order to march came quickly, and at one o'clock on the afternoon of May 17, Mackenzie's troops set out for Mexico. Included in his force of 411 men were thirty-four Seminole Negro Indian Scouts, eighteen from Fort Clark and sixteen from Fort Duncan, under the command of Bullis. The scouts rode in the advance guard behind Mackenzie. The column crossed the Rio Grande at sunset and rode the sixty-three miles to its destination during the night. By sunrise, Mackenzie's troops had moved into position to attack the three Indian villages on the south side of the San Rodrigo. Each village averaged between fifty and sixty lodges, the largest village being that of the Kickapoos, which also was situated first in the line of attack. The charge came as a complete surprise to the Indians. The Kickapoos scattered with troops in pursuit, and within minutes their village was in ruins.[52]

Mackenzie's men next turned their attention to the other two villages, but most of the Lipans and Mescaleros had escaped to the Santa Rosa Mountains during the attack on the Kickapoos. Scout Renty Grayson lassoed and captured Lipan Principal Chief Costilietos, however, as he was fleeing through the bushes. The scouts also captured the leader's daughter Teresita and took her back to Texas. Later she would bear scout James Perryman two children, including a son Warren Perryman, who served as deacon in the church at Brackettville for many years and became a leading figure in the community. Teresita died in 1881 and was buried in the Seminole Negro Indian Scouts' cemetery near Fort Clark.[53]

During the attack, Mackenzie's men killed nineteen Indians, took prisoner forty women and children, and captured sixty-five horses, some still bearing Texas brands. The troops, meanwhile, lost just one man killed and two wounded. They next destroyed the Indian villages, burning all the lodges and trappings. Mackenzie's force then set off on the return journey, choosing a more sparsely settled western route to avoid attack. The column could move only slowly as the men were tired and hampered by the prisoners, and the scouts guarded the rear and flanks against ambush. On several occasions throughout the night, they sighted hostile Indians, but the troops managed to recross safely into Texas in the early morning of May 19. The scouts had taken part in an

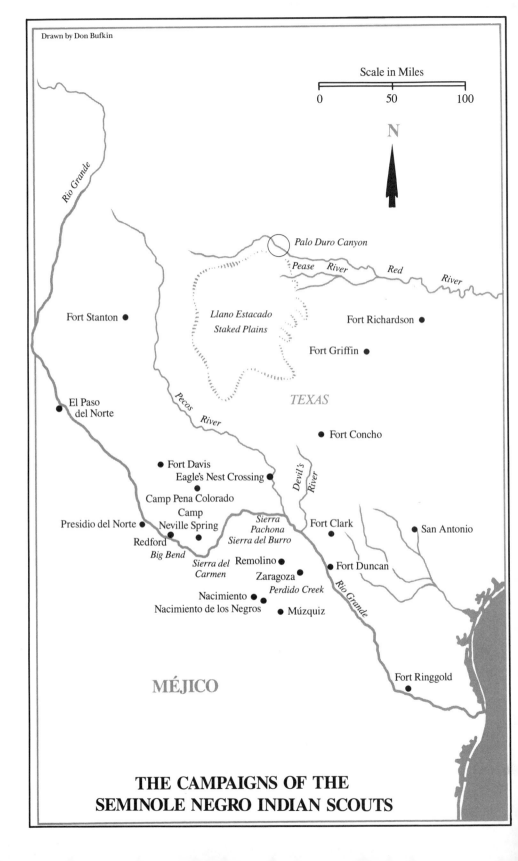

Drawn by Don Bufkin

Scale in Miles

0   50   100

N

Rio Grande

Palo Duro Canyon

Pease   River   Red   *River*

Fort Stanton ●

*Llano Estacado
Staked Plains*

Fort Richardson ●

Fort Griffin ●

*Pecos

River*

TEXAS

El Paso
del Norte ●

● Fort Concho

● Fort Davis

Eagle's Nest Crossing ●

*Devil's

River*

Camp Pena Colorado ●

Camp
Neville Spring

*Sierra
Pachona
Sierra del Burro*

Fort Clark
●

● San Antonio

Presidio del Norte ●

Redford ●

Big Bend

*Sierra del
Carmen*

Remolino ●

Zaragoza ●

Perdido Creek

Nacimiento ●
Nacimiento de los Negros   ● Múzquiz

● Fort Duncan

Rio Grande

Fort Ringgold
●

MÉJICO

THE CAMPAIGNS OF THE
SEMINOLE NEGRO INDIAN SCOUTS

expedition that had covered more than 140 miles in thirty-eight hours. Most of their riding had taken place in intense heat, and they had not slept or eaten much, yet the mission had been a complete success.[54]

The scouts had played a major role in the expedition that effectively put an end to Kickapoo raids in West Texas. In his official report of the action, Mackenzie called special attention to their contribution. Bullis was promoted to first lieutenant. The American commissioners used the prisoners taken during the attack as incentive to persuade the remaining Kickapoos in Mexico to return to the United States. They would be reunited with their kinsmen only if they agreed to remove to the Indian Territory. Continued activity by Mackenzie's troops along the border doubtless influenced most of the Kickapoos to accept the commissioners' terms. The scouts continued to patrol the north bank of the Rio Grande, camping first at San Pedro Springs and later at Elm Creek. Following these and other, monetary inducements, the first contingent of 317 Kickapoos left Múzquiz on August 28 and arrived at Fort Sill, Indian Territory, in December. They would be joined later, in 1875, by a further 145 of their tribesmen.[55]

Mackenzie's raid thus was responsible for the return to the United States of most of the Mexican Kickapoos. Those who remained behind, moreover, had witnessed the power of the United States frontier military on the border and its willingness to disregard international boundaries in pursuing its quarry. No longer could Indian raiders view Mexico as a safe haven. Indeed, Mackenzie's expedition so impressed the Mexican government that it consented to negotiate a reciprocal treaty with the United States permitting mutual pursuit and punishment of thieves and depredators across the border. Following the Remolino campaign, Indian raids in West Texas abated noticeably. Small groups of partisans began anew their depredations in 1876 and 1877, but these were short lived. By 1880, the remaining Mexican Kickapoos had abandoned their war with Texas, given up plunder as a means of support, and returned to hunting and agriculture.[56]

The scouts' next major campaign would take place in the Texas Panhandle in 1874. By that time, the southern plains Indians had become frustrated by the rapid disappearance of the buffalo and raids by renegades on their horse herds. During the spring, more than six hundred Cheyenne, Comanche, and Kiowa warriors and their families quit their Indian Territory reservations. They joined their kinsmen on the plains in an attempt to put an end to their grievances and gain recompense for lost lands and earlier defeats. On June 27, 1874, an attack on a small party of buffalo hunters at their encampment at Adobe Walls on the Canadian River by more than two hundred Native Americans under the overall command of Comanche leader Quanah Parker marked the beginning of what became known as the Red River War. By midsummer, Indian bands were attacking white settlements at every opportunity, and United States military officials felt that a major campaign was needed to return them to their reservations.[57]

In late July, General Sheridan received authorization to marshal his forces into a three-pronged attack aimed at trapping these Indians in the Texas Panhandle. As part of the maneuver, the Department of Texas sent three columns into the field. Mackenzie commanded the largest and strongest of these, the southern column. His force of 639 included eight companies of the Fourth Cavalry, five of the Tenth and Eleventh Infantry, and a scouting party consisting of thirteen Seminole maroons, twelve Tonkawas, and a few Lipans under the command of Lieutenant William Thompson. The southern column left Fort Clark for Fort Concho on August 22 with instructions to search along the headwaters of the Red River for hostile bands.[58] The blacks and Indians would serve as "advance scouts and trailers," and a special correspondent of the *New York Herald* considered them to be "quite necessary to an expedition of this kind."[59]

By September, the forces of General Nelson Miles, acting out of Fort Dodge, Kansas, had driven the main body of the Indians onto the Staked Plains in the Texas Panhandle. They took refuge in the Palo Duro Canyon near present Amarillo, built villages, and settled in for the winter. The southern column reached its supply camp at Fort Griffin on September 1 and remained there for nearly three weeks before being joined by Mackenzie. On September 19, the scouts, who had been reconnoitering far to the north, informed Mackenzie that they had discovered fresh Indian tracks in the vicinity of the headwaters of the Pease River. Mackenzie started the column in that direction early the next morning. Later that day, four of the scouts returned to camp stating that they had been attacked by twenty-five Comanches. After a short exchange, the Indians had forced them to retreat hastily.[60] One of the four was Seminole Negro Indian Scout Adam Paine, described by a contemporary as "a big black kinky headed negro, wearing horns."[61] For an individual act of gallantry during the exchange, Paine received the Medal of Honor. In his commendation, Mackenzie, not noted for lavishing praise upon his men, stated that Paine had displayed "habitual courage" and "more cool daring than any scout I have ever known."[62]

The Seminole black scouts soon would play a leading role in the Battle of Palo Duro Canyon, the most dramatic, decisive, and significant engagement in the Red River War. On September 25, the scouts informed Mackenzie that they had discovered numerous fresh Indian trails around Tule Canyon, the biggest of which had been made by a large number of horses. The following day, they reported that hostile Indians had gathered around the encampment of the southern column. Being thus forewarned, Mackenzie's troops were able to beat back an attack by an estimated 250 warriors.

Thompson and his men led a counterattack the following morning that drove the Indians from the vicinity. During the charge, one of the Seminole blacks distinguished himself by casually swinging from his saddle, taking aim, and shooting the horse from under a fleeing Comanche, who then was killed by a Tonkawa scout. The scouts pursued their attackers in an easterly direction for several hours but came to realize they were being led away from the main body of Indians and returned to camp. The southern column then set out in a northwesterly direction, and during the night, the scouts reported a large number of tipis on the floor of the nearby Palo Duro Canyon. Mackenzie's men then made ready to launch another surprise attack on the Indian villages at dawn.

At daybreak on September 28, the troops arrived at Palo Duro, just below its junction with Blanca Cita Canyon, and peered over the rim. They saw five well-equipped villages of Kiowas, Comanches, and Southern Cheyennes, which numbered over a hundred tipis and stretched for three miles along the canyon floor. A large herd of horses grazed nearby. The scouts soon discovered a narrow zigzag path leading into the canyon, and Mackenzie ordered Thompson to take his men down and begin the attack. The descent took almost an hour. At the last moment, sentries sounded the alarm. The frightened Indians fled from their dwellings and ran for a pass at the western end of the canyon, leaving behind most of their belongings in their haste. The scouts led the charge and killed three warriors, the only Native Americans found dead in the field. Mackenzie's other troops, meanwhile, set fire to the Indians' property. By the early afternoon, they had destroyed all the tipis and tons of equipment and supplies.

The Indians began to regroup and take up sniping positions among the rocks, so Mackenzie led his troops back up to the canyon rim, driving before them the entire horse herd. Only after the column had reached the safety of the supply train were the men allowed to rest and eat after some thirty-one hours in the saddle without sleep and two full days without food. Mackenzie's only casualty during the entire engagement had been one man wounded. The scouts selected the best of the Indians' horses for their own use, then the troops shot the rest, numbering over a thousand, to prevent their being recaptured.

The Palo Duro Canyon campaign was a major victory for the United States military and a crippling blow to the southern plains tribes. Although their casualties were relatively small, the Indians were left without food, clothing, shelter and, most importantly, horses to replenish their supplies. Faced with a winter of freezing temperatures on the plains, most drifted back to their reservations. A few bands still roamed the Panhandle after Palo Duro, but Mackenzie's men remained in the field, and the scouts were able to track down most of them before the southern column demobilized in December. With the exception of some minor activity by Miles's troops in the eastern Texas Panhandle and western Indian Territory during the early months of 1875, the war had ended.[63]

In his summation of the 1874 military operations, Sheridan reported, "The campaign was not only comprehensive, but was the most successful of any Indian campaign in this country since its settlement by the Whites, and much credit is due to the officers and men engaged in it."[64] The Red River War would mark the last major stand by Kiowas, Comanches, and Southern Cheyennes against white expansion. The Seminole Negro Indian Scouts had played a key role in breaking the resistance of these bands, forcing them to return to their reservations, and restoring peace to the white settlements on the southern plains.

The scouts respected and felt affection for their commander, Lieutenant Bullis, who treated them as equals in the field. In 1875, three of them risked death to rescue him from a band of hostile Indians. On April 25, while on a routine scout in the lower Pecos country, Bullis, Sergeant John Ward, Trumpeter Isaac Payne, and Private Pompey Factor struck a fresh trail of some seventy-five horses leading from the white settlements towards the Eagle's Nest crossing. The scouts followed the trail for an hour and came upon some twenty-five to thirty Comanches about to cross the Pecos with the stolen stock. Unobserved, Bullis and his men tied their horses, crept to within seventy-five yards of the Indians, and opened fire. They maintained the assault for forty-five minutes, killing three of the Comanches and wounding a fourth. Twice they managed to separate the raiders from the stolen horses, but the Indians drove them back on both occasions. Finally, however, the tide turned, and the Comanches forced the scouts to beat a hasty retreat to avoid being cut off from their mounts.

The three scouts were the first to reach their horses, but as they were about to ride off, Sergeant Ward glanced back and saw that Bullis had been separated from his mount and soon would be stranded among the Comanches, who were approaching rapidly. Ward alerted his companions and, wheeling his horse, dashed back towards Bullis through a hail of fire while Payne and Factor dismounted and provided cover. Two bullets hit the sergeant's carbine, passing through the sling and shattering the stock, but he charged on undeterred. Upon reaching Bullis, Ward scooped him onto the back of his horse, and the two rode off beyond the covering fire. Payne and Factor then quickly remounted, and all four escaped unharmed. The black scouts had displayed courage, loyalty, and quickness of wit in completing a remarkable rescue. As Bullis remarked, his men literally had saved his hair. The three were commended for valiant conduct and, on May 28, each was awarded the Medal of Honor for his part in the action.[65]

Between 1875 and 1877, Colonel William Shafter's expeditions into West Texas and Mexico utilized the scouts extensively. On these missions, the scouts rode frequently alongside black cavalry and infantry regiments, or "Buffalo Soldiers" as they were called by their Native American adversaries. During the spring of 1875, small bands of Comanches raided white settlements in West Texas, and Shafter received orders to devise a plan to intercept these Indians, search out and destroy their villages, and return them to their reservations. Shafter organized an extensive campaign at Fort Concho, and by the summer, he had his command in place. The expeditionary force that rode out onto the Staked Plains on July 14 carried supplies for four months and included six companies of the Tenth Cavalry, two of the Twenty-Fourth Infantry, one of the Twenty-Fifth, and detachments of Seminole black and Tonkawa scouts under Bullis and Lieutenant Charles Ward. The force represented the largest body of men ever sent into the field in West Texas by the United States army, and with the exception of the white officers, it consisted entirely of blacks and Indians.[66]

On October 18, Bullis and several of his scouts together with a small force of black cavalrymen discovered and charged a large Native

American encampment at Sabrinas. Though the Indians escaped, the troops captured twenty-five of their horses and mules and destroyed all of their supplies. Typical of the surprise attack, which the Seminole Negro Indian Scouts employed so successfully, this action constituted the harshest blow Shafter's command was able to inflict on the raiders. In late November, Shafter received orders to terminate the expedition and return to Fort Duncan. The entire campaign had resulted in the death of only one Indian and the capture of five others, but the command had destroyed two encampments and supplies and had captured live-stock. More significantly, Shafter reported that his forces had driven the raiders from the southern plains deep into Mexico and that there was not left "an Indian east of the Pecos and south of the Red River."[67]

The Lipans and Mexican Kickapoos resumed their raids on settlements in West Texas during the spring and summer of 1876, and the scouts remained in detached service with Shafter's command. In July, Shafter received orders to take a substantial force across the Rio Grande and attack a large Lipan village known to be in the vicinity of Zaragoza. Around July 20, Shafter's command, consisting entirely of black troops under white officers, with three companies of the Tenth Cavalry, detach-ments of the Twenty-Fourth and Twenty-Fifth Infantry, and a party of Seminole Negro Indian Scouts under Bullis, crossed over into Mexico. After marching for several days, Shafter became concerned that a Mexican force might cut off his return. To guard against this possibility and to save time, most of the troops went into camp while Shafter gave Bullis overall command of his twenty scouts and an equal number of Buffalo Soldiers from Company B, Tenth Cavalry, and instructed him to locate and destroy the Lipan village as planned.

Bullis's force set out in the late afternoon of July 29 and, early the next morning, located the Lipan village on the San Antonio River, about five miles from Zaragoza. Although the village was large, numbering some twenty-three lodges, the black troops went straight into the attack at daybreak. After the initial volley, Bullis's men became involved in a fierce hand-to-hand battle with the Lipans. As scout Charlie Daniels later explained, "We didn't had no time to load de gun, but jest turn de butt of de gun and fight 'em."[68] The battle lasted just fifteen minutes as the Indians then fled the field. Bullis's men had killed fourteen of the Lipans and captured four women as well as almost one hundred head of horses and mules. The Lipan lances had inflicted flesh wounds on three of the blacks, but none was seriously injured. Once more, the surprise attack had been highly effective. After destroying the Lipan village, Bullis's men rejoined the main column. Shafter and most of his command then recrossed safely into Texas, but the scouts received no respite, for they set out immediately on yet another expedition into the Mexican interior in search of Lipan raiders.[69]

In 1877, the scouts participated in three major campaigns against Indians based in Mexico. In late June, while riding north of the mouth of the Pecos, Bullis and thirty-seven of his men came upon the trail of a raiding party of some five Lipans and three Comanches who had been stealing stock in Gillespie County, and followed it to the Rio Grande. As the river was high, the scouts crossed over on a raft of logs tied together with lariats, and thereafter that place was known as "Bullis Crossing." The scouts continued the pursuit, but some of their horses broke down, forcing thirteen men to remain behind. Bullis and the other scouts, seven of them riding on pack mules, continued to follow the trail into the Sierra Pachona, and on July 2, they came upon the stolen horse herd grazing on the hillside. But one of the mules brayed, and the Lipans discovered their foe. The Indians took quickly to the rocks and brush in a rough sierra. In an hour-long running fight, the scouts killed one and wounded three of the Lipans, forced others to abandon their supplies, and recaptured most of the stolen horses without suffering a single casualty themselves. Bullis and his men then recrossed the Rio Grande safely, having completed another successful campaign.[70]

Bullis's command next rode into Mexico on the trail of hostile Indians in September. On the 26th, three of the scouts reported that they had located a band of Lipans known to have engaged recently in raids into Texas. The Lipans had built their village on Perdido Creek near Zaragoza. That same day, the scouts, together with detachments of the Eighth and Tenth Cavalry, crossed the Rio Grande. The force of ninety-one men under Bullis's overall command proceeded southwest for three days until it came across the Lipan village. At sunrise, the troops charged the unsuspecting Indians and after a five-mile running fight, captured three women, two children, and about twenty horses and mules. They then destroyed the village and the Indians' entire supplies. The scouts' tactics once again had paid dividends, and the Lipans had suffered yet another defeat on their home territory.[71]

In mid-October, thirty-four Seminole Negro Indian Scouts under Bullis, with the Mexican guide José Tafoya, Teresita the captured Lipan, and a surgeon left Fort Clark on a supposedly routine expedition up the

Rio Grande. On the 22nd, two other scouts, who had been on a mission for the last forty days, reported to Bullis on the Pecos that a band of Indian raiders had returned to Mexico and was moving south towards the Sierra del Carmen in the Big Bend country. Bullis and his command crossed the Rio Grande on October 28 and followed the trail for four days until they came upon the Mescalero village on the Texas side of the river. On the evening of November 1, the Mescalero raiders discovered the scouts on their trail, ran off their herds of stolen horses and cattle to safety, recrossed into Mexico, and managed to trap the detachment on a narrow ledge in a deep canyon with a mountain towering above and the river way below. For once surprised and outmaneuvered by the Mescaleros, the scouts faced their greatest crisis.

Greatly outnumbered and surrounded by their adversaries, the scouts found themselves in a position almost impossible to defend. For a time, they were "severely handled" and lost several animals and all of their rations, but they eventually managed to fight their way out and went on to complete a wondrous escape into the open country without suffering a single casualty.[72] The scouts believed that their safe deliverance from predicaments such as this came about through divine intervention, and every night while on expedition, they would give thanks for their good fortune in camp meetings featuring singing and prayer.[73] These meetings are reminiscent of Gullah night vigils, similar practices also having been found in Bantu-related cultures in the Kongo and Angola.[74]

Bullis returned to Texas shortly afterward and informed Shafter of the exchange. He received additional support in the form of detachments of the Eighth and Tenth Cavalry and returned to Mexico in mid-November. The scouts picked up the three-week-old trail and followed it back to the Big Bend country where the Mescaleros had been camped. The column trailed the Indians into the Mexican interior and surprised them in their village in the Sierra del Carmen. Bullis's men killed two of the Mescaleros, including the band leader, Alsate, described by Bullis as "the most cunning Indian on all the frontier of Texas and Mexico." The troops wounded three others and captured horses, mules, and arms, while suffering only one casualty themselves. They dispersed the Indians summarily before destroying their village; then they left this band to face the harsh winter without shelter or supplies.[75]

The expeditions of 1875, 1876, and 1877 had their desired effect upon the Indian bands based on the Mexican side of the Rio Grande; they became wary of attack and drastically reduced their raids into Texas.

In June 1878, a detachment of Seminole Negro Indian Scouts accompanied Mackenzie on an expedition into Coahuila to destroy a Lipan village near Múzquiz, but they discovered no hostile Indians in the area. Mackenzie's raid did spur the Mexican government into cooperating with the United States in making serious efforts to police its side of the border, however, and soon Indian raids in Texas began to decrease.[76]

The scouts had gained experience of exploratory missions earlier. As well as being charged with clearing the Staked Plains of hostile bands, Shafter's 1875 expedition had been asked to chart the area, detailing its natural resources and water supplies to assess its suitability for cultivation and stock-raising. Subsequently, the expedition had produced the first accurate and reliable map of the Staked Plains, greatly increased the amount of information available on the area, and dispelled forever the myth that it was devoid of water. The expedition's findings had been circulated widely and had resulted in a large influx of ranchers, sheep farmers, goat herders, and homesteaders into West Texas.[77]

As the number of Indian raids began to decline, the scouts came to be employed more frequently in this type of work. From September to November 1878, they helped to improve communications in West Texas by working with Captain John Rodgers of the Second Artillery to build a road from the Pecos River to Fort Davis. Unfortunately, during this tour of duty, Charles or "Cato" July accidentally shot and killed himself. Because of increased lawlessness in the Big Bend Country, military officials at Fort Davis authorized the establishment of Camp Pena Colorado, an outpost situated further to the south some four miles below present-day Marathon. During 1879, the scouts helped construct both the buildings and the roads leading to this post. In October, thirteen Seminole black and two Lipan scouts under Bullis set out to discover the best route for a wagon road from the new crossing of the Pecos at Pena Blanca to Pena Negra, and estimate the length of time needed for its construction. On several occasions, the scouts escorted the parties of Judge Joseph Jones during their surveys of West Texas, and between January and April 1880, they acted as guides to an expedition organized by a number of railroads to examine the mineral resources of Presidio County. As explorers, fort and road builders, escorts, and guides, the Seminole Negro Indian Scouts played a vital role in the development of West Texas and helped spur the movement of white settlers into the area.[78]

The scouts' final Indian campaign of note followed what proved to be the last major raid in Texas.[79] On April 14, 1881, a small band of Lipans crossed over from Mexico and attacked the McLauren Ranch at the head of the Rio Frio in Real County. The Indians killed two of the inhabitants, robbed the ranch and other homes in the vicinity, and made their escape with stolen horses and other plunder. Two weeks later, Bullis, thirty-four scouts, and Teresita rode out of Fort Clark with instructions either to capture or kill those Lipan raiders.

Although the Lipans had wrapped their horses' hooves with rawhide to prevent their making tracks, the scouts picked up their trail on April 27. In yet another remarkable feat, Bullis's men were able to follow the two-week-old trail over the rugged terrain surrounding Devil's River. There they discovered the Lipans had killed thirty of the captured horses they could not drive before them. The scouts crossed the Rio Grande below the mouth of the Pecos and pursued the raiding party high into the Sierra del Burro. Teresita was used as a leading guide, but she came to realize from signs on the trail that it was her band they were following and tried to lead the detachment away. One of the scouts saw through her ploy, however, and kept the unit on the right track. At this point, Teresita became violent and the scouts tied her to her horse. The detachment finally came upon the Lipan raiders on May 2 after six days of pursuit.

Bullis concealed his command until midnight when he took twenty-seven of his men and crept off towards the Lipan camp, leaving the other seven behind with the belligerent Teresita and the horses. At daybreak, the scouts attacked and routed the unsuspecting Lipans, who had not envisaged pursuit. They killed five members of the band, took prisoner a boy and a wounded woman, and recaptured the remaining stolen horses. Most importantly, the leader of the band, San-Da-Ve, was wounded mortally and died soon afterwards. Yet again, the scouts suffered no casualties themselves and were able to recross safely into Texas.[80]

News of the success of the expedition "was hailed in Texas with wild joy."[81] Within a month, the West Texas border country was deemed safe enough to allow Bullis to relinquish his command of the scouts, and he was transferred soon afterwards to Camp Supply, Indian Territory. The citizens of West Texas presented Bullis with a sword, and the state legislature commended him for helping to put an end to Indian raids. He served later as agent at the San Carlos reservation and saw service in

Cuba and the Philippines during the Spanish-American War before finally retiring as brigadier general. For the scouts, the Indian wars were at an end. In the year following their final campaign, some twelve expeditions set out from military posts in Texas, but not one encountered a single hostile Indian.[82]

The employment of the Seminole Negro Indian Scouts by the United States was an extension of the old "divide and rule policy." The maroons made excellent guides and trailers and had proved themselves in combat against both white and Indian adversaries in Florida and Mexico. The army wished to exploit these talents before returning them to the Indian Territory. By enlisting their services against Indian bands of the region, military officials tried to negate any possibility of a troublesome alliance between the two on the border. In fact, such collusion was never likely. Since the blacks had left the Indian Territory, Comanches had tortured, murdered, and sold them into slavery while crossing the plains, and Lipan and Mescalero raiders had attacked them constantly once they had settled in Mexico. The maroons, in turn, had little use for alliances with plains or border Indians and were quick to make agreements with officials of both Mexico and the United States that in exchange for land, food, tools, and money, they would take up arms against such bands.

After 1870, the Seminole Negro Indian Scouts killed, maimed, imprisoned, and destroyed the villages and property of divers bands of Kickapoos, Apaches, Cheyennes, Kiowas, and Comanches. In so doing, they played a major role in furthering the policy that had brought them back to the United States by driving these bands onto reservations or deep into the Mexican interior and facilitating white expansion into West Texas. By 1881, the scars ran so deep that reconciliation was virtually impossible. The case of the Mexican Kickapoos furnishes a good example. During the 1860s, the Kickapoos and Mascogos had come to resent each other's presence at Nacimiento. Feelings were running so high by 1873 that maroon informants and Seminole Negro Indian Scouts led Mackenzie to the Kickapoo village at Remolino, resulting in deaths, incarceration, the destruction of families and property, and the forced removal of most of the group to reservations in the Indian Territory.

The exploits of the scouts proved conclusively that the maroons were concerned solely with promoting what they considered to be their best interests, and were thinking only of themselves. As they offered the best hope for land, homes, prosperity, and peace, the promises of white

Americans were accepted at face value. If the price were war against Indians of the region, so be it. In their pursuit of freedom to control their own destinies, the Seminole maroons, yet again, were prepared to go to the most extreme lengths.

Originally, United States officials had envisaged the removal of the Mascogos to West Texas as merely the first step on their journey to the Indian Territory. They had viewed the employment of the Seminole Negro Indian Scouts, moreover, as just a short-term measure designed to provide support for the group while in transit. As the scouts gave such useful service to the frontier army, however, the maroons' removal to their former home became, at best, a low priority. Not only had the military removed the threat of an alliance between the minorities on the border, but also the scouts had proven to be remarkably efficient in combating hostile Indian bands. As time went by, the Seminole blacks would become the subject of a fierce argument over who had authorized their return from Mexico in the first place, whose responsibility it was to care for the group in Texas, and ultimately, what precedents existed for removing a band of Mexican maroons to the Indian Territory. Old agreements soon would be forgotten as government departments began to pass the buck around Washington.

5

Classifying Seminole Blacks

In the early 1870s, most of the maroons who had removed to Mexico with John Horse returned to the United States. United States officials had led them to believe that they would be restored to their former homes in the Indian Territory as soon as possible. While awaiting clearance to begin the journey northward, the maroons settled in temporary camps on the military reservations of West Texas garrisons, and the able-bodied men enlisted as scouts. But the United States failed to honor its commitments and soon began to deny responsibility for the welfare of the group. After 1870, the Seminole blacks in Texas would try hard to return to the Indian Territory, but only a handful would succeed in making the journey.

During the 1870s and 1880s, the maroons became the subject of a fierce intra- and interdepartmental wrangle within the United States government between the Indian bureau, the interior and war departments, and the adjutant general's office over who had authorized their return to Texas and which was responsible for their upkeep and ultimate removal to the Indian Territory. Although all had favored and played a part in bringing about the return of the Mascogos to the United States, each began to deny responsibility once the group had settled in Texas. High-level government officials tended to treat the matter as low priority as the Seminole Negro Indian Scouts were playing such a vital role in helping to clear West Texas of Indian bands hostile to white settlement. Ironically, the scouts' excellent military record served only to undermine their best interests.

At first, genuine confusion over the racial makeup of the group led some United States officials to believe erroneously that the maroons were a Seminole Indian band with black intermixture. Since 1850, the activities of the maroons and Seminoles in Coahuila had given rise to exaggerated reports and misinformation, fueled by Wild Cat's intrigues

among the tribes of the southern plains. The population of the colony
had fluctuated constantly both in size and makeup. The Kickapoos had
abandoned the enterprise early and recrossed the Rio Grande. Other
black emigrants from the Indian Territory had joined the colony, as had
Texas runaways and Mexican blacks. All of the Seminoles had returned
to the Indian Territory by 1861, leaving behind just the Mascogos, but
this was not widely known. To complicate matters still further, by 1865
other Southern Kickapoo bands had removed to Coahuila.

Lacking detailed information on the group, the Indian bureau and the
army had planned originally to remove the maroons to their former
homeland under the policy of relocating border bands on reservations
in the Indian Territory. The military then enlisted the men as Indian
scouts, confusing the issue still further. The detachment came to be
known as the Seminole Negro Indian Scouts; but did this mean Seminole
Negro-Indians who were scouts, or Seminole Negroes who were Indian
scouts? While such weighty questions were being debated in the halls of
government, the maroons struggled to raise enough corn, beans, chickens, and goats to survive and learn the outcome.

As they came to realize that the great majority of the community
consisted of blacks only formerly associated with Seminoles, the Indian
commissioners began to argue that they could find no precedent for
relocating "negroes" at government expense or providing them with
land. Having pacified the group, government officials would attempt
for fifteen years thereafter to classify the Seminole blacks in ways that
would facilitate denial of any further responsibility towards them. Never
defined as Seminoles, at various times the maroons were deemed to be
"Negro-Indians" (and therefore not Indians), Creek blacks (but not
Creek citizens), and freedmen without Indian affiliation (or just blacks,
without cause for special consideration). The earlier promises to these
people, as well as the needs and wishes of the group, soon would be
forgotten as government officials constructed a rationale whereby they
neither could remove nor subsist the group.

The controversy dated back to the time the Mascogos first returned
to the United States. In April 1870, Commissioner of Indian Affairs Ely
Parker recounted that in his annual report of the previous year he had
recommended that the group be returned to the Indian Territory, but
added hastily that his department did not have the means to bring this
about. If the military would conduct them to the Seminole Nation and
arrange for their subsistence en route, however, the Indian bureau then

would assume responsibility and provide for their resettlement. The adjutant general gave an official copy of Parker's report to the commander of the Department of Texas on May 10 with the remark that the secretary of war declined to give any orders under the circumstances. As a result, on May 21, the department instructed the commanding officer at Fort Duncan to bring about the removal of the Mascogos to Texas, encourage them to remain at his post, and issue them rations until he received further orders.[1]

In early October, Secretary of War William Belknap applied to the interior department for means to pay the expenses of the John Horse party, which he expected would remove to Texas shortly.[2] In reply, the Indian bureau stated that it had at its disposal an appropriation of twenty-five thousand dollars made at the last session of Congress to enable the secretary of the interior to "collect bands of Kickapoo or other Indians roving on the borders of Texas and Mexico and to relocate and subsist them in the Indian Territory," which would "cover the case in question."[3] Belknap interpreted this statement to mean that the interior department was prepared not only to bear the cost of removals but also to subsist the Seminole maroons while they remained in Texas as they were supposedly en route to the Indian Territory. Military officials in Texas continued to issue rations regularly to the entire group from army supplies, but recorded the expenses with a view to receiving reimbursement from the interior department. On the mistaken assumption that the appropriation would cover these expenses in full, the war department continued to support this arrangement for more than two years without complaint.[4]

In the summer of 1872, the Office of the Adjutant General issued General Order 54, which forbade the regular issuance of army rations to Indians. The chief commissary of subsistence in the Department of Texas believed that the order included the Seminole blacks. In early August, Major Henry Merriam, the commanding officer at Fort Duncan, was asked to furnish a report. Merriam recommended that the army continue to issue rations to the group. The maroons had expected to be removed to the Indian Territory at any time and were not prepared to provide for themselves. If the Department of Texas withdrew their rations, they would be driven to support themselves by illegal means, or would return to Mexico where they would pose a threat to the frontier. In the light of Merriam's recommendation, the army continued to issue the group supplies while the interior department considered the case.[5]

Belknap informed Acting Secretary of the Interior B. R. Cowen in early September that the war department had to discontinue issuing the group with army supplies as the military received no benefit from this expensive practice.[6] He then referred back to the arrangements made with the interior department in 1870 and requested that it direct the Indian bureau to assume its responsibilities and take up the burden of the maroons' subsistence. Belknap reminded Cowen that the bureau now had at its disposal over sixty thousand dollars to collect, relocate in the Indian Territory, and subsist bands of Indians living on the border. Cowen believed, however, that he had no authority to use these funds to subsist the Seminole blacks while they remained at Forts Duncan and Clark. By that time, the group had been living in Texas for more than two years and no longer could be considered to be en route to the Indian Territory. Instead, Cowen authorized the latest commissioner of Indian affairs, Francis A. Walker, to ascertain whether the maroons were willing to return to the Indian Territory.[7] If they were, immediate measures should be taken to achieve that result, and Walker suggested that once they had removed, "the appropriation [would] be made available for relieving their present necessities."[8]

In response to inquiries from the Indian bureau, Merriam reported in late October that the maroons were ready to make the journey to the Indian Territory and that this had been their intention in returning to Texas. Indeed, they had been waiting to remove for over two years and more than once had shown impatience at the delay. All they needed were instructions, transportation, and subsistence for the duration of the journey. In mid-November, General Philip Sheridan, commanding the Military Division of the Missouri, endorsed the report with the recommendation that they be removed forthwith.[9]

Upon receiving Merriam's report, however, Walker chose to reconsider the case and reversed completely his earlier recommendation to make the funds at his disposal available to the immigrants if they chose to return to the Indian Territory. Walker could find no evidence that his department had authorized their return from Mexico and believed they should not have removed at all. Under the circumstances, the Indian bureau had no obligation to them. Walker, apparently, had become aware of the group's racial makeup as he next stated that the appropriation had not been intended to pay the expenses of removing and subsisting "these persons." The Indian bureau wished to steer well clear of creating the precedent of paying the removal expenses of blacks, and was quick to divest itself of any further responsibility towards the group.

The commissioner's final argument rested upon the mistaken supposition that the intention was to resettle the Seminole blacks among the Creeks. Walker pronounced that the maroons had failed to return to the Creek Nation within the year specified by the 1866 Reconstruction treaty, thus did not qualify for rights and privileges equal to native citizens, and therefore should not be forced upon that tribe. In short, the commissioner had refused to subsist the blacks in Texas or to allow them to remove to the Indian Territory. Walker admitted that he did not know what could be done for the maroons, but he was adamant that they should not become the charge of the Indian bureau. Cowen concurred with Walker's assessment, forwarded his decision to Belknap, and passed the case back to the war department. As 1872 drew to a close, it began to seem unlikely that the maroons' removal to the Seminole Nation ever would come about.[10]

Early in the new year, Belknap asked Sheridan to consider the case.[11] Sheridan concluded that both the military and the Indian bureau had been instrumental in bringing about the removal of the Mascogos to Texas and that both, therefore, had obligations to the group. He believed it would be "a very cruel thing to drive these negro Indians back into Mexico" and recommended that the army assign the group a permanent tract of land at Elm Creek from the military reservation at Fort Duncan. The military could spare the land easily and should allot it to the heads of families so that they could establish farms. Sheridan expressed astonishment at the Indian bureau's unequivocal denial of support for the group and requested that it reconsider its decision.[12] Belknap referred Sheridan's report to the new secretary of the interior, Columbus Delano, and expounded further upon the role played by the commissioners of Indian affairs in bringing about the Mascogos' return from Mexico. In early March, Delano admitted that the rulings of the Indian bureau had been contradictory and recommended that the case be investigated by the assistant attorney general, but never followed through. The question of what should be done with the Seminole maroons remained unanswered and, once again, the subject fell into abeyance.[13]

Frustrated by the endless machinations of government, the leaders of the group began to give vent to their demands and grievances. In late June, shortly after the Remolino raid, Elijah Daniels, John Ward, and

James Bruner, the leading members of the Daniels band at Fort Clark, filed a petition with Colonel Ranald Mackenzie, then in command of the post, for a piece of land of their own in the Indian Territory, where they could build permanent homes. The petitioners requested that some of their old men first be allowed to view the tract before the group set out. If the delegation found the land satisfactory, the maroons would require subsistence during the journey and arms and rations upon arrival until they could plant a crop. Once having established homes, however, the group would ask nothing more of the government than to be treated the same as Indians.

Both Mackenzie and Sheridan supported the petition and recommended that the group remove to Fort Sill. The maroons should resettle on part of the land occupied by the Kiowas and Comanches at the post, for, being industrious, they would exercise a beneficial influence on the Indians and be more likely than their neighbors to establish farms and support themselves. Some of the men could be enlisted, also, if needed. In spite of the strong support the idea received from the military, however, a mixture of vested interest and inertia on the part of governmental agencies would see to it that the proposed removal of the Daniels band to the Indian Territory never came about.[14]

The maroons soon were to come up against the greatest crisis they had faced since their return from Coahuila. In early December, the Department of Texas ordered that, with the exception of regularly enlisted men, the army should not issue rations to the group after Christmas week. The women, children, old, and infirm had been receiving rations even if they did not belong to the families of enlisted scouts and had come to rely almost completely upon those supplies for their subsistence. Beginning in the new year, the entire community would have to survive on the wages and rations of the scouts and the few laundresses employed by the military, supplemented by whatever the women could earn in the neighboring towns and the few crops they could raise around their makeshift settlements. As 1873 drew to a close, many faced the dreadful prospect of poverty, starvation, and destitution.[15]

Quickly, the maroons determined to appoint a delegation to lobby for a reversal of the decision. They viewed the choice of delegates as vital. Elijah Daniels was the undisputed leader of the band at Fort Clark, and John Kibbetts had been acknowledged as head of the scouts since their first enlistment. After John Horse had removed to Texas, however, there had been some contention over who should be considered overall leader of the group at Fort Duncan, and this factionalism accounts largely for the transfer of Daniels and his supporters to Fort Clark. In early December, the 130 Seminole blacks at Fort Duncan held an election and voted Kibbetts headman over Horse by a majority of seventeen.[16] The aging but knowledgeable and experienced John Horse assumed a patriarchal role thereafter and frequently gave advice on important issues affecting the group. On this occasion, in view of the seriousness of the decision to terminate their rations, the maroons sent both Kibbetts and Horse to San Antonio to appeal their case before Brigadier General Christopher Augur, the commander of the Department of Texas.

The two maroon leaders presented a long and varied list of requests and grievances to Augur. John Horse had sole possession of the title to the group's land grant at Nacimiento and asked to have it recorded and guaranteed in the United States. If Horse were to die, Augur should confer with Horse's son Joe Coon, who also was familiar with the claim. Horse requested further that the government reimburse his followers for the losses they had incurred in removing from Mexico, as it had promised. Kibbetts spoke at length on behalf of his men. He asked that the army permit the scouts to keep their horses at their camp on Elm Creek instead of at the picket line at Fort Duncan, some three miles distant. Their quota of forage for horses employed in military service, which had been reduced, also should be restored in full. Furthermore, scouts ordered out at night should not ride alone but in pairs to protect against Indian attacks. Finally, army officers should not ask his men to work on menial tasks around the post, such as wood-cutting, when not on expedition, but should employ them exclusively for scouting duty. Of most immediate and vital concern to the group as a whole, however, were the questions of removal and the stoppage of rations, and the two leaders devoted most of their petition to these matters.

Kibbetts and Horse requested that the department restore full rations to all of the Seminole maroons, as there was little hope of their finding work in the vicinity, and the wages of the scouts were insufficient to support the group as a whole. They asked, also, that Augur allow the men who had married into the group to enlist so as to bolster the total income of the community. As he was head of the scouts and received a sergeant's pay, Kibbetts was not inclined personally to quit Fort Duncan, but he expressed the sincere hope that the authorities would permit all those who could not enlist to remove to a better location. John Horse and most of the group, meanwhile, were anxious to leave the military reservation and were prepared to move to Florida, the Indian Territory, or elsewhere. Horse concluded by asking Augur to petition the president on their behalf to provide the necessary land for a permanent home where they could live in peace, educate their children, and practice their religion.[17]

In a few sentences, John Horse had explained the key to the Seminole maroons' way of thinking. They had viewed the old alliance with the Seminoles in Florida, the Indian Territory, and Coahuila primarily as an arrangement designed to secure or preserve their liberty. Once the United States had abolished slavery, they no longer had need for such an alliance. From the late 1860s on, the maroons expressed a wish to return to the Seminole Nation, but this was spurred by the potential for land and opportunity and not the wish to reestablish relations with the Seminoles.

After the Civil War, the Seminole Nation became a highly desirable location for blacks, and the former emigrants were well aware of this. They hoped to capitalize on their links with the tribe to acquire land in the freedman communities, as well as economic benefits, education for their children, and other privileges associated with Seminole citizenship. But the maroons also were prepared to accept land in other locations, provided they could remain together as a group. Thus, during the course of his lifetime, John Horse sought land for his people in Florida, the Indian Territory, Coahuila, Texas, and even Africa. At various times, the maroons also showed willingness to accept land in the Oklahoma Territory or sections of the Indian Territory outside the Seminole country. United States officials tended to concentrate their efforts on resettling them in the Seminole Nation, not because that was the only location they would consider, but because it offered the only practical alternative to their either remaining as squatters on the military reservations or returning to Mexico to reconstitute a threat to the West Texas settlements. What the maroons wanted most was a place of their own where they could live their lives peacefully and independently. They were interested in reviving their association with the Seminoles only because it offered the best prospect of providing such a place.

Though he could see both the justice of their cause and the tragedy of their predicament, Augur could offer no hope to John Horse and John Kibbetts. He informed them that the Indian bureau had refused to help and the war department could do nothing beyond enlisting the men who were fit for service. They asked what would become of the women, children, aged, and sick who were not members of the families of scouts. To this, Augur admitted later, "I was unable to make any satisfactory answer."[18] Seeing that it was hopeless to pursue the matter further at that time, Kibbetts and Horse returned to Fort Duncan with the grim news that the group faced a bleak new year.

The military terminated the rations of the majority of the Seminole maroons on January 10, 1874. The thirty-seven women and forty-eight children among the group at Fort Duncan had continued to receive issues until then, but from that day forward, the army would furnish rations only to the enlisted scouts and laundresses. On February 8, Kibbetts complained that the government had turned its back upon the agreement it had made with the Mascogos in 1870 in which it had promised to provide rations for all if the able-bodied men would enlist as scouts. Fort Duncan was so isolated that the women and children were not able to find work and were starving. The scouts were unable to bear the burden of supporting the entire community, and Kibbetts asked that the military restore their rations in full.[19]

Kibbetts's petition received strong support from both Augur and Lieutenant John Bullis. Bullis, in close touch with the situation at Fort Duncan, recommended earnestly that his superiors take action to alleviate the suffering of the women and children. Augur went still further: if the government did not agree either to remove them to the Indian Territory or to furnish them subsistence where they were, the maroons would be driven to steal from local white communities in sheer desperation to prevent starvation. Retaliation by white settlers inevitably would follow, and the cost of restoring peace would outweigh by far that of the supplies requested by Kibbetts. Furthermore, Commissioner Walker's earlier decision to disavow responsibility for the group had been hasty and ill-considered. The maroons were subject not to the Creek but to the Seminole treaty of 1866. This had no limit as to when they could return, and Augur believed there could be no doubt "as to their entire right to return there now." Their only requirements would be transportation, and subsistence during the journey and for a short time after their arrival. Trying to be as accommodating as possible, Augur offered to provide teamsters to remove the maroons during the summer, should his superiors approve his suggestions.[20]

After considering Kibbetts's petition and the recommendations of Bullis and Augur, the acting commissary general reported that the military would require a special appropriation before it could feed the Seminole maroons legally. He believed it would be far more appropriate for the commissioner of Indian affairs to supply them with rations. In early April, therefore, Belknap referred these proposals once again to the secretary of the interior with the request that he instruct the Indian bureau to provide subsistence for the maroons and make arrangements for their removal to the Indian Territory.[21]

The commissioner of Indian affairs, Edward P. Smith, decided that he needed more information before he could make a recommendation, and in late July he asked special commissioners Atkinson and Williams, who were in the vicinity of Forts Duncan and Clark trying to bring about the removal of the remaining Mexican Kickapoos, to furnish a report. In the meantime, the commanding officer at Fort Duncan had found it necessary to feed ten destitute maroons to prevent them from starving. The military issued these ten with rations during June and July, but determined that it could not bear the responsibility of feeding them beyond the end of August. Both the commissary general and Belknap recommended that the Indian bureau take up the burden of their subsistence, but Acting Commissioner H. R. Clum replied that he could not do so while they remained in Texas. By the beginning of September, therefore, these utterly dependent Seminole blacks found themselves abandoned once more by the government.[22]

In mid-November, Atkinson forwarded his report to Smith. The special commissioners agreed with Sheridan's earlier assessment that both the military and the Indian bureau had been responsible in part for the return of the Mascogos from Mexico. A number of the old men, women, and children were destitute. In view of this and the maroons' apparent right by treaty to the care and protection of the government, Atkinson recommended that the bureau remove them to a reservation in the Indian Territory and furnish them subsistence until they could provide for themselves. The expense could be covered by the funds Smith had at his disposal for collecting, subsisting, and removing roving bands from the border country. By December 20, however, it had become clear that the Indian bureau was disinclined to act upon this recommendation, and Atkinson informed Smith that the condition of the Seminole blacks had worsened considerably since his report and that many were now completely destitute. They were anxious to remove to the Indian Territory, and Atkinson proposed that his superiors authorize Williams and himself to take them there. But again the interior department took no action, and the maroons spent yet another winter cold and hungry on the military reservations.[23]

From March to May 1875, United States officials took censuses of the Seminole maroons at Forts Duncan and Clark under orders from Atkinson and the latest commander of the Department of Texas Brigadier General Edward Ord. Atkinson instructed Lieutenant Alfred Markley and Bullis to conduct surveys at Duncan and Clark respectively with a view to determining the feasibility of returning the maroons to the Indian Territory and discovering their views on the proposed move. In late April, moreover, Ord had felt it necessary to issue Department of Texas Special Order 80 without consulting his superiors. Section 3 provided that the army would issue rations to the group at Fort Duncan whenever this was deemed necessary to prevent suffering. The department commander believed he needed more precise information on the population and condition of the communities at both Duncan and Clark before he could proceed further on the question of issuing rations, and ordered additional surveys. These censuses, together with their accompanying reports, provide the most detailed statistical information ever assembled on the Seminole maroon communities in Texas.[24]

Markley's findings at Fort Duncan were the first to be presented to both Atkinson and Ord. His census of May 9 listed 107 Seminole maroons living on Elm Creek. The group was divided into twenty-five family, or household, units headed by that of John Kibbetts; one scout, Henry Vaughn, and one old woman, Juana Washington, the sister of John Horse, were listed alone. Nineteen of the men were enlisted scouts, and another two, Dan Johnson and Peter Bruno, were young and strong, but the military had rejected them as worthless. These Markley deemed to be totally independent. Fifty-five women and children, moreover, were either self-supporting or members of the scouts' families, and needed no help.

Of the others in the group, three men and four women were old and helpless and required continuous assistance. These included Cuffee Payne[25] and his wife Betsy, Cyrus Bowlegs and his wife Mina, Calo Wilson and his wife Lucy, and Juana Washington. Two men, four women, and eleven children, moreover, required occasional help. Markley's assessment here seems misguided, for in March he had described eight of the seventeen as being either destitute or old and worn out. He had listed John Horse as "decrepit" and his wife Susan as infirm. Scout George Washington, the son of Juana and nephew of John Horse, was hospitalized with a gunshot wound, and his wife Tina and their six children also required temporary help. Thus, by early May 1875, thirty-one of 107, or almost thirty percent of the Seminole blacks at Fort Duncan, were in need of some degree of assistance from the government.

Although there was widespread destitution within the group, the maroons at Fort Duncan now showed a decided unwillingness to return to the Indian Territory. During his March census, Markley asked each if he or she wished to remove, and with the exception of John Kibbetts, who was uncertain, they all replied that they definitely did not. The very old, who were among the most destitute, were the most adamant, answering that they did not wish to make a fresh start but preferred to die in Texas. It seems likely that these old maroons still harbored hopes that the government would provide for them, but as Markley predicted, they had only starvation or charity to look forward to. A mixture of lethargy and skepticism, induced by so long a wait, apparently had undermined temporarily the resolve of the Kibbetts band to return to the Indian Territory.[26]

In May, Shafter, the commander at Fort Duncan, recommended that with the exception of the scouts, the army should issue rations to the maroons only after an assessment of each individual application as they all could help to support themselves. Previously, when the entire group had received rations, the scouts would not reenlist but would "run about the country" for up to three months, returning to military service only when they were desperate for money. Now, with their families totally dependent upon them for support, the scouts were anxious to be retained in continuous service and were proving to be more useful than ever before. Shafter believed that with the exception of the entirely helpless and occasional assistance to the sick and women and children who had no man to provide for them, the military should not issue rations to the unenlisted blacks. Although he suggested only limited assistance to the most dependent members of the maroon community, Shafter's recommendations would appear most humane and generous in the light of the action subsequently taken by the government.[27]

The census of the Daniels band at Fort Clark was not as detailed as that completed at Duncan, but nevertheless, it contained the most important statistics on the community. Bullis listed 151 Seminole maroons living on Las Moras Creek. The group included twenty-nine scouts, seven unenlisted but able-bodied men, and twenty-six women who lived with them, whom Bullis deemed to be independent. Twenty-two others obviously needed assistance as eleven men and eleven women were described as old and destitute. Sixty-seven children also were listed, fifty-five aged under twelve and totally dependent, and twelve aged between twelve and sixteen. Around thirty-three to forty percent of the group's total population probably was in need of some degree of assistance from the government, however, as it was reported that some seven families, or between fifty and sixty of the old men, women, and children, were prepared to remove to the Indian Territory as they were unable to work and were destitute.

Since the stoppage of rations, the maroons at Fort Clark had been most dissatisfied. Their needs were not matched by their means, and they had been driven to steal cattle from neighboring ranches in order to survive. Bullis recommended action to remove the old people and children to the Indian Territory as the other members of the group then would feel more at ease in Texas. For those who were to remain behind, the government should purchase a reservation where they could build farms; after a little initial support, they soon would thrive. Major Albert Morrow, post commander at Fort Clark, agreed that the government should allow the destitute to remove to the Indian Territory and added that if it did not, the army once again should issue them with "the Indian ration."[28]

In spite of the recommendations of Shafter, Bullis, and Morrow, the government neither removed nor granted assistance to the destitute among the Seminole maroons. During the second week of May, they received a crushing blow when Belknap declined to approve Special Order 80, Section 3, as he knew of no applicable appropriation. Ord wrote to the adjutant general requesting that the Indian bureau be asked to assume responsibility for removing the destitute and helpless at Fort Duncan to the Indian Territory. The commissioner presumably could make arrangements with the quartermaster's and commissary departments for their transportation and subsistence en route. Sheridan supported Ord's recommendation, and on June 10 Belknap referred these reports to the secretary of the interior.[29]

Again in late May 1875, Bullis described the plight of the Daniels band. The group was destitute, and local ranchers were complaining that the maroons were stealing stock to stave off starvation. Recently, many of the younger blacks had been set to return to Mexico and only just had been prevented from doing so by the older members of the group. Stressing the important role the scouts were playing on the border, Bullis implied that the government should take action to put an end to their misery. Morrow recommended that his superiors grant him authority to issue rations to the destitute as otherwise their only choice would be "stealing or starving." Ord concurred, adding that the scouts' families had no means of subsistence while the men were in the field and should receive rations during those periods. The old and destitute, moreover, "should be fed or sent to reservations." Sheridan forwarded these recommendations to the adjutant general "as a last hope that some action will be taken to meet the wants of a deserving people whose service has been and can still be made so valuable to the Government."[30]

The commissary general reported back that his department still had no applicable appropriation and was unable to proffer assistance to the maroons. Consequently, as the supplies of the war department were exhausted, Belknap asked Delano to instruct the Indian bureau to make provision for the Daniels band. On June 23, Clum returned his decision on Ord's earlier recommendation regarding the Kibbetts band at Fort Duncan. As the maroons had expressed unwillingness to remove to the Indian Territory, and his department had no funds at its disposal to subsist them while they remained in Texas, the Indian bureau was not in a position to help in any way. Delano then extended the decision to include the Daniels band at Fort Clark. Belknap retorted that his department had no applicable appropriation at its disposal and could not be held liable either for their subsistence or any outbreak of hostilities that might result. Yet again, the interior and war departments had refused to remove or subsist the destitute maroons, and both had denied responsibility for their future well-being.[31]

In early August, the Daniels band presented various requests to Colonel Edward Hatch, the latest commander at Fort Clark. The maroons asked that the authorities grant them land suitable for cultivation around the post or allow them to remove to their old homeland in Florida so that they could become self-supporting once again. In Texas, all the workable acreage was already in the hands of large capitalists and beyond the means of poor people such as themselves. In Florida, however, they could rent good land and eventually purchase it from the fruits of their labor. Large areas of the state still were vacant, and the beneficial climate and productive soil would assure their success.

Hatch believed it would be humane and economical to comply with their wishes. Their removal to Florida would not be expensive, and they soon would thrive and prove an asset to that state. They had experience of growing cotton, sugar, and corn, and as their old men pointed out, if all else failed, the Florida fisheries could provide them with a living. The maroons were "entirely distinct from the Seminole Indians" and were like other blacks except that they were "accustomed to arms," "brave and daring," and "superior to the Indians of this region in fighting qualities." If the government did not grant them their requests, they probably would return to Mexico, furnish an asylum for renegades both black and white, and engage in depredating excursions into Texas. Ord concurred, noting that the old and very young were so destitute that they were forced to live by stealing cattle from local ranches and begging from relatives. The secretary of war approved these recommendations in late August and then referred them through the interior department to the commissioner of Indian affairs for a decision.[32]

While commissioner Smith was considering the case, Charles Jones, United States senator for Florida, wrote to him protesting against this latest proposal. The maroons had lived too long on the uncivilized Mexican frontier and had developed bad habits. If they resettled in Florida, racial conflict and strife would be the likely result. Furthermore, the government had neither the right nor the authority to remove "paupers" from one state to another without the consent of the latter. The proposition did not include a provision for their subsistence after removal, and they would be dependent upon the state government for support. The older members of the group, moreover, had resided in the state earlier as slaves, not citizens, and their children had been born in a foreign country. Florida, therefore, had no obligation to the maroons and had the right to prevent their immigration. Jones requested that Smith decide against the recommendations of the war department and make arrangements for "these semi-barbarous people" in a more suitable location.[33]

On September 20, Smith returned a somewhat surprising decision, based upon his belief that there were at least three good reasons why the government should support the Seminole blacks. First of all, it had a responsibility to them. The government had removed the maroons from Florida to the Indian Territory as part of the Seminole tribe, but kidnappings and abductions had forced them to seek refuge in Mexico. In that inhospitable country, they had failed, and many of the old and very young now were destitute and in great need of assistance. Second, if they did not receive land, the group could become hostile and force an increase in expenditure for guarding the border country. Finally, the maroons were familiar with agricultural practices and anxious to become self-supporting, and they most certainly should be encouraged and assisted in this endeavor.

Clearly influenced by Senator Jones's objections to their resettlement in Florida, Smith recommended authorizing the return of the maroons to the Indian Territory, arguing that Article 2 of the treaty of March 21, 1866, allowed for their permanent relocation in the Seminole Nation. He then proposed that his superiors allow him to submit an estimate for an appropriation of up to forty thousand dollars to defray the costs of removal. There could be no question as to the humanity and economy of such an action.[34] The interior department approved Smith's suggestions, and the commissioner incorporated them into his annual report for 1875 as legislation recommended. Events were moving rapidly. In late December, Shafter even put forward the name of his brother as a candidate to collect the two maroon bands and conduct them to the Indian Territory.[35]

The military transferred most of the Kibbetts band to Fort Clark during the early part of 1876 in a move apparently envisaged as the first step in the removal of all of the maroons to the Indian Territory. Only a few scouts remained at Fort Duncan, and they completed the transfer a year later. The Kibbetts band settled below the village of the Daniels band, and the homes and gardens of the Seminole maroons came to extend along both sides of Las Moras Creek from near the present site of the scouts' cemetery upstream towards the post. John Horse and his family made their home at the lower settlement, just above the cemetery.[36]

At first, the earlier settlers resented the presence of the Kibbetts band. In early March, Elijah Daniels wrote to Mackenzie, then in command at Fort Sill, to request that he allow the band to remove forthwith. Twice before, in July 1873 and March 1875, Mackenzie had suggested that the government relocate Daniels and his supporters at Fort Sill, but upon receiving this latest petition, he now recommended that they be assigned lands in the Seminole Nation. Their removal would be inexpensive, and they would become self-supporting within a year. Once again, however, the authorities in Washington did not see fit to implement Mackenzie's proposals.[37]

The maroons already had encountered hostility from citizens of Texas[38] and had made a dangerous enemy in the notorious outlaw John "King" Fisher. A favorite haunt of the scouts at Fort Duncan was the Old Blue Saloon in nearby Eagle Pass. Around Christmas time 1874, Corporal George Washington became involved in an argument with Fisher at the bar over payment for drinks. A gunfight broke out in which Fisher received a scalp wound and Washington was shot in the stomach. Other maroons may have been involved as Dan Johnson was noted as having a gunshot wound the following March. Washington died after suffering in hospital for several months, but although he was indicted, Fisher was cleared of the murder charge.[39] Never one to forget an injury, Fisher would shoot a Seminole Negro Indian Scout from his horse many years later as he tried to strike the outlaw "King" with his quirt following another barroom incident in Eagle Pass.[40]

The acts of violence reached a climax in the spring of 1876. In late April, thirty-five citizens of Kinney County complained to the secretary of war about the maroons at Fort Clark. They argued that the army employed few of the group as scouts, and the remainder continually stole property from local white settlers. Because he had no authority over the unenlisted blacks, the commanding officer at the post could offer no assistance. There was some contention also over the land the group was using on Las Moras Creek. The maroons may have tried to increase their agricultural production by moving outside the limits of the military reservation. The Texans claimed that they had located on private property and were causing damage both to it and to the surrounding countryside. By the third week in May, the government appeared to be taking no action, and the local whites decided to take matters into their own hands.[41]

During the evening of Friday, May 19, in a move clearly designed to scare the Seminole maroons into returning to Mexico, assassins ambushed John Horse and Titus Payne as they were riding just south of the post hospital. Payne was shot and killed instantly. His body was dragged from the road and remained undiscovered until the Monday morning when he was found with his gun laid across his chest. John Horse was wounded in four places and his mount American also was hurt badly, but the old warriors managed to make the maroon settlement, and Horse lived to tell the tale of his narrow escape from yet another attempt on his life.[42]

Both the Seminole blacks and the local whites grew fearful after the attack. The maroons became afraid to pass from their settlement to the post or the nearby town of Brackettville where some had found work, and both men and women took to carrying arms. The Texans, in turn, feared retaliation.[43] This led to renewed calls for the maroons' removal from Ord, Sheridan, and Colonel John Irvin Gregg, the latest commanding officer at Fort Clark. Ord suggested again that positive good could come from this if their relocation were planned carefully, for the blacks' "simple manners" and "religious tendency" would have a beneficial effect on neighboring Native Americans such as the Sioux or the Apaches. Sheridan forwarded these recommendations to Washington in early June in the hope that the threat to white lives and property might at last spur the government into action.[44]

Once again, the efforts of these military officials proved futile. In early June, the latest commissioner of Indian affairs, John Q. Smith, returned a decision against either removing or supporting the maroons. Smith felt unable to support his predecessor's recommendation for an appropriation to relocate and subsist the group in the Indian Territory and would not submit an estimate for the consideration of Congress. In fact, in a complete reversal of his namesake's line, Smith found himself in full accord with the conclusions reached by Commissioner Walker in December 1872.

The commissioner argued that the Indian bureau neither had authorized the return of the Mascogos to the United States nor benefitted from the move and that his department had no obligation to them. Also, these maroons clearly had no legal title to any portion of a reservation, either in the Indian Territory or elsewhere. Under the terms of the 1866 treaty, the permission of the tribal authorities would be required before the group could relocate in the Seminole Nation, and this was unlikely to be forthcoming as the blacks had been described as "fierce and lawless." In the same vein, the government hardly could be expected to purchase a separate tract of land for an independent band of maroons elsewhere in the Indian Territory and bear the expense of removing them there. Finally, the group included a number of former Texas runaways who had no history of Indian association and had no more right to consideration than any other freedmen. Smith concluded that the Seminole blacks held no just claim to support from the government.[45]

Smith's decision to revert to the policy of Commissioner Walker instead of supporting the initiative of his immediate predecessor brought to an end four years of continuous and intense debate and sealed the fate of the Seminole maroons living on the border. Evidence had been presented, propositions put forward, and recommendations made. It seemed that little else remained to be said on the subject. Interest waned as time passed, and Smith's decision proved to be final. For a time, Ord continued to lobby on their behalf, but his pleas went unheeded.[46] The commissioner of Indian affairs had made it clear once and for all that he would not sanction the removal of the group to the Indian Territory and that it could expect no further support. Though the maroons had kept their part of the bargain, having removed to Texas and their men having served the frontier army admirably as scouts, the government chose to renege on its earlier agreements and instead abandoned the group to starvation and destitution.

This episode illustrates ways in which individuals, agencies, and institutions construct identities of others for their own purposes. It relates strongly to other white attempts at classifying blacks associated with Native Americans during the nineteenth century. Motivation tended to stem from vested interest or expediency. Thus the Texas situation closely parallels both Jesup's removal policies in Florida in the 1830s and the work of the Dawes Commission in the late 1890s and early 1900s. Just as commissioners of Indian affairs attempted to define the Texas Seminole maroons in ways that would legitimize a refusal to establish the precedent of removing or subsisting blacks at government expense, so Jesup tried to separate the races to end the Second Seminole War and the Dawes Commissioners classified and divided by race the societies of the Five Civilized Tribes to expedite white settlement of the Indian Territory. All three episodes would prove destructive to those subjected to the process. Jesup's policies led to fragmentation, factionalism, and displacement within postremoval Seminole society, the work of the Dawes Commission left freedmen citizens of the Five Civilized Tribes subject to segregation and institutionalized racism without recourse in the new state of Oklahoma, and the decisions of interior and war department officials left the Texas Seminole maroons in limbo for half a century and eventually cost them their homes.

6

In Search of Home

In view of the implications of commissioner John Q. Smith's decision not to remove or support the group, several parties of Seminole maroons soon would choose to return independently to Coahuila or the Indian Territory. These people had grown tired of broken promises, of fighting Indian wars, of threats of further violence, of poor prospects for their children. More than a quarter of a century had passed since they had left the Indian Territory, but the maroons still had not managed to establish a permanent, secure settlement where they could raise their families, build farms, and maintain their customs and traditions. In this sense, freedom remained elusive. Beginning in the late 1870s, many would meet the challenge by seeking elsewhere a better life than that offered on the military reservations. Others would elect to continue the struggle in Texas, but all would be united in a search for home.

The maroons had been disturbed greatly by the attack on John Horse and Titus Payne in May 1876, but the violence reached a new peak early in the morning of New Year's Day, 1877. Adam Paine, who had won the Medal of Honor for his part in the Red River War, had been discharged from the scouts on February 19, 1875, at the end of his term of service. Instead of reenlisting, Paine had taken to frequenting the border towns and was suspected of stealing horses and cattle and running them into Mexico. Of more importance, he was wanted in Brownsville for stabbing a private of the Eighth Cavalry. On the afternoon of December 31, Brackettville law enforcement officers received word that he had returned to Fort Clark. Paine was attending a New Year's dance in the Bowlegs's yard at the maroon settlement when, shortly after midnight, Deputy Sheriff Claron Windus blasted him with a shotgun at such short range, it has been said, that his clothes were set afire.

A number of the maroons, including the influential Medal of Honor winner Pompey Factor, Joseph Philips, and Dindy Factor, had seen enough and crossed over into Coahuila to rejoin their kinsmen at Nacimiento. John Horse is known to have returned to the hacienda shortly after the attempt upon his life and also may have removed at this time. The emigrants failed to fulfill the fears of United States military officials that they might join other bands on the border and engage in raids on Texas, however. In Mexico, they again had to defend their settlement and its environs and once more took up arms against depredating Indian bands.[1]

By the summer of 1880, it seemed probable that, in the light of declining Indian hostilities, the military would curtail the duties of the scouts and reduce their numbers. Several of the leading enlisted men were not prepared to face the uncertainty of life on the military reservation or in Coahuila and hoped to secure a more stable future for their families by removing to the Seminole freedman settlements in the Indian Territory. In June, First Sergeant David Bowlegs, Sergeants Sampson July and Bob Kibbetts, and Privates Isaac Payne and Pompey Perryman asked Bullis to relay the message to Ord that they wished to visit the Seminole Nation as representatives of the group to inspect the country and ascertain what rights and privileges they would receive if they were to return there with their families.[2]

Bullis, Colonel David Stanley, commanding officer at Fort Clark, and Ord supported the proposal. Stanley believed that the maroons' removal would lead them away from "the temptations of the Mexican Frontier," and Bullis stated that once settled in the Seminole Nation, they would "become industrious and make good citizens." Ord even offered to remove the maroons if the interior department would resettle and supply them upon arrival in the Indian Territory. Acting Commissioner of Indian Affairs E. J. Brooks replied that if they were transported there, his department would "find them suitable homes on the Seminole Reservation."[3]

The following summer, David Bowlegs, "the most influential of their number," visited the Seminole Nation. Bowlegs liked what he saw of the thriving black communities, was impressed particularly by the educational opportunities afforded the children of Seminole freedmen, and took back to Texas a favorable report of his findings. Later, in an interview with Stanley, Bowlegs stated his reasons for wishing to remove:

> If I had no one but myself and my wife I would rather soldier than do anything else I know of, but I have a large family growing up,

and we are here where we own nothing, and can get no work. My children will grow up idle and become criminals on this frontier. I have been raised like an Indian, but want to go to my people and settle in a home, and teach my children to work, and most of my people are like me.[4]

Bowlegs's account of life in the Seminole Nation excited many members of the group, and they eagerly awaited the call to remove there.

In the spring of 1882, still not having received permission to commence the journey, the maroons determined to spur the government into action. Several of the scouts, including David Bowlegs, received their discharge papers in May and instead of reenlisting, prepared to remove. By mid-June, fifty-seven maroons were ready to leave. They had some transportation of their own, but asked for another four army wagons to enable them to make the journey. Stanley suggested that he provide the wagons and that the party travel via either Fort McKavett or Fort Concho so that the teams could be relieved. They also would need rations en route as they were poor and needy. Once again, Sheridan strongly supported these proposals and forwarded them to the secretary of war for his consideration.[5]

The Indian bureau referred the proposition to Union Agent John Q. Tufts for a report.[6] In mid-July, Tufts wrote to John Jumper, principal chief of the Seminoles, asking for his opinion. Jumper called a meeting of the Seminole authorities and delivered their verdict to Tufts on August 2: "The Council are unanimously opposed to the coming of the said Bowlegs and party. [There] is no foundation in fact for the assertion that the Seminoles here were willing for them to come among them to settle." These maroons had "voluntarily abandoned their Tribe" many years before and had no just claim to the rights and benefits of citizenship under the 1866 treaty. Moreover, the group contained individuals of "doubtful identity" and notorious outlaws who were deemed to be undesirable immigrants.[7] In view of the Seminoles' emphatic refusal to receive the Bowlegs party into the nation, Commissioner of Indian Affairs Hiram Price recommended that no action be taken to remove the group at that time.

Despite the opposition of the Seminoles and the Indian bureau, Bowlegs, his wife Fanny, and their nine children removed independently to the Seminole Nation in December. Relatives welcomed the immigrants, who settled so easily into the freedman community that

Seminole and United States authorities failed to detect their presence for more than a year.[8] In May 1883, it was reported that more of the scouts wished to remove the following spring if the military no longer required their services. Some were growing old, and all wished to settle down and have homes of their own. They would need transportation to the Indian Territory and some assistance upon arrival until they could raise their first crop. The scouts would not be needed beyond the end of the fiscal year and Augur, in command of the Department of Texas, recommended that arrangements be made to send them there at that time. Price then instructed Tufts to ask the Seminoles if they would be willing to accept the maroons into the nation.[9]

Tufts again received a very definite negative reply from Chief Jumper on September 17. Jumper made it clear why the Seminoles would not welcome the return of the maroons: the majority had been owned by the Seminoles, had chosen freely to leave for Mexico, and had become citizens of that country. Moreover, because they had removed before the 1856 and 1866 treaties, which had created separate Seminole reservations, they had not been included in those treaties' provisions. Therefore, the emigrants could not claim Seminole citizenship by "blood, tribal organization or treaty" and had no right to land or other benefits in the nation.

Jumper argued that there was insufficient arable land for the population already living in the Seminole Nation, and that the established residents could not afford to make room for the would-be immigrants. He portrayed the maroons as "turbulent," "lawless," and a threat to the already troubled nation. Jumper put the case in a nutshell: "To sum it all up, they have no rights here, we have no room for them, and we protest against their being sent here as we have done before."[10] With this in mind, Tufts proposed that the maroons remain in Texas where they could be controlled more easily. Consequently, on October 18, Price repeated his earlier opinion that the bureau should not remove the group, and the secretary of the interior approved his recommendation the following day.[11]

In October 1883, however, another party of twenty-seven maroons removed independently from Texas to the Seminole Nation. When added to the Bowlegs family, this made a total of thirty-eight Seminole blacks who had immigrated without permission in less than a year. These latest arrivals settled amongst their kinsmen in the freedman community and began immediately to make improvements on the land. But their presence became known to Chief Jumper, and on March 1, 1884, he wrote an uncompromising letter to Tufts demanding that they be ejected forthwith as intruders.[12]

Intruders in the Indian Nations consisted typically of white squatters who took up residence there without legal justification. The nations' authorities had the right to call upon their agents to have such persons expelled. Jumper's latest initiative would mark the beginning of a determined, year-long effort by Seminole leaders to use this power to have the Texas maroons removed from the nation. Tufts sent notice to the immigrants to leave at once or state their case to him in person. In response, their leading men, together with several freedmen and Seminole leaders, traveled to Muskogee and appeared before the agent on March 25.

From their various testimonies, it emerged that the immigrants felt they had a perfect right to remain in the nation. David and Fanny Bowlegs had been born enslaved to an Indian in the Seminole country and had left for Coahuila in 1849. Seminoles had forced the members of the second immigrant group to quit the reservation even earlier. These included Joseph Bagby (or Bagly), his "state-raised" wife, their ten children, and their two sons-in-law, Henry Coleman and Thompson; David Bowlegs's sister Dolly, her state-raised husband, and their nine children; and Polly Marshall and her Creek black husband, who had been sold by his Indian owner to a Texas white in 1847. Bagby, Dolly, and Polly had been born in the Seminole country and their Indian owners had sold them into bondage in Texas in 1847 and 1848. Bagby and Polly, moreover, were children of Seminole freedmen John Cudjo and Jacob Davis, respectively, and they maintained that they and their families should enjoy rights in the nation as descendants of recognized citizens under Article 2 of the 1866 treaty. The immigrants seemed prepared to remain in the nation in defiance of the ruling of the Seminole council.

Being unsure of how to proceed, Tufts referred the facts to Price, requested instructions, and suggested that he allow the blacks to settle in the Oklahoma Territory. In the meantime, the Union agent issued them a permit to settle in the Seminole Nation and raise a crop until his superiors decided the matter.[13] Jumper attacked Tufts's initiative immediately in a letter to delegate John F. Brown, who was representing the Seminole Nation in Washington. He instructed Brown to visit the Indian bureau and put the views of the Seminoles before the commissioner. To Jumper's way of thinking, the immigrants had no right to return to the nation, were "not at all servicable [sic] as examples of industry" to recognized citizens, and should not be allowed to remain while the matter was being settled. Both parties had stated their case, and now it remained for the secretary of the interior to settle the issue.[14]

Commissioner Price believed that Tufts should eject the Bowlegs family but allow the Bagby party to stay. He could see no reason why maroons who had left the reservation voluntarily years before the 1866 treaty should be included in its provisions. If they had no rights in the Seminole Nation, they had none in the Oklahoma Territory either, even if it were considered a suitable resettlement area for blacks such as Chickasaw and Choctaw freedmen. The leaders of the Bagby party, on the other hand, had been sold and removed forcibly from the Seminole country. They and their descendants should be entitled to all the benefits of Seminole citizenship under the terms of the treaty.[15]

Secretary of the Interior Henry M. Teller took issue with Price's assessment, and arrived at different conclusions. The 1866 treaty had not been designed to include maroons who had removed from the Seminole country eighteen years before it was signed, whether others had forced them to leave or not, especially as they had not returned until long after the barrier stopping them from doing so had been removed. The treaty clearly referred to blacks "who were living among the Seminoles at the date of the treaty, and *their descendants born after that date.*" All of the claimants had lived in Texas for a number of years and likely had exercised the rights of American citizens there. As such, they had no claim under the Seminole treaty and should be treated as intruders.[16] It was indeed unfortunate that the decision which effectively denied the immigrants the support of the government and anticipated their removal from the Seminole Nation was based largely on the mistaken assumptions that they had chosen not to return earlier and that they had become United States citizens.

On May 17, Commissioner of Indian Affairs E. L. Stevens relayed the opinion to Tufts with instructions on how to proceed. If the Seminoles were unwilling to allow them to remain, Tufts should give the immigrants a reasonable amount of time in which to dispose of their improvements and quit the nation. If they failed to do so, he should eject them as intruders. Tufts sent notice to the immigrants to leave and fixed a time for their removal. The blacks ignored the order, however, and boldly remained where they were. Again, Jumper protested to Tufts who told him that he had recommended that troops remove them forcibly. The Indian bureau took no action, however, and left the immigrants undisturbed.[17]

On February 12, 1885, Brown wrote a letter of complaint to the Indian bureau demanding that it take steps quickly to remove the intruders. Price instructed Tufts to order the immigrants to leave the Seminole Nation by May 1, and advise them that he would have his police expel them forcibly if they had not left by the deadline.[18] Once again, however, the Union agent failed to bring about their removal. Tufts's superiors never received a report of his actions, and correspondence upon the subject ceased. The agent's failure to act may have been prompted by the impossibility of enforcing removal orders in the Indian Territory and the fearsome reputation of the Seminole black towns.[19] Whatever the reason, the immigrants seem not to have been troubled further by either the Seminole authorities or United States officials but to have settled peacefully into the freedman communities. These people, at least, finally had found home. They would be joined later by still other returnees from Texas: Jake, Jim, and Joe Bruner, and Cato and Johnny Wilson, all being reported as having resettled in the Seminole Nation around that time.[20]

Although they continued to reside in the Seminole Nation, the immigrants removed themselves effectively from the center of attention. None was included in Seminole census records for the 1890s, which were compiled for annuity payments, or indeed in the final rolls of the Seminole Nation drawn up for land allotment under the Dawes Commission. This would suggest that they never became Seminole citizens or derived any direct benefit from their tribal association in the way of monetary disbursements or land ownership. Rather, they seem to have lived upon and worked the land of relatives.[21]

The immigrants did not disappear completely, however. On May 16, 1885, Stanley, by now a brigadier general and in command of the Department of Texas, reported that they had been welcomed into the Seminole Nation and were living there still. And in February 1888, the maroons at Fort Clark, recounting their numbers, stated that three families were residing in the Indian Territory. Interestingly enough, David Bowlegs's army discharge papers were filed with the Seminole County Clerk in Wewoka in October 1935 and now are housed in the Western History Collections at the University of Oklahoma. Seminole freedman George Noble recalled in 1942 that Bowlegs often told stories of his scouting days before he died near Noble town, and Kenneth

Porter reported in 1951 that the descendants of the immigrants in Seminole County still maintained visiting relations with the Brackettville and Nacimiento communities.[22]

One implication of this affair is that it highlights facets of Seminole-black relations in the Indian Territory during the 1880s. The immigrants were indeed unfortunate in their timing. Had they returned to the Seminole Nation a few years earlier, they would have found a more sympathetic leadership in Principal Chief John Chupco and his conservative Seminole and freedman counselors. Chupco had fought side by side with blacks during the Second Seminole War in Florida and for the Union during the Civil War in the Indian Territory and actively had promoted their incorporation into the nation on an equal footing during Reconstruction. Had Chupco still been chief, the petitions of the immigrants might have been received more favorably.

As it was, John Jumper and his supporters were again in control of the government. Though he was a fullblood, Jumper was an educated Christian, with white and mixed-blood associates, who favored rapid acculturation. During the antebellum period, he had acquired substantial holdings in slave property and had dealt widely in blacks. He had become a Confederate colonel in the Civil War and had led the Seminole Battalion against Union black troops during military engagements in the Indian Territory. Defeated and exhausted, Jumper and his associates were anxious for peace and supported the status quo by not contesting the rights of blacks in the nation during Reconstruction. The scars ran deep, however, and little love was lost between the Jumper party and the freedmen. Faced with a crisis situation, Jumper responded by giving vent to the strong racial consciousness of his supporters in opposing the immigration of the Texas maroons into the nation, no matter how strong their claim to citizenship. The freedman population already was increasing rapidly, and Jumper's actions seem to have stemmed from a fear that the Seminoles would be swamped by blacks.

The Seminole freedmen were the ones who wanted the maroons to return to the nation. The immigrants were "well received" by their black kinsmen, not the Seminole Indians. From the start, the tribal leadership opposed their projected removal and after it had been completed, insisted upon their ejection. At first sight, several of Chief Jumper's arguments appear to have had a sound basis. The immigrants, after all, did not have an indisputable right by treaty to enjoy the same benefits as Seminole citizens. Moreover, little was known of these people and the fear that they might constitute a threat to the peace of the nation seems understandable in the light of their having lived so long on the dangerous and lawless Texas-Coahuila border. The shortage of arable land in the nation was another source of great concern to the Seminole leadership during Reconstruction. Jumper, in fact, went so far as to purchase additional acreage for the Seminoles from the Creeks. The immigrants also removed without receiving permission from either the Seminole or federal authorities, and this could have set a precedent for a flood of illegal intruders. But the maroons had a strong claim to be allowed to remain in the nation, and Jumper's unequivocal denial of their petition seems both unreasonable and discriminatory.

All of the thirty-eight immigrants either had been enslaved by Seminoles or were descended from former slaves. Some had fled to Coahuila to escape servitude or kidnappers whereas the owners of others had sold them into slavery in Texas. Many were direct descendants of recognized Seminole freedman citizens and had kinsmen living in the nation. A provision in the 1866 treaty, moreover, allowed the Seminoles to admit such individuals.[23] The tribal leadership made a definite decision not to exercise its discretionary powers in this case. Furthermore, a precedent had been set earlier for granting these people permission to return to the nation: Wild Cat's Indian followers also had left voluntarily in 1849, had been exposed to lawless border conditions, and had not been present when the 1856 treaty was signed. Under Jumper's own reasoning, therefore, they could have made no just claim and had constituted a potential threat to law and order. Yet Jumper not only had allowed them to return between 1859 and 1861, but also had encouraged them openly to do so. A dual system was being operated by the Seminole leadership: what applied to Indians did not necessarily apply to blacks.

This assertion is supported by the whole tone of Jumper's reaction to the immigrants. The Seminole leader stressed that several of their number had been slaves, labeled them as "persons of African descent and blood," and referred to them on more than one occasion as "these negroes."[24] An uncompromising attitude dominated his response and there was no hint of guilt, remorse, or compassion in his statements. With the emphasis being placed so heavily upon the importance of "blood," there seems little doubt that if the immigrants had been Seminole Indian rather than Seminole black, Jumper would have granted them admission into the nation.

Apart from Chief Jumper, an axis of former Confederate sympathizers headed by delegate John F. Brown dominated the Seminole authorities at this time. An acculturated mixed-blood who had led the opposition to the incorporation of the freedmen during the 1866 treaty negotiations, Brown would succeed Jumper and dominate Seminole affairs for the next twenty years. Brown wholeheartedly supported the Jumper line and after his accession, adopted it as his own. He honored the rights of the freedmen, but strongly opposed the efforts of the maroons to return to the nation. Racial tension and mutual suspicion continued to figure prominently in relations between blacks and the former Confederate Seminole leadership during the postbellum period.

Seminole Reconstruction, as it affected blacks, undoubtedly was extremely successful. The Seminoles incorporated the freedmen into the nation, granted them rights and privileges as citizens, and left them to their own devices. The lot of the Seminole freedman was infinitely superior to that of most blacks associated with the other Civilized Tribes at that time. Significantly, the immigrants chose to return during a period when the Choctaw and Chickasaw freedmen, in particular, were experiencing widespread discrimination, segregation, the threat of forced removal from the nations, and outright persecution. The maroons clearly perceived the Seminole Nation to be a desirable place to live after the Civil War.

Yet it was the freedman settlements, and not those of the Indians, that attracted the Texas group. The immigrants wished to reestablish relations with their kinsmen, not with the Seminoles. The Indians and blacks continued to consider themselves separate groups. The freedman settlements were so isolated and independent, in fact, that they continued to constitute maroon societies, the Indians being generally unaware of what took place there. Thus, it took an entire year for the Seminoles to realize that illegal immigrants from the border country had made their homes within the black towns. The tribal authorities then were powerless to eject them from the almost autonomous freedman communities.

The freedmen welcomed the maroons into the nation, hid and supported them, and risked censure by the tribal and federal authorities for doing so. Clearly, the ties that bound the Seminole blacks in the Indian Territory to those in Texas and Mexico were far stronger than those linking the freedmen to the Seminoles. In May 1885, a military official observed astutely that the Texas maroons had "no idea of individual enterprise and responsibility" but regarded "their whole people as a unit."[25] While the Seminoles considered themselves to be Seminole and Indian, their maroon associates thought of themselves not as Seminole, Indian, or black, but Seminole black.

While the Bowlegs affair was following its course, matters affecting the maroons in Texas took a marked turn for the worse, resulting in renewed efforts to bring about their removal to the Indian Territory. In August 1884, military officials decided that the number of Seminole Negro Indian Scouts should be cut from forty to six at the end of the month.[26] Stanley, who was forced to issue the order, was appalled by his charge:

> Thirty-four men—all with wives and children—who have served as soldiers for the average of thirteen years; without any trades or property; and with habits essentially Indian, are thrown upon a community, itself poor, and hostile to these harmless vagabonds. [How] they are to live, or what is to become of them, I cannot imagine.[27]

The decision came as a devastating blow as the entire group of 234 had continued to rely almost completely upon the wages and rations of the scouts. Worst of all, they were given less than two weeks notice to find alternative means of subsistence in an area where work was scarce and the inhabitants hostile. The maroons were unprepared to face this latest crisis, lacked even "the transportation to carry their families and effects to where they might hope to earn a living," and faced almost certain destitution.[28]

Again, local military officials who were familiar with the situation rallied to the maroons' support. Lieutenant Edward Ives, in command of the scouts, asked his superiors to modify the order so as to permit local officers to discharge them gradually, or keep them in service until at least the end of September to allow them to find other ways of providing for the group. If the military did not exercise restraint, the maroons likely would be reduced to stealing or begging. Lieutenant Colonel Bliss, once again in command at Fort Clark, supported Ives's assessment. The maroons were "in an almost helpless condition, with many widows and orphans." Some feared that they would be ejected from the military reservation and asked permission to remain until spring, when they would seek other work in Texas. Some thirty others wished to remove to the Seminole Nation or a separate reservation of their own in the Indian Territory.

Bliss believed the government should pursue the latter option as, if it could provide land and transportation, almost all of the maroons would relocate. He recommended that the military keep the scouts in service for another month and that during that time, the government procure a suitable tract for the group in the Indian Territory. These blacks were not troublesome or dangerous but "better than the same class of their color now living in Texas." They had served the army well and were entitled to consideration. Both Stanley and Major General John Schofield, the latest commander of the Military Division of the Missouri, agreed that the government should resettle the group in the Indian Territory, and the secretary of war passed the matter on to the interior department for a decision. No action was taken, however, and the maroons suffered through another winter at Fort Clark.[29]

In the spring of 1885, two of the group's leading men, Sergeant Bob Kibbetts and ex-Sergeant Sampson July, decided to appeal their case directly to the department commander. The two presented a well-balanced combination. Kibbetts was in his mid-thirties by now, and was recognized as head of the remaining scouts. Mature, intelligent, energetic, and determined, he showed great potential and was the obvious choice to succeed eventually to the overall leadership. July, in contrast, was aging, represented the views of the older generation of maroons, and was "looked upon as the Patriarch of the tribe."[30] The two also had been prominent in previous efforts to secure the removal of the group to the Indian Territory. Kibbetts had made an investigative trip to the Seminole Nation in 1869 while the maroons still were living in Coahuila, and he and July had been part of the Bowlegs delegation that had sought permission to undertake a similar mission in 1882.

On May 13, Kibbetts and July visited Stanley at his headquarters in San Antonio. They discussed their troubles and needs and found the department commander to be sympathetic. Stanley recommended that the group "be cared for." If the Seminole authorities objected to the maroons' resettlement in the nation, which they had "no good right to do," the government should procure a separate reservation for the blacks elsewhere. Again, Schofield supported Stanley's suggestions, requesting urgently that his superiors comply. But yet again, the Department of the Interior chose not to act, and still another year went by.[31]

Undaunted, Kibbetts determined to go even higher. In March 1886, he traveled to Washington alone, "at considerable personal expense," to lay the maroons' case before top government officials.[32] Kibbetts first visited the Office of Indian Affairs, requested that the commissioner allow the group to return to the Seminole Nation under Article 2 of the 1866 treaty, and presented some documents he had brought with him, including Sheridan's recommendations, to support his petition.[33] He then appeared before the Senate Committee on Indian Affairs, headed by Chairman Henry Dawes, and "made a favorable impression [as] a man of intelligence [capable] of being of some service to his race." Taking a positive approach, Kibbetts wanted to know whether the maroons did not have a right to return to the nation under existing treaties. If they did not, he asked that the government find homes for them in the Oklahoma Territory. Dawes forwarded these requests to the secretary of the interior so that he could furnish a report. Through his enterprise, Kibbetts had gained the attention of high-ranking government officials and had set the wheels of the decision-making process in motion.[34]

Immediately after Kibbetts's visit to the Indian bureau, the acting commissioner wrote to Chief Jumper asking if he would allow the maroons to return to the nation. Though he realized that they were not included directly under the terms of the 1866 treaty, the acting commissioner believed these blacks to be "a portion of the people whose rights were intended to be secured" by it. If the Seminole authorities would allow them to return, it would constitute "an Act of Justice as well as generosity towards a remnant of the people formerly held in slavery." Jumper chose not to reply to this communication, however. As the consent of the tribal authorities was a prerequisite of any initiative to relocate the maroons in the nation, the Seminole leader's silence was tantamount to a refusal and put an end to the proposal.[35]

Taking his cue from Jumper, Commissioner of Indian Affairs John DeWitt Clinton Atkins went still further. As they had been granted Mexican citizenship long ago and were not resident in the United States when slavery was abolished, these maroons were "in no sense *freedmen*" and had no right to consideration under existing laws and treaties.[36] In short, United States officials finally had found the answer to the problem of defining the government's relationship with the Seminole maroons. From now on, they were to be considered neither Indian nor black but just plain Mexican and therefore ineligible for further support.

The secretary of the interior informed Dawes that new laws would be needed before they could resettle the maroons in the Oklahoma Territory, but the Senate committee proposed no such legislation. Bob Kibbetts's long and expensive journey to the East on behalf of his people had proven fruitless, and it came to mark the last major attempt to resettle the entire Texas group in the Indian Territory.[37]

Elderly men had dominated the leadership of the maroons since their return from Coahuila. John Horse, John Kibbetts, and Elijah Daniels, for instance, were all over sixty years old by the 1870s. John Horse and Sampson July, moreover, were credited with having assumed patriarchal roles within the community. As in other small-scale societies, a council of male elders likely met periodically and furnished advice to the leader on important matters affecting the group. This would explain the origin of a petition drawn up by eight of the group's leading older men in February 1888 and addressed to President Grover Cleveland. The petitioners, with their approximate ages, included John Wilson, 80; Hardy Factor, 84; Friday Bowlegs, 60; Sampson July, 60; Dick Johnson, 70; and Ben Wilson, 60. Dembo Factor, who claimed to have been a warrior at the "Dade massacre" and a subchief at the Battle of Lake Okeechobee during the Second Seminole War, headed the list of signatories. Dembo described himself as 86 years of age, "the oldest living of the tribe," and was "regarded as the Seminole Chief." The old leader doubtless had determined a course of action in concert with his principal advisers.

The petition displayed for the first time the pragmatic realization that the group as a whole never would be allowed to return to the Seminole Nation. In fact, the signatories reversed the usual tack by asking not to be sent there, because of the climate. Instead, they requested that the president set aside a reservation for the maroons at Fort Clark. The tract should include the village they had built on Las Moras Creek. In addition, the government should purchase the well-watered land to the southwest so as to make the total area around fifteen thousand acres, "adapted for farming and grazing." The petitioners also requested stock, seed, agricultural implements, and a sum of money to create and maintain a school. They hoped to establish "a well behaved, contented and prosperous community," and preserve the unity of the group as a whole.

The maroons were tired of wandering and sought a permanent home. The promise of land had persuaded them to return to Texas, after all, and they felt their petition worthy. Though the commissioner of Indian affairs earlier had decided that they were ineligible for a reservation as they were not Indian, they pointed out that many of their number had Indian blood flowing through their veins and that their claim had been "illogically and unjustly" dismissed in the light of their historic association with the Seminoles. Finally, the petitioners argued that the group contained many old people, orphans, and women with dependent children, who were not members of the scouts' families, were incapable of labor, and were in great need of assistance. President Cleveland did not grant these requests, however. The reservation never materialized, and the maroons continued to squat at Las Moras Creek for another quarter of a century.[38]

In the spring of 1894, former scout William Warrior asked Major Edward Hayes, the commander at Fort Clark, to inquire of Governor Brown if the Seminoles would allow the maroons based at the post to return to the nation. Brown stated in his reply of May 5 that it had been decided earlier in Washington that the group had no right to Seminole funds and lands. His position then was spelled out: "The Seminole people do not want the 'Seminole Negro Indians' among the(m) *at all* and it is useless to think of being received by them." Brown's governorship would see no change in Jumper's policy of unequivocal opposition to the immigration of Seminole maroons from Texas.[39]

Most of the group had come to realize long before that they never would be allowed to return to the Indian Territory and had tried to develop a more settled lifestyle at Fort Clark. They built a church of simple plan and maintained a cemetery for the scouts, established some four miles south of the post in 1872, that has survived to this day. Of the able-bodied unenlisted men, some found work as hands on local ranches, others worked the land and became small farmers, a few found jobs around the fort, and the remainder lived by hunting and fishing. Eagerly, the group would await the scouts' return to Fort Clark from expedition, when the men would ride off to Brackettville to celebrate in the town's saloons. Typically, the women took care of the home, raised the children, planted fruit and vegetable gardens, and tended to the farm animals and livestock. Some found employment as laundresses at the post, and a few others found local work around Brackettville.[40]

The able-bodied remained handicapped by the large number of young, old, and helpless who were dependent upon them for support and by the limitations of the small amount of land made available to them. The maroons rarely were able to raise sufficient crops to match their needs and constantly were poverty-stricken. The government typically refused to help, even during times of their greatest need. During the summer of 1899, however, heavy rains caused Las Moras

Creek to rise and flood the maroons' settlement, leaving them "entirely destitute." Though the commissioner of Indian affairs decided that they were ineligible for relief, on that occasion the maroons were provided with subsistence until they could support themselves. Nevertheless, for the majority of the community, life on the military reservation continued to be a grim struggle for survival.[41]

The scouts continued to bear the brunt of supporting the group. Although the Indian threat to West Texas had been removed effectively by 1881, outlaws remained a problem and the army retained the unit in part-time service on a reduced scale. From then on, the scouts' home base continued to be Fort Clark, but they also completed detached service at Fort Davis, Camp Pena Colorado, and Camp Neville Spring in the Big Bend country, and Fort Ringgold, situated a mile from Rio Grande City in Starr County. Though their assignments would become much more mundane, the scouts would continue on active duty for over thirty more years.

After the construction of Camp Pena Colorado in 1879, the military assigned there detachments of the Tenth Cavalry and a unit of twenty Seminole Negro Indian Scouts. In November and December 1884, these scouts saw action in what became known as "the Petty Incident," during which black soldiers under Captain Robert Smithers crossed the border in pursuit of Mexican raiders in blatant violation of the reciprocal treaty of 1882. This affair led to the construction of yet another post in the Big Bend country. The scouts found an ideal location with good water some ten miles west of Tornillo Creek the following February, and on March 5, 1885, Camp Neville Spring became officially a second subpost of Fort Davis.

Later that year, the army mobilized the scouts in anticipation that Geronimo's band of Chiricahuas might attempt to cross over into Texas to escape from the pressure that the forces of General George Crook were exerting. Crook ordered all military units in the Big Bend to be on the alert and instructed specifically that the scouts keep close watch over the river crossings between Presidio del Norte and Presidio de San Vicente to prevent the Apaches from entering Texas. For the rest of the year, the scouts patrolled the Big Bend border country, reporting on one occasion that several Chiricahuas had been sighted attempting to cross near Presidio del Norte. Though this served to keep the troops vigilant, there is no record that Geronimo's band actually crossed over into Texas at this time.

Following the surrender of Geronimo to General Nelson Miles in early September 1886, the army curtailed the activities of the scouts drastically. Thereafter, those based at Camp Neville Spring engaged mostly in routine patrols along the border. In his annual report the following year, post commander Second Lieutenant John Cunningham reported that the scouts had covered an area of 150 miles around Neville Spring without seeing a single Indian. The camps of cattle punchers now extended throughout the Big Bend area, and Cunningham felt it no longer necessary to send out his men on even routine patrols. On April 7, 1891, the scouts finally received instructions to abandon the post and relocate even closer to the border at Polvo (present-day Redford). By that time, their duties had become mostly constabulary. From then until their disbandment, the scouts helped maintain law and order in West Texas from the Big Bend to the Gulf, bringing outlaws and horse thieves to justice.[42]

Beginning in 1909, military officials thought that the unit had outlived its usefulness and began to phase it out. By 1914, most of the old scouts from the days of the Indian wars had passed away, and only eight enlisted men remained in active service. On May 7, the order came down that these were to disband and leave the Fort Clark reservation along with the rest of the group. On July 10, Captain Sterling Adams, in command at the post, put the order into effect. The army would discharge Privates Curly Jefferson, Fay July, Sam Washington, and Charles July on July 31 and require them to remove from the reservation with their families, stock, belongings, and a third of the remaining group before August 15. First Sergeant John Shields and Privates Isaac Wilson, Antonio Sánchez, and William Wilson received discharge orders for September 31, and after that date the detachment would cease to exist. Adams ordered these scouts to remove from the reservation with the remainder of the Seminole maroons and all of their property before October 15. There were just a few exceptions: Adams permitted Joseph Philips, Renty Grayson, Eva Payne, Dolly Bowlegs White, Pompey Perryman, Jim Perryman, Phyllis Kibbetts, Ann Williams, Julie Ward, and their dependent children to remain, along with Adam Smith and Joe Thompson, until the elderly passed away or the war department decided otherwise. Once the removals had been completed, all of the maroons' homes, except those belonging to the twenty-four individuals allowed to stay, were to be destroyed.[43]

The order to quit their settlement on Las Moras Creek was the ultimate expression of the deplorable treatment the United States government had dished out to the Seminole maroons since their return from Mexico. The group living at Fort Clark had come to include 207 individuals, of whom 113 were adults and 94 children, divided into 52 families. Six families from Nacimiento, or 31 others, also were residing temporarily at the post. A great many were incapable of supporting themselves, and most of the others were unskilled. The group considered itself a social unit, moreover, and United States officials had treated it as such since 1870. These maroons could not be expected to integrate easily into the local settlements and simply were not prepared for life outside the military reservation.[44]

The maroons also had a considerable stake in the post, having lived there for over forty years and made numerous improvements to the land. Five years earlier, Major-General James F. Bell had written this detailed description of the community:

> A settlement or village in which these people live has been permitted to grow up on the military reservation of Fort Clark without any evidence of protest or interference on the part of the Government. This village now contains 93 buildings, including a church. The buildings are for the most part constructed of logs or pickets with chinks stopped with mud and with grass roof. Some have shingle roofs, but all are one story. The village, including the yards, occupies about 150 acres, of which but little is cultivated. The inhabitants of the village appear to own about 5 farm wagons, 3 spring wagons, 9 buggies and 2 spring carts, also the following live stock: 93 horses, 10 mules, 18 burros, 10 cattle, 790 goats and 18 pigs, all of which stock is fed upon the military reservation.[45]

By the time the maroons received notice to remove, their village had come to encompass some 225 acres. Yet again, appeals on their behalf proved unsuccessful. The army decided that, as they no longer would include military personnel among their number, the blacks could not remain at the post. Moreover, the Seminole rolls had closed on March 4, 1907, so they had no right to tribal funds or lands in the Indian Territory. The secretary of the interior thus summarized the position as he saw it: "No allotments can be made to them as Seminoles and, of course, there is no provision of law for making allotments to them as Negroes." With these few words, the government washed its hands of the Seminole maroons for the last time. It would be left to nearby Brackettville and Del Rio to provide a home for the group.[46]

Those who had resettled at Nacimiento soon faced a grave crisis. In 1879, the heirs of the original owners of the hacienda, the Sánchez Navarro family, sold it to an Englishman, John Willett, but would not guarantee the transference of the four *sitios* at Nacimiento in the possession of the Mascogos and Kickapoos, or their water rights. The land in question had ceased to be part of the Sánchez Navarro estate when the Mexican government had granted it to the settlers in 1852, and President Juárez had reaffirmed the Mascogos' and Kickapoos' title in 1866 and 1867. Willett, however, claimed that he could find no trace of any such title and considered the maroons and Indians to be merely squatters upon his property. He then appealed to Evaristo Madero, the governor of Coahuila, to remove the Mascogos.[47]

In December 1881, Willett's agent told the maroons to leave the hacienda, and on February 12, 1882, Madero threw his support behind the initiative by ordering both the Mascogos and the Kickapoos to remove themselves immediately. The leaders of the two groups protested the order before Madero in person on May 8, making clear the strength of their resolve to remain on the grant. Taking a leaf from Wild Cat's book of diplomacy, the Mascogos stated that they would defend their land by force if necessary, "uniting themselves with Indians from the Indian Nations of Arkansas and Texas." But they hoped to secure their title by more peaceful means.[48]

The maroons and Kickapoos determined to send a representative to put their views before President Porfirio Díaz. Old John Horse was the obvious choice. He had been present when the Mexican government first had granted the land to the immigrants in 1852, had been recognized by the Mexicans as the leader of the Mascogos in the 1850s and 1860s, and had received a commission as colonel in the Mexican army. He thus was respected in national circles. He also was an excellent diplomat and had represented the interests of his people successfully on many previous occasions. Since his return from Texas, he had remained active in the leadership and had appealed personally to Madero on behalf of the Mascogos in May 1881.

Consequently, John Horse, possibly accompanied by his son Joe Coon and by Hardy Factor, set out for Mexico City in early August 1882. The outcome of his interview is unknown, however, as Horse died before he could reveal the details of his mission. Accounts vary as to the cir-

cumstances surrounding his death, some even saying that he was murdered in a *cantina* on the return journey. From the best available
evidence, however, it seems likely that he died of a sudden bout of
pneumonia in the military hospital in Mexico City in the early afternoon
of August 9, 1882. The authorities did not record his place of burial.[49]

John Horse had been the dominant personality in Seminole maroon
affairs for half a century, and his death marked the end of an era. His
remarkable life had been one of epic proportions. He had been an adviser
and confidant of Seminole chiefs, an intermediary for the United States
government, and an officer in the Mexican army. He had served the
maroons as warrior, diplomat, leader, and sage, and had represented their
interests from Washington, D. C., to Mexico City. He had taken up
arms against the United States, the French, and hostile Indians. He had
survived three wars and at least four attempts on his life and had escaped
from the grasp of renowned slave hunters. A truly colorful frontier
character and one of legendary if not mythical dimensions, this maroon
leader, it has been said, dressed in Indian fashion, spoke at least four
languages, drank hard liquor, aimed a straight shot, and rode the
Mexican border country on a white horse, mounted upon a saddle
embellished with silver and gold.

The life of John Horse had been one long struggle to find freedom
and a homeland for his people where they could live in peace and their
communities could thrive. On this heroic quest he had led the Seminole
maroons from Florida to the Indian Territory, to Coahuila, to Texas,
and then back to Mexico in search of the promised land. He even had
sought to relocate his followers in Africa if that were what it would take.
In the words of Alice Walker's character Fanny, "All his life he was
looking for a little bit of land the whites didn't covet, a little bit of peace.
He got neither. But that was the dream."[50] It was only fitting that he
should have died while still in pursuit of this dream.

Most significantly, Horse's life had witnessed the changes that had
taken place in Seminole-black relations. When he was born, around
1812, a strong, mutually beneficial, primarily military and economic
alliance had linked Seminoles and Africans in Florida. By the time of his
death some seventy years later, many of the blacks were living in isolated
maroon communities in Texas and Mexico, hundreds of miles from their
former Seminole allies in the Indian Territory. As a young man, Horse
had seen the relationship come under intense pressure. The wish of the
Indians and Africans to preserve their individuality, independence, and

identity had led to their almost continuous separation and gradual estrangement. The United States military authorities had exploited this weakness in removal negotiations during the Second Seminole War, and slave speculators and kidnappers had widened the divisions still further. Mutual suspicion had arisen within the Seminole and maroon camps, the two groups determining to pursue their best interests independently.

In the Indian Territory, John Horse had encountered many of the problems faced by Seminole blacks at that time. He had seen members of his family kidnapped by slave hunters and his life, home, and property threatened by angry Seminoles. Though technically he had been free, he had been a target for reenslavement attempts and forced to live as a virtual prisoner at Fort Gibson for five years. Unwilling to live in slavery no matter how mild the system of servitude, or submit to Creek codes and an unsympathetic Seminole leadership, Horse had managed to forge a tenuous alliance between his supporters and the followers of Wild Cat that had resulted in their joint exodus from the Indian Territory.

Once relocated in Coahuila, however, Horse had seen the gradual deterioration of the alliance as the Seminoles had sought to exert their will over the increasingly independent maroons. He had been there when the Seminoles had ridden out of Nacimiento on their return journey to the Indian Territory, severing at a stroke the ties that linked the two groups. Since that time, Horse's followers had lived in isolated border communities and pursued independent courses of action. There would be no reestablishment of relations with the Seminoles in John Horse's lifetime. During the 1870s, it emerged that the maroons would not be returning to the Indian Territory. The Seminole leadership made it clear that they would not be welcome. At exactly the time John Horse was setting out for Mexico City to defend the Mascogos' land grant at Nacimiento, John Jumper was rejecting the petition of the Bowlegs party to relocate in the Seminole Nation. By the time of Horse's death, the maroons' historic association with their former Seminole allies was clearly a thing of the past.

Apparently, Horse's final mission succeeded, for President Díaz protected the Mascogos from 1885 through 1891 against the persistent efforts of Governor José María Garza Galán of Coahuila to evict them from the hacienda. The result was the reaffirmation of the Mascogos' and Kickapoos' joint title to four *sitios* at Nacimiento in 1892 when engineer Mijar y Haro drew up a plat of the area and deposited it in the agrarian department. Mijar's plans gave no specifications of the landholdings of each group, however, and a boundary dispute arose between the Mascogos and Kickapoos that has continued until recent times.[51]

The dispute came about because the Kickapoos resented the more numerous maroons' taking the greater part of the grant at Nacimiento. The extra land did not bring immediate benefit to the Mascogos, however. It was reported in 1907 that they were the better farmers and planted the larger area, but like the sharecroppers of the deep South, the three hundred maroons living at the hacienda constantly ran into debt and were forced to sell their yields in advance; hence, they were "always destitute." While they did not plant so large an acreage, the Kickapoos at least were able to keep what they raised for their own use. Moreover, the Mascogos and Kickapoos leased out water rights to Mexicans and other settlers who put nearly one thousand acres at Nacimiento under cultivation. The maroons and Indians subsequently "loaned and spent the money and when this was gone had a pretty hard time." It would be left to the Mexican government to expel the renters and insist that the grantees themselves work the land from then on. Though their landholdings at the hacienda had been secured, the Mascogos' troubles, clearly, were far from over.[52]

The lives of the maroons at Nacimiento would be no easier than those of their kinsmen in Texas, faced as they were with jealous Kickapoo neighbors, an unsympathetic state government, frequent national revolutions, and the constant problem of producing the crops necessary for survival in an area noted for its harsh climate and difficult terrain. Nevertheless, it was home. These blacks had followed a long, hard road. Through constant upheavals and dislocations, wars, and destitution, they had maintained their dignity and had remained committed to the quest for independence, peace, and security. The Seminole maroons in Texas and Coahuila could look back with pride at having won the right to personal liberty and self-determination. In the face of adversity, they had established settlements and retained their identity by preserving a strong sense of culture and community. In this sense, they truly had found freedom on the border.

7

Either Side of a Border

The descendants of the Florida maroons had come a long way since slavery days. To escape from the enslaver or enhance their ability to control their own lives, these people had gone to the limit. They had engaged in international intrigue and diplomacy, traveled far and crossed national boundaries, and campaigned in foreign, Indian, and civil wars. They had entered into alliances with European powers, Native Americans, Mexico, and the United States to defend their liberty, preserve their communities, or otherwise further their interests. International frontiers had taken on different connotations for the Seminole maroons. For many years, different sides of borders represented either enslavement or freedom. After slavery was abolished in the United States, however, the only boundaries of major significance became ones separating them from food, homes, and kin.

Once the remaining Seminole Negro Indian Scouts had disbanded in the summer of 1914, military officials ordered the maroons to abandon their settlement on Las Moras Creek and leave the Fort Clark reservation. The army exempted only a few of the old and infirm and their dependents, and within a few years all had left the post. Thrown into an unfamiliar and unsympathetic world without land, money, or jobs, the maroons managed to purchase a small tract in nearby Brackettville, and most of the group settled there.

The dwellings they constructed were of the same design as their former homes on the reservation and became known as "chink houses." Such a structure was designed to accommodate a family and consisted of a double framework of wood packed with a mixture of clay, pebbles, and rock, topped with a thatched roof. Sometimes it would be plastered over, whitewashed, and decorated with wood. Often the kitchen was detached from the rest of the house. Although in their most basic form they deteriorated rapidly under heavy rain and needed frequent repairs, these insulated homes were warm in winter, cool in summer, and easily constructed, offering an attractive alternative to adobe.[1]

Of the two hundred to three hundred Texas Seminole maroons, many of the men found work as wranglers and hands on local cattle, sheep, and goat spreads and became well known in the Big Bend and border country for their horsemanship and ranching skills. Some of the women took in laundry or found work at Fort Clark until the post was deactivated in 1946. Other members of the group ran small businesses, farmed, or planted gardens. For most, however, life remained difficult.[2]

Continuing problems with the Kickapoos and the constant battle against heat and drought ensured that those maroons who had remained behind or resettled in Coahuila would have no easier a time. Nevertheless, the group adjusted well. In the early 1940s, Kenneth Porter reported that as many as four hundred to five hundred Mascogos were living at the hacienda and that most were prosperous, "well-fed, well-housed, and well-dressed." They lived in adobe houses with thatched roofs and engaged in agricultural pursuits and stock-raising. The Mascogos utilized irrigation ditches and had developed extensive corn fields; vegetable gardens; herds of cattle, horses, and swine; and flocks of goats and chickens. The settlement also boasted a village school, two praise-houses, and a government hospital.[3] In view of the problems, this was some achievement. The existence today of two Seminole black communities on the border—one at the small West Texas town of Brackettville and the other at Nacimiento de los Negros, near Múzquiz, Coahuila—offers testimony to the tenacity of a proud people who beat the odds.

Solidarity was the key factor in ensuring survival. The strength of group identity and tremendous pride in their unique history, culture, and traditions would act as solid buffers to the trials and tribulations they would experience. Richard Price has argued that the Saramaka maroons of Surinam are "acutely conscious of living in history, of reaping each day the fruits of their ancestors' deeds . . .."[4] This is true also for the Texas Seminole maroons.[5] The group always had its storytellers, its "tribal historians." Today, that mantle rests with the knowledgeable duo of Miss Charles Emily Wilson, granddaughter of Sampson July, and William "Dub" Warrior, great-grandnephew of John Horse's son Joe Coon. In the words of Miss Charles (as she is known in the community):

Wild Cat and John Horse just picked up everybody and went to the border. Everybody wanted to feel free. They didn't want to be slaves, but they were good people. They said, "Give us land and implements for gardens and let us raise animals and we'll rid your country of those Indians." They were good fighters.[6]

There could be no more eloquent, precise, or succinct a recounting of the maroons' history.

The Brackettville group has maintained the scouts' cemetery to this day. Over the years, the site has become for the community a dramatic symbol of historic time and place, the final resting place of powerful spirits, a link with the ancestors. The group still digs its graves so that the dead face eastward, as do the Gullahs and certain Central and West African cultures. As Margaret Creel has stated, "Gullahs and Africans shared a concept of the cosmos. The world followed the sun from east to west."[7] The Seminole maroons also subscribed to this philosophy. The graveyard still serves as the primary focus of group pride. Indeed, the Seminole Indian Scout Cemetery Association remains a central social organization within the community, and the offices of president, vice president, and secretary-treasurer are considered positions of leadership within the group as a whole. Billy Joe Pierce, the current president, is an energetic and enterprising individual, and his creative ideas bode well for the future.[8]

The Texas group moved its Mount Gilead Baptist Church from the Fort Clark reservation to Brackettville after the scouts' disbandment. Here, they continued to practice a syncretic religion, traceable to Florida, which pointed to their diverse background and the effects of cultural transmission. The group had combined elements of Africanisms and Seminole ceremonials with Presbyterianism, Southern Baptism, and Roman Catholicism to form an exotic West Texas hybrid. In 1924, it was reported that the churchgoers called themselves Mount Zion Baptists yet commemorated Advent, prayed continually for the dead, held wakes, had a hog meat taboo, believed in the literal breaking of bread, and put great store upon revelations, an important officer in the church being the interpreter of dreams.[9]

The retention of their unique language was a second manifestation of the strength of group identity and solidarity. After removal, "Afro-Seminole" continued to be the language spoken in the maroon communities in the Indian Territory, Coahuila, and Texas. The language is disappearing rapidly, but older residents of the Brackettville community still speak it on occasion, using it mostly for "funnin'" with each other.[10] This practice seems to add weight to Molefi Kete Asante's assertion that "African-Americans retain their essential Africanness" through the communicative process as a whole rather than just the lexicon, but more research is needed in this area.[11]

The maroons also retained their unique system of naming. Utilization of West African day names remained a significant feature. The prominent Factor family also tended to use first names with African derivations, such as Dembo, Dindy, and Arty (Hardy), reflecting the family's prestige within the community. The widespread use of nicknames for both men and women within the present-day Texas and Oklahoma groups suggests the retention of African patterns more complex than merely occasional employment of names with African provenance.[12]

The maroons kept their famous biblical and historical first names, and surnames derived from former Indian owners. Seminole transmission was most readily apparent in their use of the busk name Warrior, the English translation of Tustenuggee, and its variant, Ward. Fittingly, Winfred Warrior, who was killed in Vietnam in 1969, was the latest soldier to be buried in the scouts' cemetery.[13] Dub Warrior of Del Rio, meanwhile, is a former president of the Seminole Indian Scout Cemetery Association and remains active in the leadership of the Texas group. Historically, Seminole black names often included a colorful composite of these diverse elements. Names that figured prominently in the Texas and Coahuila groups included, for example, Sampson July, Friday Bowlegs, Pompey Factor, and Cuffee Payne.

Thus, these maroons had moved far away from the Seminole Indians in time, space, and culture. Since their alliance with the Seminoles had drawn to a close and the two finally had separated in 1861, the Texas and Coahuila groups had lived in remote communities on the border and had pursued independent courses of action. Though they had incorporated elements of their earlier association with Native Americans into their culture, much more had been left out. There seem to have been no clans among the maroons, for example. Seminole black culture also reflected the resilience of Africanisms within maroon societies and included elements from the group's plantation past, as well as from their experience since separating from the Seminoles. Their history, their mores, and their lifestyle were truly their own, and theirs alone.[14]

The descendants of the maroons living in West Texas today still call themselves Seminoles, though they are aware of their racial makeup and cultural complex. In 1942, Rosa Fay stated, "We are colored people— we aren't Indians; there may be some intermixture, but we are colored," and Sara Daniels added simply, "The Mascos are the colored people and the Seminoles are the Indians."[15] But for many years they were careful to draw lines between themselves and other blacks. The use of the term *Seminoles* asserted then and confirms today their Native American heritage and denial of slavery while fostering group pride and identity. The same can be said for the maroon descendants at Nacimiento who have sought to maintain distinctiveness from others by calling themselves *Indios Mascogos*.[16] Members of the Texas group today also refer to the old language as *Seminole*, though they know it is not the native language of the Seminole Indians and that it is composed mainly of non-Indian elements. The use of *Seminoles, Seminole,* and *Indios Mascogos* maintains links with the past and confers exclusivity, providing security and continuity for group members.

Interestingly enough, the Seminole Indians of Oklahoma made several attempts earlier this century to reclaim Wild Cat's old land grant at Nacimiento with a view to returning there. The idea first took shape in the early 1900s when tribal members began to realize that the allotment of their lands in severalty during the years just prior to Oklahoma statehood would put them in closer contact with white settlers and expose them to robbery and corruption. Leading Seminoles instigated the moves and found their strongest support among the conservatives, who wished to return to a simpler way of life in a more remote location. The first attempt came in 1903 when a pilot delegation of prominent Seminoles journeyed to Múzquiz to discuss the grant with the local authorities. The party included Chief Hulbutta Micco; Alice Brown Davis, later appointed chief of the Seminoles, who acted as interpreter; and about thirty other delegates. Some progress was made during the discussions, and the Seminoles returned to the Indian Territory with the intention of taking up the matter with the Mexican government at a later date.[17]

In early 1905, Hulbutta, Davis, Isaac Jones, Pasokee Harjochee, and other prominent tribal members traveled to Mexico City in an effort to substantiate their claim. During the ensuing negotiations, the Seminoles established their title to land at Nacimiento. The Mascogos and Kickapoos, however, had occupied all four *sitios* at the hacienda granted earlier to the three groups. To dispossess them would cost more than the land was worth, and the Seminoles were not prepared to settle among the maroons even if the Mexicans were to permit them to do so. Before further discussions could take place, a revolution broke out in Mexico, forcing the Seminoles to return home. Alice Brown Davis attempted to revive the case by returning to Coahuila in 1910, but her efforts proved unsuccessful, and the Seminoles' claim fell into abeyance for a decade.[18]

In the winter of 1920–21, Chief Papicua of the Mexican Kickapoos visited Louis C. Brown, son of the late Governor John F. Brown, and encouraged the Seminoles to remove to Nacimiento at once, offering every assistance within his power. Apparently, the Mexican Kickapoos preferred their neighbors to be Seminole Indian rather than Seminole black. Consequently, the Seminoles put together another delegation to investigate the possibility of removing to the hacienda. The party of five included Louis Brown, C. C. Patten, Wallace Cully, Isaac Jones, and Ahalakochee, the grandson of Wild Cat, who had returned to the Indian Territory with the other Seminoles from Mexico sixty years earlier.[19]

The delegation left Wewoka for Múzquiz on January 16, 1921, carrying with it a bronze medal that had been cast as proof of Wild Cat's treaty with the Mexican government in 1852. The Seminoles knew that the Mascogos were now in possession of most of the old grant at Nacimiento, but the delegates hoped to interview them to "learn their attitude and disposition" towards the proposed removal.[20] With dramatic irony and almost poetic justice, the situation had turned full circle. For years the tribal authorities had thwarted the attempts of the maroons to return to the Seminole Nation. Now the Mascogos were to have a say in determining the fate of Seminole efforts to relocate on their domain.

During the journey, Ahalakochee told stories of his earlier experiences after leaving the Indian Territory in 1849 and furnished valuable information on the Seminole and maroon migration to Mexico. The fullbloods' dream of a less complicated existence in a bygone age found embodiment in his nostalgic descriptions of Nacimiento in the 1850s, and as the party approached Mexico, the delegates' hopes ran high. Once they crossed the border, however, they found "[a] wild and desolate country infested with bandits and laid waste by revolution."[21] By January 30, Jones and Cully had seen enough and were ready to return home.[22] The last straw came when the delegates reached Múzquiz. Patten described the scene: "Here as everywhere we have travelled in

Mexico, evidences of long years of destructive wars are seen on every hand, and desolation is resting upon every village and farm."[23] The thoroughly disillusioned delegation returned home during the first week of February, having given up on the idea of finding a suitable reservation in Coahuila. Its demise effectively marked the end of any real likelihood of a reestablishment of relations between the Seminoles and maroons on the border.

Following a number of unauthorized investigative missions to Mexico by prominent individuals in the years following the 1921 expedition, the Seminole leadership made two final attempts to reclaim the lands at Nacimiento in the late 1930s. In June 1937, a delegation of four prominent Seminoles, Peter Tiger, Edward Harjo, Peter Miller, and John Morgan, journeyed to Múzquiz to appeal the case before local officials.[24] Upon reaching Nacimiento, however, "They found that the land was inhabited by a band of negroes who called themselves Seminoles." Once again, the delegates showed unwillingness to share land with the Mascogos, and the Mexican government offered to grant the Seminoles another tract elsewhere. The leadership was not impressed by this proposal, however, and substantial support for the move was not forthcoming.[25]

Significantly, as the interest of the Seminole Indians waned when they learned that the maroons were residing on the grant, that of the Seminole freedmen increased. In December, it was reported that the Caesar Bruner band was thinking of removing to Nacimiento.[26] Whereas the Seminoles were opposed to any renewed association with the Mascogos, the freedmen still felt they had strong ties with the maroons in Coahuila despite their long separation.

The delegation must have gained the support of President Lázaro Cárdenas, for in 1938, he offered to grant the Seminoles another piece of land. Other representatives journeyed to Mexico to inspect the tract, but widespread support for the move again was lacking, and none was made.[27] Recent leaders have been aware of the Seminole claim to land at Nacimiento, and in the late 1970s, proposals still were being put forward occasionally to send representatives to Mexico to pursue it further.[28] Whether the Seminoles will renew their interest in Wild Cat's old land grant is open to conjecture, but the likelihood of their actually relocating there is remote. As the Mascogos and Kickapoos have occupied land at the hacienda for so long, the Mexican authorities likely will not displace them. Moreover, in the light of their recent dispute with the freedmen over disbursement of the multimillion-dollar award for Florida lands lost under the terms of the 1823 Treaty of Moultrie Creek, the Seminoles likely will not agree to share land with the Mascogos even if permitted to do so.[29]

While relations between the maroons living on the border and the Seminoles ended long ago, close ties continue to link the Texas and Coahuila groups. The Brackettville and Nacimiento communities always were extremely mobile and a great deal of interchange took place between 1870 and 1914. The two retained strong associations after the scouts had disbanded. In the summer of 1918, for example, it was reported that a number of former scouts had returned to Coahuila, but wished to cross the border frequently to visit relatives at Brackettville. The group members' citizenship status remained problematic, but both the United States and Mexican governments allowed free passage between the settlements into the mid-1930s. It even has been suggested that Pompey Factor used his Medal of Honor as a passport to cross the border at one time.[30] The maroons' long search for freedom, coupled with the retention of a strong sense of community, ultimately transcended externally imposed definitions of nationalities, cultures, and their identity as a people, and they found home on either side of a border. In a striking display of cultural adaptability, many became bilingual and transnational, pursuing a lifestyle with roots on both sides of the Rio Grande.

The Seminole maroon communities shared a fierce pride in their heritage and for many years remained aloof from "state negroes." This led to a shortage of potential marriage partners, and the two groups tended to intermarry extensively, strengthening bonds still further. According to Laurence Foster, into the 1930s, most members of the Brackettville and Nacimiento groups preferred that "their children wed 'Seminoles' as they are fond of calling themselves." Foster observed further, "There is [still] a very close relationship between the two groups. They make frequent visits to one another and also correspond with each other very often."[31] Kinship ties, a shared past, and a strong sense of community would help them overcome discrimination, hardship, and geographic separation.

Today, most of the descendants of the Seminole maroons in Texas and Coahuila are related in some way or other, as indeed are the Seminole freedmen of Oklahoma. There are now only some 100 to 150 Seminole blacks in West Texas, with perhaps the same number living in or around

Nacimiento. Nevertheless, family and group reunions take place in Brackettville each June and September during the annual Juneteenth and Seminole Day celebrations, with members traveling from as far away as California, New England, and even overseas. On these weekends, a traditional American parade precedes retirement to a shaded area on the grounds of the Seminole Indian Scout Cemetery Association building for speeches, programs, food, and drink. The visitor to these festivities will see colorful clothing and jewelry reminiscent of Africa and Mexico, smell the aroma of Texas barbecue, and hear the sounds of jazz, blues, spoken Spanish, and even on occasion, "Afro-Seminole." In this small slice of African American pie, one of the "New Peoples" discloses in most dramatic fashion some of the secret ingredients of its gourmet recipe.[32]

Certain individuals within the Oklahoma group had maintained visiting relations with their kinsmen in Texas and Coahuila throughout this century, but in June 1981, an historic group reunion took place in Brackettville. Seminole freedmen from the Little River country made their way to West Texas along the interstate highways to celebrate Juneteenth with old relatives and new friends.[33] It was indeed a far cry from the journey their forefathers had made 132 years earlier. The Oklahoma Warriors learned that they had kinsmen in Del Rio, descendants of Seminole Negro Indian Scouts William, Scott, and Carolina Warrior, and Medal of Honor winner Sergeant John Ward. And their Texas cousins learned that a Warrior still sat on the Seminole tribal council in Oklahoma as leader of the Dosar Barkus band of freedmen. Though the Seminole blacks will be quick to tell you they were never slaves, it was highly appropriate that their reunion should take place during emancipation festivities on the border. The search for freedom had divided the maroons in 1849; it was only fitting that a joint celebration of a proud history built on liberty should bring them together again.

Notes

Introduction

1. Kevin Mulroy, "Classifying the Texas Seminole Maroons, 1870-1886: Seminoles, Freed-men, 'Negro-Indians,' or Just Plain Mexicans?" Paper read at the annual conference of the American Society for Ethnohistory, Toronto, Canada, November 1990, and at the annual convention of the Pacific Coast Branch of the American Historical Association, Kona, Hawaii, August 1991. The use of so many different names simply serves to highlight the group's marginal status.
2. William C. Sturtevant, pers. com., Toronto, November 3, 1990. Price and Sturtevant, in fact, have been advocating the use of "Seminole maroons" for many years. See Sturtevant, Review of *Africans and Seminoles: From Removal to Emancipation,* by Daniel F. Littlefield, Jr., *American Anthropologist* 81(1979): 916-17.
3. Richard Price, ed., *Maroon Societies: Rebel Slave Communities in the Americas* (Baltimore: Johns Hopkins University Press, 1979), 1-30.
4. Ibid. For a recent groundbreaking comparison along these lines, see Rebecca B. Bateman, "Africans and Indians: A Comparative Study of the Black Carib and Black Seminole," *Ethnohistory* 37(1990): 1-24.
5. Edward M. Coffman, *The Old Army: A Portrait of the American Army in Peacetime, 1784-1898* (New York: Oxford University Press, 1986), vii.
6. Kevin Mulroy, "Ethnogenesis and Ethnohistory of the Seminole Maroons," Paper read at the Eleventh Oklahoma Symposium on Comparative Frontier Studies, "Ethnogenesis: A Frontier Phenomenon?", University of Oklahoma, March 7, 1992. This essay is to be published in the *Journal of World History.* See also Jacqueline Peterson and Jennifer S. H. Brown, eds., *The New Peoples: Being and Becoming Métis in North America* (Lincoln: University of Nebraska Press, 1985), 3-4; and Bateman, "Africans and Indians," 1.

1. Florida Maroons

1. F. Harper, ed., *The Travels of William Bartram, Naturalists' Edition* (New Haven: Yale University Press, 1958 [1791]), 240; John K. Mahon, *History of the Second Seminole War, 1835-1842* (Gainesville: University of Florida Press, 1967), 2-7; Kenneth Wiggins Porter, "The Cowkeeper Dynasty of the Seminole Nation," *Florida Historical Quarterly* 30(1952): 348-49; John R. Swanton, *Early History of the Creek Indians and Their Neighbours* (Washington D.C.: Government Printing Office, 1928), 120-23, 389-99, 414; Peter H. Wood, "The Changing Population of the Colonial South: An Overview by Race and Region, 1685-1790," in Peter H. Wood, Gregory A. Waselkov, and M. Thomas Hatley, eds., *Powhatan's Mantle: Indians in the Colonial Southeast* (Lincoln: University of

Nebraska Press, 1989), 51-56. The best studies of the genesis of the Seminoles are Howard
F. Cline, *Notes on Colonial Indians and Communities in Florida, 1700-1821*, vol. 1 of
Florida Indians, 3 vols., *Garland American Indian Ethnohistory Series* (New York:
Garland, 1974); Charles H. Fairbanks, *Ethnohistorical Report on the Florida Indians*, vol.
3 of *Florida Indians* (1974); Richard A. Sattler, "Siminoli Italwa: Socio-Political Change
Among the Oklahoma Seminoles Between Removal and Allotment," unpublished Ph.D.
diss., University of Oklahoma, 1987, chapter one; and William C. Sturtevant, "Creek Into
Seminole," in Eleanor B. Leacock and Nancy O. Lurie, eds., *North American Indians in
Historical Perspective* (New York: Random House, 1971), 92-128.

2. Sturtevant, "Creek Into Seminole," 105.

3. William Bartram, *Travels Through North and South Carolina, Georgia, East and West
Florida* (Philadelphia: 1794), 401. On the *sabana* system, see Amy Turner Bushnell,
"Ruling 'the Republic of Indians' in Seventeenth-Century Florida," in Wood, Waselkov,
and Hatley, *Powhatan's Mantle*, 134, 140, 142-43.

4. Bartram, *Travels*, 401.

5. Irene Wright, "Dispatches of Spanish Officials Bearing on the Free Negro Settlement of
Gracia Real de Santa Teresa de Mose, Florida," *Journal of Negro History* 9(1924): 145-46,
150-53; Verne Elmo Chatelain, *The Defenses of Spanish Florida, 1565 to 1763*(Washington
D.C.: Carnegie Institute of Washington Publication 511, 1941), 160-61 n. 4.

6. Jane Landers, "Black Society in Spanish St. Augustine, 1784-1821," unpublished Ph.D.
diss., University of Florida, 1988, 14-15.

7. Jane Landers, "African Presence in Early Spanish Colonization of the Caribbean and the
Southeastern Borderlands," in David Hurst Thomas, ed., *Archaeological and Historical
Perspectives on the Spanish Borderlands East. Columbian Consequences vol. 2* (Washington
D.C.: Smithsonian Institution, 1990), 321.

8. Governor José de Zuniga y Cerda, Orders for Apalachee Province, 1704. I am grateful to
Amy Turner Bushnell for providing this reference.

9. Amy Turner Bushnell, *The King's Coffer: Proprietors of the Spanish Florida Treasury
1565-1702* (Gainesville: University Presses of Florida, 1981), 67; Wright, "Dispatches,"
166, 173.

10. Quoted in Kenneth Wiggins Porter, *The Negro on the American Frontier* (New York: New
York Times and Arno Press, 1971), 164. On black runaways to Spanish Florida, see Jane
Landers, "Spanish Sanctuary; Fugitive Slaves in Florida, 1687-1790," *Florida Historical
Quarterly* 62(1984): 296-313; and John J. TePaske, "The Fugitive Slave: Intercolonial
Rivalry and Spanish Slave Policy, 1687-1764," in Samuel Proctor, ed., *Eighteenth-Century
Florida and Its Borderlands* (Gainesville: University of Florida Press, 1975), 1-12.

11. For a recent in-depth study of Fort Mose and its inhabitants, see Jane Landers, "Gracia
Real de Santa Teresa de Mose: A Free Black Town in Spanish Colonial Florida," *American
Historical Review* 95(1990): 9-30. On the Stono Rebellion, see Herbert Aptheker,
American Negro Slave Revolts(New York: Columbia University Press, 1943), 86; and Peter
Wood, *Black Majority; Negroes in Colonial South Carolina from 1670 through the Stono
Rebellion* (New York: Knopf, 1974), 308-26.

12. Landers, "Gracia Real," 19-22; Porter, *Negro on the Frontier*, 169-70.

13. Quoted in Porter, *Negro on the Frontier*, 170.

14. Landers, "African Presence," 323.

15. The notion that ethnicity can serve as an early and important structural principle in the formation of new societies is taken from Nancie L. Solien González, *Sojourners of the Caribbean: Ethnogenesis and Ethnohistory of the Garífuna* (Urbana: University of Illinois Press, 1988), 6.

16. Mulroy, "Ethnogenesis," passim.

17. Mahon, *Second Seminole War*, 20.

18. Landers, "Black Society," 74-77.

19. Quoted in J. W. Pratt, *Expansionists of 1812* (New York: Macmillan, 1925), 117. See also Landers, "Black Society," 204-5.

20. Charles H. Coe, *Red Patriots: The Story of the Seminoles* (Cincinnati: Editor Publishing Co., 1898), 11-13; Landers, "Black Society," 85-89; Porter, *Negro on the Frontier*, 183-203; Pratt, *Expansionists,* 202-9.

21. Quoted in Nicholas Halatsz, *The Rattling Chains: Slave Unrest and Revolt in the Antebellum South* (New York: McKay, Van Rees, 1966), 108.

22. Winifred Vass, *The Bantu Speaking Heritage of the United States* (Los Angeles: UCLA Center for Afro-American Studies, 1979), 48.

23. James Leitch Wright, "A Note on the First Seminole War as Seen by the Indians, Negroes, and Their British Advisers," *Journal of Southern History* 34(1968): 567.

24. J. G. Forbes, *Sketches, Historical and Topographical of the Floridas, more particularly of East Florida*, rpt. ed. (Gainesville: University of Florida Press, 1964 [1821]), 121, 200-5. See also William S. Coker and Thomas D. Watson, *Indian Traders of the Southeastern Spanish Borderlands: Panton, Leslie and Company and John Forbes and Company, 1783-1847* (Pensacola: University of West Florida Press, 1986), 302-8; Grant Foreman, *Indian Removal* (Norman: University of Oklahoma Press, 1932), 316; Joshua R. Giddings, *The Exiles of Florida* (Columbus, OH: Follett, Foster and Co., 1858), 33; E. P. Southall, "Negroes in Florida Prior to the Civil War," *Journal of Negro History* 19(1934): 81.

25. Coker and Watson, *Indian Traders,* 309; George Klos, "Blacks and the Seminole Removal Debate, 1821-1835," *Florida Historical Quarterly* 68(1989): 60-61.

26. See Captain Young's "Sketch Map, 1818" of Bowlegs's Town, reproduced in J. Leitch Wright, Jr., *Creeks and Seminoles: The Destruction and Regeneration of the Muscogulge People* (Lincoln: University of Nebraska Press, 1986), 206.

27. Porter, *Negro on the Frontier*, 221-36.

28. William Hayne Simmons, *Notices of East Florida, with an Account of the Seminole Nation of Indians,* rpt. ed. (Gainesville: University of Florida Press, 1973 [1822]), 76.

29. Wiley Thompson to Lewis Cass, April 27, 1835, National Archives Microfilm Publications, Microcopy M234, Record Group 75, Records of the Bureau of Indian Affairs, Letters Received by the Office of Indian Affairs, 1824-1881, 962 rolls (hereafter cited as M234), Roll 806, Seminole Agency Emigration 1827-1846, frame 103; George A. McCall, *Letters from the Frontiers* (Philadelphia: J. B. Lippincott and Co., 1868), 160.

30. Porter, *Negro on the Frontier,* 302-3.

31. Simmons, *Notices of East Florida,* 76; Thompson to Cass, April 27, 1835, M234-806, frame 103; John L. Williams, *The Territory of Florida,* rpt. ed. (Gainesville: University of Florida Press, 1962 [1837]), 239-40. See also Myer M. Cohen, *Notices of East Florida and the Campaigns* (Charleston: Burges and Honour; New York: B. B. Hussey, 1836), 78.

32. Simmons, *Notices of East Florida,* 76; Thompson to Cass, April 27, 1835, M234-806, frame 103; McCall, *Letters from the Frontiers,* 160.

33. Simmons, *Notices of East Florida*, 76-77.

34. Ibid., 50; Thompson to Cass, April 27, 1835, M234-806, frame 103; Woodburne Potter, *The War in Florida* (Baltimore: Lewis and Coleman, 1836), 45-46; Williams, *Territory of Florida*, 239-40.

35. James Leitch Wright's assertion that North American maroon communities tended to constitute "an amalgamation of Indians and Africans" certainly does not apply to the Seminole black settlements. See his *The Only Land They Knew: The Tragic Story of the American Indians in the Old South* (New York: Macmillan, 1981), 274.

36. Rebecca B. Bateman, "We're Still Here: History, Kinship, and Group Identity Among the Seminole Freedmen of Oklahoma," unpublished Ph.D. diss., Johns Hopkins University, 1990, 23-27, 144-59.

37. Mary Helms, "Black Carib Domestic Organization in Historical Perspective: Traditional Origins of Contemporary Patterns," *Ethnology* 20(1981): 82-83; Price, introduction, Bryan Edwards, "Observations on [the] Maroon Negroes of the Island of Jamaica," and A. J. F. Köbben, "Unity and Disunity: Cottica Djuka Society as a Kinship System," in Price, ed., *Maroon Societies*, 19, 241, 346-47, 354.

38. In a letter to Cae (or Coi) Harjo, September 11, 1837, Abraham signed his Seminole busk name, Souanaffe Tustenukke (Tustenuggee). The letter is quoted in full in Porter, *Negro on the Frontier*, 333-34. John Kibbetts, the leader of the Seminole Negro Indian Scouts in the 1870s, also would use his busk name Sittertastonacky (Chitto Tustenuggee), or Snake Warrior, on occasion. The existence of black Warriors among the Oklahoma and Texas groups offers further evidence of this practice. Nevertheless, I disagree strongly with Wright's argument (*Creeks and Seminoles*, 278, 80, 95, 256) that "many Indian-Negroes were essentially Indians and not Africans," that "mixed marriages were common among Creeks and Seminoles," and that blacks joined Seminole clans because "it was difficult to preserve the African heritage." There is no evidence that the maroons ever participated in busk rituals on a large scale, adopted the matrilineal clan system of the Seminoles, or intermarried extensively with Indians; and post-removal Seminole-black relations seem to suggest the opposite. See Kevin Mulroy, "Relations Between Blacks and Seminoles After Removal," unpublished Ph.D. thesis, University of Keele (England), 1984, 591-98, 618-24; Bateman, "Africans and Indians," 13; Bateman, "We're Still Here," 23, 35 n. 1; and Arthur Gallaher, Jr., "A Survey of the Seminole Freedmen," unpublished M.A. thesis, University of Oklahoma, 1951, 111-13. The Seminole maroons' tenacious retention of Africanisms, meanwhile, is documented throughout this work.

39. Ian F. Hancock, "Creole Features in the Afro-Seminole Speech of Brackettville, Texas," *Society for Caribbean Linguistics Occasional Papers* 3(1975): passim; Ian F. Hancock, "Further Observations on Afro-Seminole Creole," *Society for Caribbean Linguistics Occasional Papers* 7(1977): passim; Ian F. Hancock, "Texas Gullah: the Creole English of the Brackettville Afro-Seminoles," in Joseph L. Dillard, ed., *Perspectives on American English* (The Hague: Mouton, 1980), 305-33; Ian F. Hancock, *The Texas Seminoles and Their Language* (Austin: University of Texas African and Afro-American Studies and Research Center, 1980), passim. See also, Joseph L. Dillard, *Black English: Its History and Usage in the United States* (New York: Random House, 1972), 150-55.

40. Laurence Foster, "Negro-Indian Relationships in the Southeast," Ph.D. diss., University of Pennsylvania, 1935, 51-57; Eugene D. Genovese, *Roll, Jordan, Roll: The World the*

Slaves Made (New York: Pantheon Books, 1974), 197-98, 475-81; Simmons, *Notices of East Florida,* 44.

41. As Peter Wood has suggested, "[Slave names] which survived most readily from Africa were the ones which were particularly commonplace, or significant, or familiar in a variety of regions, and day-names suited all these categories," (*Black Majority,* 183). On black naming practices, see also Dillard, *Black English,* 123-35; John C. Inscoe, "Carolina Slave Names: An Index to Acculturation," *Journal of Southern History* 49(1983): 527-54; and Charles Joyner, *Down by the Riverside: A South Carolina Slave Community* (Urbana: University of Illinois Press, 1984), 217-22. On naming patterns among the Seminole freedmen of Oklahoma see Bateman, "We're Still Here," 343-54.

42. Giddings, *Exiles of Florida,* 324.

43. Nancie L. Solien González, "New Evidence on the Origin of the Black Carib, with Thoughts on the Meaning of Tradition," *New West Indian Guide* 57(1983): 157. See also Nancie L. Solien González, "The Neoteric Society," *Comparative Studies in History and Society* 12(1970): 1-13; and González, *Sojourners,* 4. James Clifford's argument that, "Groups negotiating their identity in contexts of domination and exchange" utilize alliances and processes of appropriation, compromise, subversion, masking, invention, and revival in order to remain whole is supported by the experience of the Seminole maroons. As with the Mashpee, "Their history was a series of cultural and political transactions, not all-or-nothing conversions or resistances." James Clifford, *The Predicament of Culture: Twentieth-Century Ethnography, Literature, and Art* (Cambridge: Harvard University Press, 1988), 338-39, 342.

44. Jedidiah Morse, *Report to the Secretary of War of the United States on Indian Affairs* (New Haven: S. Converse, 1822), 306-9; Swanton, *Early History of the Creek Indians,* 400 n. 1, 406-7. On women slaveholders among the Seminoles in the Indian Territory, see Daniel F. Littlefield, Jr., *Africans and Seminoles: From Removal to Emancipation* (Westport, CT: Greenwood Press, 1977), 84, 111, 118 n. 27, 150-51, 162-72 and Mulroy, "Relations," 397-418.

45. Joseph E. Holloway, introduction to Holloway, ed., *Africanisms in American Culture* (Bloomington: Indiana University Press, 1990), xvii. Brent Weisman has suggested recently that forthcoming archaeological digs at Pilaklikaha; Kettle (formerly Boggy) Island, home of Sitarkey's blacks after they had left the Alachua Savannah; and other African settlements in northern peninsular Florida, soon may unearth significant new evidence on these maroon communities. Brent Richards Weisman, *Like Beads on a String: A Culture History of the Seminole Indians in North Peninsular Florida* (Tuscaloosa: University of Alabama Press, 1989), 103, 174; and Weisman's comments in Denise Mathews, producer and writer, "Black Warriors of the Seminole," WUFT–TV Channel 5 Production, Gainesville, Florida, 1989.

46. McCall, *Letters from the Frontiers,* 160.

47. John M. Goggin, "The Seminole Negroes of Andros Island, Bahamas," *Florida Historical Quarterly* 24(1946): 201-6; Harry A. Kersey, Jr., "The Seminole Negroes of Andros Island Revisited: Some New Pieces of an Old Puzzle," *Florida Anthropologist* 34(1981): 169-76; Kenneth Wiggins Porter, "Notes on the Seminole Negroes in the Bahamas," *Florida Historical Quarterly* 24(1945): 56-60.

48. Landers, "Black Society," 96.

49. Charles J. Kappler, comp., *Indian Affairs, Laws and Treaties,* 3 vols. (Washington D.C.: Government Printing Office, 1904-1913), vol. 2, 141-44.

50. Ibid., 249-51, 255-56, 290-91.

51. United States Congress, *American State Papers,* 38 vols. (Washington D.C.: Government Printing office, 1832-1861), Military Affairs, vol. 6, 454, 458, 464.

52. Grant Foreman, ed., "The Journal of Elijah Hicks," *Chronicles of Oklahoma* 13(1935): 75; Littlefield, *Africans and Seminoles,* 11; Potter, *War in Florida,* 106. For a discussion of the life of the Dade command's black guide, see Kenneth Wiggins Porter, "Louis Pachecho: The Man and the Myth," *Journal of Negro History* 28(1943): 65-72.

53. American State Papers, Military Affairs, vol. 7, 820-22.

54. Thomas S. Jesup to Roger Jones, March 6, 1837, *Negroes, &c., Captured from Indians in Florida,* 25 Cong., 3 Sess., House Doc. 225 (hereafter cited as House Doc. 225), 51.

55. Porter, *Negro on the Frontier,* 182-357.

56. Giddings, *Exiles of Florida,* 97.

57. During the course of his lifetime, John Horse would be known by a remarkable number of names. He took the surname of his owner Charles Cavallo in Florida. This later was corrupted to Cowaya and other variants, such as Coheia. In Florida and the Indian Territory, he also became known by the nickname Gopher John. Once settled in Mexico, however, and from then on, he was referred to as Juan Caballo or, more commonly, John Horse, its English translation. Even then, the multiplicity of names did not stop. After 1856, he frequently was called Capitán Juan de Dios Vidaurri, a mixture of his Mexican military title and his adopted confirmation name. For an amusing explanation of how he acquired the name Gopher John, see Kenneth Wiggins Porter, "Davy Crockett and John Horse: A Possible Origin of the Coonskin Story," *American Literature* 15(1943): 10-15. For consistency and continuity, John Horse will be the name used throughout this work. Wild Cat also was known as Coacoochee. In Mexico, the Seminole leader often was referred to as Gato del Monte and even, on occasion, "Captain Catamount."

58. "Capitulation of the Seminole Nation of Indians and Their Allies, March 6 1837," House Doc. 225, 52.

59. American State Papers, Military Affairs, vol. 7, 835.

60. Mahon, *Second Seminole War,* 201-4.

61. Jesup to Joel R. Poinsett, June 16, 1837, National Archives Record Group 94, Records of the Office of the Adjutant General 1780s-1917, General Jesup's Papers (hereafter cited as Jesup Papers), Letters Sent.

62. Jesup to Poinsett, September 23, 1837, Ibid.

63. Jesup to William L. Marcy, April 3 and July 1, 1848, National Archives Microfilm Publications, Microcopy M574, Record Group 75, Special Files of the Office of Indian Affairs, 1807-1904, 85 rolls (hereafter cited as M574), Roll 13, File 96, "Seminole Claims to Certain Negroes 1841-1849."

64. Jesup to Marcy, July 1, 1848, Jesup to Poinsett, March 14, 1838, and Jesup to William Wilkins, May 22, 1844, Ibid.

65. Kenneth Wiggins Porter, "Billy Bowlegs (Holata Micco) in the Seminole Wars," *Florida Historical Quarterly* 45(1967): 229.

66. Robert K. Thomas, "Afterword," in Peterson and Brown, eds., *New Peoples,* 247.

2. Emigrants from Indian Territory

1. *Annual Report of the Commissioner of Indian Affairs for 1841* (Washington, D.C.: Government Printing Office, 1842), (hereafter cited as ARCIA, followed by the year), Report 34, William Armstrong to T. Hartley Crawford, September 30, 1841, 327; *ARCIA 1842*, Report 25, Armstrong to Crawford, September 10, 1842, 450-51; Kappler, *Indian Affairs*, vol. 2, 249-51, 290-91.
2. *ARCIA 1841*, Report 34, Armstrong to Crawford, September 30, 1841, 337, and Report 36, J. Logan to Armstrong, September 30, 1841, 341; *ARCIA 1842*, Report 27, Logan to Armstrong, June 30, 1842, 456; *ARCIA 1845*, Report 17, Logan to Armstrong, September 20, 1845, 515-17; *ARCIA 1846*, Report 11, Logan to Armstrong, October 1, 1846, 274; *Arkansas Intelligencer*, August 2, 1845; Josiah Gregg, *Commerce of the Prairies*, 2 vols. (New York: H. G. Langley, 1844), vol. 2, 303; Daniel F. Littlefield, Jr., *Africans and Creeks: From the Colonial Period to the Civil War* (Westport, CT: Greenwood Press, 1979), 159-61; Littlefield, *Africans and Seminoles*, 176.
3. Kenneth Wiggins Porter, "Lament for Wild Cat," *Phylon* 4(1943): 39-43; Porter, *Negro on the Frontier*, 253-54; Kenneth Wiggins Porter, "Seminole Flight from Fort Marion," *Florida Historical Quarterly* 22(1944): 114-15, 119-20.
4. Armstrong to Crawford, April 12, 1842, Thomas L. Judge to Crawford, October 22, 1843, M234-800, Seminole Agency 1824-1845, A1223-42, J1350-43; *ARCIA 1842*, Report 25, Armstrong to Crawford, September 10, 1842, 450-51; *ARCIA 1843*, Report 90, Thomas L. Judge to Armstrong, September 15, 1843, 418-19, and Report 87, Armstrong to Crawford, September 30, 1843, 408; Crawford to Armstrong, April 10, 1844, M574-13, File 96, frames 247-56; Ethan Allen Hitchcock, *Fifty Years in Camp and Field: The Diary of Major General Ethan Allen Hitchcock*, ed. by W. A. Croffut (New York: G. P. Putnam's Sons, 1909), 138; Littlefield, *Africans and Seminoles*, 76; Edwin C. McReynolds, *The Seminoles* (Norman: University of Oklahoma Press, 1957), 232; Porter, "Seminole Flight from Fort Marion," 132 n. 4.
5. *Niles Weekly Register*, May 5, 1838; Porter, *Negro on the Frontier*, 258-60; Porter, "Seminole Flight from Fort Marion," 129, 133 n. 7; John T. Sprague, *The Origin, Progress and Conclusion of the Florida War* (New York: Appleton and Co., 1848), 195.
6. W. W. J. Bliss to R. B. Mason, April 11, 1842, and Bliss to S. Kearny, May 13, 1842, National Archives Record Group 393, Records of the United States Army Continental Commands, 1821-1920, Fort Gibson (hereafter cited as Fort Gibson), Letters Received, Box 1; Mason to R. Jones, November 3, 1844, Fort Gibson, Letters Sent; L. Thomas to Mason, December 18, 1844, Fort Gibson, Letters Received, Box 2; Fort Gibson, Indian Affairs, 1-2, 8; Report of Pierce M. Butler, Cherokee Agency, April 16, 1845, M234-800, B2452-45; Grant Foreman, *The Five Civilized Tribes* (Norman: University of Oklahoma Press, 1934), 226, 258.
7. Butler to Crawford, March 7, 1844, M234-800, B1988-44; J. L. Berger to Gustavus Loomis, April 3, 1844, Fort Gibson, Letters Sent; J. L. Dawson to N. Boone, April 10, 1844, Fort Gibson, Letters Received, Box 2; *ARCIA 1844*, Report 76, Butler to Crawford, September 30, 1844, 476; *Arkansas Intelligencer*, March 30, 1844; Littlefield, *Africans and Creeks*, 170-71.
8. Micco Nupper (Micanopy) et al. to Commissioner of Indian Affairs, April 20, 1844, M234-800, M194-44.

9. Alligator et al. to Crawford, May 16, 1844, M234-800, M1624-44. See also Jesup to William Wilkins, May 30, 1844, Ibid., J1482-44; and Foreman, *Five Civilized Tribes,* 237.

10. Mason to Jones, July 10, 1844, M234-800, M1973-44.

11. Ibid.; Butler to Crawford, July 25, 1845, Ibid., B2528-45; Jesup, endorsement of August 2, 1844, Ibid., M1973-44. Seminoles also attacked other blacks for cooperating with the United States forces in Florida. See Armstrong to Crawford, May 22, 1843, Ibid., A1457-43.

12. Mason to Jones, July 10, 1844, Wilkins's instructions to General Mathew Arbuckle, August 2, 1844, and Judge to Boone, August 31, 1844, Ibid., M1973-44, A1457-43, and J1684-45; Jones to Arbuckle, August 3, 1844, Fort Gibson, Letters Received, Box 2; Statement of Boone, Fort Gibson, Indian Affairs, 25.

13. *ARCIA 1844,* Report 80, Judge to Armstrong, August 26, 1844, 476, and Report 75, Armstrong to Crawford, October 1, 1844, 458.

14. Seminole Memorial, December 28, 1844, M234-800, frame 626; *ARCIA 1845,* Report 15, Armstrong to Crawford, September 30, 1845, 530; Foreman, *Five Civilized Tribes,* 243.

15. Kappler, *Indian Affairs,* vol. 2, 407-9.

16. *ARCIA 1845,* Report 20, Marcellus Duval to Crawford, September 30, 1845, 530.

17. Report of Butler, Cherokee Agency, April 16, 1845, Judge to Crawford, April 27, 1845, and Butler to Crawford, July 25, 1845, M234-800, B2452-45, J1684-45, and B2528-45; Foreman, *Five Civilized Tribes,* 258; Littlefield, *Africans and Seminoles,* 104.

18. Antonio J. Waring, ed., *Laws of the Creek Nation* (Athens: University of Georgia Press, 1960), 17-27.

19. Judge to Crawford, April 27, 1845, M234-800, J1684-45.

20. Application of Gopher John through J. C. Casey, May 28, 1845, Ibid., C2309-45.

21. Duval to William Medill, March 24, 1846, M234-801, Seminole Agency 1846-1855, D1059-46; Duval to J. K. Polk, December 21, 1846, M574-13, File 96, frames 194-200; Annie H. Abel, *The American Indian as Slaveholder and Secessionist: An Omitted Chapter in the Diplomatic History of the Southern Confederacy* (Cleveland: Arthur H. Clark Co., 1925), 25; Foreman, *Five Civilized Tribes,* 243. The old commissary building has been restored recently. See *Mistletoe Leaves* (Newsletter of the Oklahoma Historical Society) 21, #10 (Oct. 1990): 8.

22. Jesup to Arbuckle, April 8, 1846, M574-13, File 96, frame 92.

23. Mason, Statement, March 11, 1845, William A. Gordon, Statement, April 13, 1846, Loomis to Duval, May 3, 1846, and R. W. Kirkham to Jesup, August 20 and August 26, 1846, Fort Gibson, Indian Affairs, 9, 17-19, 21; Duval to Medill, June 2, 1847, and Jesup to Medill, July 13, 1848, M234-801, D38-47, and J96-48; Duval to Loomis, June 7, 1847, Fort Gibson, Letters Received, Box 3; Captain A. Cady to Jones, March 18, 1846, and Loomis to Casey, June 11, 1847, Fort Gibson, Letters Sent.

24. Loomis to F. F. Flint, October 29, 1846, National Archives Record Group 393, Records of the United States Army Continental Commands, 1821-1920, Second and Seventh Military Departments (hereafter cited as Second and Seventh), Letters Received, Box 6; Loomis to Flint, July 20, 1847, Fort Gibson, Indian Affairs, 26; Littlefield, *Africans and Seminoles,* 112-14.

25. Loomis to Jesup, December 7, 1847, and Arbuckle to Jones, January 29, 1848, M574-13, File 96, frames 31-33.

26. Loomis to Jesup, December 7, 1847, and Benjamin Marshall, Tuckabatchee Micco et al. to Medill, April 26, 1848, Ibid., frames 31-33, 52-54.

27. Gopher John to Jesup, June 10, 1848, M234-801, J102-48.

28. J. Y. Mason to President Polk, June 28, 1848, M574-13, File 96, frames 57-78.

29. Gopher John to Jesup, June 10, 1848, M234-801, J102-48; Jesup to B. L. E. Bonneville, July 28, 1848, Medill to Gopher John, August 2, 1848, and Statement of Coacoochee, August 21, 1848, Fort Gibson, Indian Affairs, 36-38; W. L. Marcy to Arbuckle, August 5, 1848, and Medill to Duval, August 5, 1848, Fort Gibson, Letters Received, Box 3.

30. Flint to W. S. Ketchum, August 21 and September 25, 1848, Fort Gibson, Letters Received, Box 3; D. S. Miles to Flint, November 17, 1848, and Duval to Arbuckle, December 1 and 11, 1848, Second and Seventh, Letters Received, Box 7.

31. *ARCIA 1845*, Report 15, Armstrong to Crawford, September 30, 1845, 506-7, and Report 20, Duval to Crawford, September 30, 1845, 529-31.

32. *ARCIA 1846*, Report 15, Duval to Medill, September 5, 1846, 280; *Arkansas Intelligencer*, May 24, 1845; *Cherokee Advocate*, May 22, 1845; Grant Foreman, *Advancing the Frontier 1830-1860* (Norman: University of Oklahoma Press, 1933), 229.

33. *ARCIA 1846*, Report 9, Armstrong to Medill, October 10, 1846, 266, and Report 15, Duval to Medill, September 5, 1846, 279; *Arkansas Intelligencer*, October 3, 1846; *Cherokee Advocate*, July 30, 1846; Foreman, *Five Civilized Tribes*, 244-45, 260-61 and n. 12; Foreman, ed., "Journal of Elijah Hicks," 71, 75, 80-81; McReynolds, *Seminoles*, 256-57.

34. Wild Cat to Secretary of War, May 12, 1847, M234-801, C82-47; *ARCIA 1846*, Report 20, Duval to Medill, September 5, 1846, 279-80; *ARCIA 1848*, Report 22c, R. S. Neighbors to Medill March 2, 1848, 576-86; Rupert N. Richardson, *The Comanche Barrier to South Plains Settlement: A Century and a Half of Savage Resistance to the Advancing White Frontier* (Glendale, CA: Arthur H. Clark Co., 1933), 170-71 and n. 317.

35. Carolyn T. Foreman, "The Jumper Family of the Seminole Nation," *Chronicles of Oklahoma* 34(1956): 284; McReynolds, *Seminoles*, 260-61; Kenneth Wiggins Porter, "Seminole in Mexico, 1850-1861," *Chronicles of Oklahoma* 29(1951): 154; Sattler, "Siminoli Italwa," 114, 169; For an excellent treatment of Wild Cat's use of southeastern Indian border strategies in the Southwest, see Susan A. Miller, "Wild Cat and the Origins of the Seminole Migration to Mexico," unpublished M.A. thesis, University of Oklahoma, 1988; and Susan A. Miller, "A New Border for an Old Use: Seminole Indians at the Rio Grande," paper read at the annual conference of the Western History Association, Austin, Texas, October 1991.

36. Arbuckle to Jones, July 31, 1848, Flint to J. Drennen, September 10, 1849, and F. N. Page to Douglas E. Twiggs, November 18, 1854, *Indians—Creek and Seminole*, 33 Cong., 2 Sess., House Exec. Doc. No. 15 (hereafter cited as *Creek and Seminole*), 22, 29, 10-11; Miles to Flint, November 17, 1848, Second and Seventh, Letters Received, Box 7.

37. Arbuckle to Jones, July 31, 1849, *Creek and Seminole*, 22.

38. "List of Negroes handed over to the Seminole Chiefs at Fort Gibson, Cherokee Nation, 2 January 1849," William G. Belknap to Arbuckle, January 3, 1849, and Arbuckle to Jones, January 8, 1849, M574-13, File 96, frames 143-54, 164, 140-41; Arbuckle to Jones, July 31, 1849, and Flint to Drennen, August 13, 1849, *Creek and Seminole*, 22, 26.

39. Belknap to Arbuckle, January 3, 1849, M574-13, File 96, frame 164.

40. "'I'm in the Wewoka Switch': Heard in the Oil Fields Over the World," *Chronicles of Oklahoma* 41(1963): 457; Mary Ann Lilley, "The Autobiography of Mary Ann Lilley," unpublished typescript, 64pp., Section 10, Indian Archives Division, Oklahoma Historical Society, Oklahoma City, 47-48; Littlefield, *Africans and Seminoles,* 133-34.

41. Duval to Belknap, June 7, 1849, Fort Gibson, Letters Received, Box 3; Duval to Arbuckle, July 16, 1849, Arbuckle to Jones, July 31, 1849, and Page to Twiggs, November 18, 1854, *Creek and Seminole,* 19, 22, 10.

42. Page to Twiggs, November 18, 1854, *Creek and Seminole,* 11.

43. "Pass," April 8, 1849, Fort Gibson, Indian Affairs, 45.

44. Duval to Belknap, June 7, 1849, Fort Gibson, Letters Received, Box 3.

45. Duval to Arbuckle, July 16, 1849, Drennen to Arbuckle, July 20, 1849, and Arbuckle to Jones, July 31 and August 14, 1849, *Creek and Seminole,* 19-20, 22, 25.

46. Duval to Arbuckle, July 16, 1849, Drennen to Arbuckle, July 20, 1849, Flint to Drennen, July 26, 1849, Arbuckle to Jones, July 31, 1849, Flint to Belknap, August 2, 1849, Flint to Drennen, August 13, 1849, and Arbuckle to Jones, August 14, 1849, Ibid., 19-26.

47. Drennen to Arbuckle, August 18, 1849, Ibid., 27.

48. Page to Twiggs, November 18, 1854, Ibid., 11.

49. Flint to Drennen, September 10, 1849, Flint to Philip H. Raiford, September 10, 1849, Arbuckle to Jones, September 14, 1849, and Page to Twiggs, November 18, 1854, Ibid., 28-31, 11.

50. Armstrong to Crawford, June 4, 1843, M234-800, A1464-43; Foreman, *Advancing the Frontier,* 243.

51. Francisco F. de la Maza, *Código de Colonización y Terrenos Baldíos de la República Mexicana 1451-1892* (Mexico City: Oficina de la Secretaria de Fomento, 1893), 356.

52. *U.S. Statutes at Large, 1789-1863* (Boston: 1852-1867), vol. 9, 930-31; James F. Rippy, "The Indians of the Southwest in the Diplomacy of the United States and Mexico, 1848-1853," *Hispanic American Historical Review* 2(1919): 376-79.

53. Maza, *Código de Colonización,* 400-6. See also Dieter G. Berringer, "Mexican Attitudes Towards Immigration 1821-1857," unpublished Ph.D. diss., University of Wisconsin, 1972, 139-42; and Odie B. Faulk, "Projected Mexican Military Colonies for the Borderlands, 1848," *Journal of Arizona History* 9(1968): 39-47.

54. Duval to O. Brown, May 30, 1850, M234-801, D392-50; Foreman, *Advancing the Frontier,* 244-48.

55. J. Lynde to Flint, October 12, 1849, Second and Seventh, Letters Received, Box 7; Page to Twiggs, November 18, 1854, *Creek and Seminole,* 11.

56. Duval to Brown, November 5, 1849, M234-289, Florida Superintendency 1838-1850, D247-49; Foreman, *Five Civilized Tribes,* 248; McReynolds, *Seminoles,* 266.

57. Raiford to Drennen, November 15, 1849, M234-924, Western Superintendency 1847-1851, D274-49 enc.; Duval to Brown, May 30, 1850, M234-801, D392-50; Page to Twiggs, November 18, 1854, *Creek and Seminole,* 11; Giddings, *Exiles of Florida,* 333; "They Packed Up at Night and Stole Away" in Kenneth Wiggins Porter, "Freedom Over Me: A Folk-History of the Wild Cat-John Horse Band of Seminole Negroes 1848-1882," unpublished typescript based on interviews and correspondence with the Seminole maroons in Texas and Coahuila during the 1930s and 1940s, Kenneth Wiggins Porter Papers, Archives Division, Schomburg Center for Research in Black Culture, New York City, Box 2 (hereafter cited as "Freedom Over Me"); *San Antonio Western Texas,* June 6,

1850; Sattler, "Siminoli Italwa," 395-96 n. 66; Frost Woodhull, "The Seminole Indian Scouts on the Border," *Frontier Times* 15(1937): Statement of Charlie Daniels, 119.

58. "My Mama Come with Wild Cat" and "Picayune John" in Porter, "Freedom Over Me."

59. *Daily Oklahoman,* January 23, 1921, Statement of Ahalakochee; Duval to Brown, May 30, 1850, M234-801, D392-50; John H. Rollins to Brown, May 8, 1850, M234-858, Texas Agency 1847-1859; Rollins to Peter H. Bell, October 30, 1850, Governors' Papers, Peter Hansborough Bell, 1849-1853, Archives Division, Texas State Library, Austin, Folder 2, Correspondence: Indian Affairs 1850-1852 (hereafter cited as Bell Correspondence).

60. Rollins to Bell, October 30, 1850, Bell Correspondence; *San Antonio Western Texas,* June 6, 1850; *Cherokee Advocate,* June 10, 1850; *Fort Smith Herald,* July 20, 1850; Arrell Morgan Gibson, *The Kickapoos: Lords of the Middle Border* (Norman: University of Oklahoma Press, 1963), 179-81.

61. Dianna Everett, *The Texas Cherokees: A People Between Two Fires* (Norman: University of Oklahoma Press, 1990), 67-71; Odie B. Faulk, "Projected Mexican Colonies in the Borderlands, 1852," *Journal of Arizona History* 10(1969): 115; *Report of the Committee of Investigation Sent in 1873 by the Mexican Government to the Frontier of Texas. Translated from the Official Edition Made in Mexico* (New York: Baker and Godwin Printers, 1875), 323-24; Rippy, "Indians of the Southwest," 386; Joseph A. Stout, Jr., *The Liberators: Filibustering Expeditions into Mexico, 1848-1862, and the Last Thrust of Manifest Destiny* (Los Angeles: Westernlore Press, 1973), 29-30; Ronnie C. Tyler, "Fugitive Slaves in Mexico," *Journal of Negro History* 57(1972): 1-2.

62. Quoted in Felipe A. LaTorre and Dolores L. LaTorre, *The Mexican Kickapoo Indians* (Austin: University of Texas Press, 1976), 13-14. See also *El Siglo Diez y Nueve,* August 26, 1850; and *Report of Committee of Investigation,* 408.

63. Rollins to Bell, October 30, 1850, Bell Correspondence; Jesse Sumpter, "Life of Jesse Sumpter, the Oldest Citizen of Eagle Pass, Texas," unpublished typescript, 70pp., 1906, Manuscripts Division, Barker Texas History Center, University of Texas at Austin, 2. See also *Cherokee Advocate,* September 3, 1850.

64. Cora Montgomery, *Eagle Pass; Or, Life on the Border* (New York: Putnam's Semi-monthly Library for Travellers and the Fireside, 1852), 73-74. Cora Montgomery was the pen name of Jane Maria (McManus) Cazneau, or Mrs. William Leslie Cazneau.

65. *Informe de la Comisión Pesquisidora de la Frontera del Norte* (Mexico City: Imprenta del Gobierno en Palacio, 1877), 257; *Memoria de la Secretaria de Estado y del Despacho de Guerra y Marina* (Mexico: 1851), 17-18; Porter, *Negro on the Frontier,* 427; *Report of Committee of Investigation,* 408.

66. "They Stopped at Las Moras Springs" in Porter, "Freedom Over Me."

67. Foster, "Negro-Indian Relationships," 42-43.

68. Hubert Howe Bancroft, *History of Mexico.* 6 vols. *Works of Hubert Howe Bancroft,* v. 9-14 (San Francisco: History Company, 1886-1888), vol. 5, 575 n. 48; *Depredations on the Frontiers of Texas,* 43 Cong., 1 Sess., House Exec. Doc. No. 257, Deposition 545, John Kibbets [sic], 22; Ben E. Pingenot, *Paso del Aguila: A Chronicle of Frontier Days on the Texas Border as Recorded in the Memoirs of Jesse Sumpter, 1827-1910* (Austin: Encino Press, 1969), 11-12 n. 11; Porter, *Negro on the Frontier,* 429; Ralph A. Smith, "The Mamelukes of West Texas and Mexico," *West Texas Historical Association Year Book* 39(1963): 69. "Mascogos" probably derived from "Muskogees." In many ways a curious term, "Mascogos" nevertheless conferred exclusivity on the maroons from an early stage.

3. *Los Mascogos*

1. Duval to Brown, May 30 and 31, 1850, M234-801, D392-50.
2. William Bowlegs to Seminole Chiefs, April 12, 1850, Second and Seventh, Letters Received, Box 8.
3. Roley McIntosh to Belknap, June 12, 1850, *Creek and Seminole,* 16-17.
4. Dent to Flint, July 15, 1850, Ibid., 17-18.
5. Ibid.; Duval to Arbuckle, July 29, 1850, and Belknap to Page, August 6, 1850, Second and Seventh, Letters Received, Box 8; Duval to Bell, October 20, 1850, Bell Correspondence.
6. Rollins to Bell, October 30, 1850, Bell Correspondence.
7. Rodney Glisan, *Journal of Army Life* (San Francisco: A. L. Bancroft and Co., 1874), 65-66; United States. War Dept., *Exploration of the Red River of Louisiana in the Year 1852* (Washington, D.C.: Robert Armstrong, Public Printer, 1853), 101; Randolph B. Marcy, *Thirty Years of Army Life on the Border* (New York: Harper and Bros., 1866), 30-31, 55-56; Woodhull, "Scouts on the Border," Statement of Renty Grayson, 123.
8. Echo Hadjo [Harjo] et al. (Canadian Creek Chiefs) to McIntosh, September 20, 1850, and McIntosh to Belknap, September 23, 1850, *Creek and Seminole,* 31-32; Duval to L. Lea, September 21 and 30, 1850, M234-801, D451-50, and D455-50; Duval to Bell, October 20, 1850, Bell Correspondence.
9. McIntosh to Belknap, September 23, 1850, and Belknap to Page, October 15, 1850, *Creek and Seminole,* 32-33; Duval to Lea, September 30, 1850, M234-801, D455-50; C. J. Atkins to Commander of Fort Gibson, September 30, 1850, Fort Gibson, Letters Received, Box 3.
10. Duval to Bell, October 20, 1850, Bell Correspondence; Duval to Lea, December 9, 1850, M234-801, D481-50; *ARCIA 1851,* Report 40, Duval to Lea, October 25, 1851, 405; Page to Twiggs, November 18, 1854, *Creek and Seminole,* 13.
11. Page to Twiggs, November 18, 1854, *Creek and Seminole,* 12; *Cherokee Advocate,* November 19, 1850; *Fort Smith Herald,* November 1 and 11, 1850; Glisan, *Journal of Army Life,* 65-66; Porter, "Lament for Wild Cat," 39.
12. Rollins to Bell, October 30, 1850, Bell Correspondence; Page to Twiggs, November 18, 1854, *Creek and Seminole,* 13-14; Gibson, *Kickapoos,* 181-82.
13. John H. Brown, *History of Texas from 1685-1892,* 2 vols. (St. Louis: L. E. Daniell, 1892-1893), vol. 2, 159; Harry S. and E. S. O'Beirne, comps., *The Indian Territory; Its Chiefs, Legislators and Leading Men* (St. Louis: C. B. Woodward Co., 1892), 172; Kenneth Wiggins Porter, "Farewell to John Horse: An Episode of Seminole Negro Folk History," *Phylon* 8(1947): 269, 271; Kenneth Wiggins Porter, "The Hawkins Negroes Go to Mexico," *Chronicles of Oklahoma* 24(1946): 55-58; Kenneth Wiggins Porter, "A Legend of the Biloxi," *Journal of American Folklore* 59(1946): 168-73; Porter, "Seminole in Mexico," 165, 167 and n. 38; Andrew J. Sowell, *Rangers and Pioneers of Texas* (New York: Argosy Antiquarian, 1964 [1884]), 187-89; Henderson K. Yoakum, *History of Texas from Its First Settlement in 1685 to Its Annexation to the United States in 1846,* 2 vols. (New York: Refield, 1855), vol. 1, 328.
14. Duval to Bell, October 20, 1850, Bell Correspondence; Duval to Bell, October 21, 1850, in Dorman H. Winfrey and James M. Day, eds., *The Indian Papers of Texas and the Southwest 1825-1916,* 5 vols. (Austin: Pemberton Press, 1966), vol. 5, 92-93.

15. Duval to George Brooke, October 21, 1850, and Duval to Lea, December 9, 1850, M234-801, D481-50, and enc.; Bell to Brooke, November 8, 1850, and Bell to Duval, November 9, 1850, in Winfrey and Day, *Indian Papers of Texas,* vol. 3, 127-28; Brooke to Bell, November 12, 1850, Bell Correspondence.

16. Brooke to Bell, November 12, 1850, Bell Correspondence; "Circular de 18 de Octubre de 1850: Admitiendo en Calidad de Colonos a los Indios de las Tribus Seminoles, Quikapus, y Mascogos," in Maza, *Código de Colonización,* 474-78; Latorre and Latorre, *Mexican Kickapoo Indians,* 123; Montgomery, *Eagle Pass,* 143; Pingenot, *Paso de Aguila,* 11-12 n.11; *Report of Committee of Investigation,* 303-4. Porter, in *Negro on the Frontier,* 429-52, used a wealth of primary documentation and oral history to bring this chapter of Seminole maroon history to light. Several of the references below draw upon this important work, but for brevity, it will not be listed further in this chapter.

17. *La Patria,* March 22, 1851.

18. "Memorandum of a conversation between Wild Cat or Coacoochee and Colonels Cooper and Temple, Eagle Pass, Texas, 27 March 1851" [sent to Secretary of War Charles M. Conrad], copy in Grant Foreman Papers, Manuscripts Division, Thomas Gilcrease Institute of American History and Art, Tulsa, OK, Box 32, vol. 65, 601-8.

19. Page to Twiggs, November 18, 1854, *Creek and Seminole,* 14; Gibson, *Kickapoos,* 183; *La Patria,* June 7, 21, 28, July 12, 19, August 9, 23, 30, 1851; *Report of Committee of Investigation,* 325-27, 408-9; Smith, "Mamelukes," 72-73.

20. Montgomery, *Eagle Pass,* 144-45.

21. Bancroft, *History of Mexico,* vol. 5, 603-6; *Fort Smith Herald,* November 8 and December 6, 1850; T. B. Holabird to R. W. Johnson, August 12, 1854, *Creek and Seminole,* 4; William J. Hughes, *Rebellious Ranger: Rip Ford and the Old Southwest* (Norman: University of Oklahoma Press, 1964), 100-1; *La Patria,* November 8, 22, December 6, 13, 27, 1851; Vicente E. Manero, comp., *Documentos Interesantes, sobre Colonización: Los ha reunido, puesto en orden Cronológico y los Pública* (Mexico: Imprenta de Hijos de Murguia, 1878), 31; Stephen B. Oates, ed., *Rip Ford's Texas by John Salmon Ford* (Austin: University of Texas Press, 1963), 196-97, 214; *Report of Committee of Investigation,* 188-90, 331; James Fred Rippy, "Border Troubles Along the Rio Grande, 1848-1860," *Southwestern Historical Quarterly* 23(1919): 96-97; Ernest Shearer, "The Carvajal Disturbances," *Southwestern Historical Quarterly* 55(1951): 201-30; *Texas Monument,* October 16 and December 4, 1850; Tyler, "Fugitive Slaves," 4-5.

22. Duval to Commissioner of Indian Affairs, April 24, 1851, M234-801, D605-51; "Official Request of Governor Bell relative to certain runaway negroes" September 17, 1851, Bell Correspondence.

23. General Luis Alberto Guajardo, comp., "Apuntes Datos y Noticias para la Historia de Coahuila," *circa* 1613-1911. Typewritten transcripts August 18, 1852, November 29, 1866, February 20, 1867, taken from the official archives of Monclova, Saltillo, and Santa Rosa (or Múzquiz), together with Guajardo's notes, assembled for a projected history of Coahuila, Western Americana Collections, Beinecke Rare Book and Manuscript Library, Yale University, New Haven; *La Patria,* November 22, 1851; *Report of Committee of Investigation,* 331.

24. Coe, *Red Patriots,* 168; William H. Emory, *Report on the United States and Mexican Boundary Survey,* 2 vols. (Washington, D.C.: Cornelius Wendell Printer, 1857. Reprinted in 34 Cong., 1 Sess., House Executive Doc. 135), 43; Charles H. Harris III, *A Mexican*

Family Empire: The Latifundio of the Sánchez Navarros, 1765-1867 (Austin: University of Texas Press, 1975), 173; Indian Pioneer Papers, 116 vols., Indian Archives Division, Oklahoma Historical Society, Oklahoma City (hereafter cited as Indian Pioneer Papers), vol. 58, no. 7011, Nina Tanyon, July 20, 1937, 394-96; Woodhull, "Scouts on the Border," Statements of Charlie Daniels and Renty Grayson, 123. Though it constitutes a work of propaganda and should be treated with caution, a major source on the experience of the Seminoles and Mascogos in Coahuila during this period remains the *Report of Committee of Investigation,* especially 188-94, 303-4, 325-27, 409-11. Several of the references below draw upon this document, but for brevity, it will be listed further in this chapter only if it constitutes the sole citation.

25. Julius Fröbel, *Aus Amerika, Efrahungen, Reisen und Studien,* 2 vols. (Leipzig: J. J. Weber, 1857-1858), vol. 2, 220-21.

26. *Daily Oklahoman,* January 16, 1921; *El Siglo Diez y Nueve,* September 3, 1852; Guajardo, "Historia de Coahuila," August 18, 1852; *Informe de la Comisión Pesquisidora,* 260-62; Copy of Agreement between the Leaders of the Seminoles, Mascogos, and Kickapoos, and the Secretaria del Gobierno del Estado de Coahuila, Saltillo, August 18, 1852, Múzquiz Records, Western Americana Collections, Beinecke Rare Book and Manuscript Library, Yale University, New Haven (hereafter cited as Múzquiz Records). The Múzquiz Records include letters received and copies of letters sent by officials of the municipality of Múzquiz, Coahuila. References hereafter will be listed either LR (letter received) or LS (letter sent) followed by the correspondent and date.

27. *Depredations on the Frontiers of Texas,* Deposition 545, John Kibbets, 22; Giddings, *Exiles of Florida,* 335.

28. *Daily Oklahoman,* January 16, 1921; Montgomery, *Eagle Pass,* 143.

29. Ronnie C. Tyler, ed., "Exploring the Rio Grande: Lieutenant Duff C. Green's Report of 1852," *Arizona and the West* 10(1968): 60.

30. Drennen to Lea, September 27, 1852, Lea to A. H. H. Stuart, November 10, 1852, Duval to Lea, November 15, 1852, and Duval to Commissioner of Indian Affairs, April 8, 1853, M234-801, I131-52 and enc., D223-52, and D298-53; *ARCIA 1852,* Doc. 37, Report of Drennen, 103.

31. Pingenot, *Paso del Aguila,* 70 and nn. 2 and 3; *San Antonio Western Texas,* September 18, 1851, November 18 and December 2, 1852; Sumpter, "Oldest Citizen," 33; Tyler, "Fugitive Slaves," 5.

32. "Contra Gato Del Monte de la Nación Extranjera Seminole por Haber Vendido unos Negros Libres de los Immigrados al Territorio Mexicano," Legajo Número 45, 1853, Exp. Número 1719, Archivo de la Secretaría de Gobierno, Saltillo, Coahuila, 1848-1876, Vol. 44, 185-91, Manuscripts Division, Bancroft Library, University of California, Berkeley, M-A 10, vol. 44 (photocopy).

33. "My Mama Come with Wild Cat" in Porter, "Freedom Over Me." In the 1971 Warner Brothers' comedy "Skin Game," James Garner and Lou Gossett, Jr. star as two confidence tricksters traveling around the antebellum South posing as master and slave. At each town they come to, Garner "sells" Gossett and then helps him escape, the two later splitting the proceeds.

34. Smith, "Mamelukes," 79.

35. Holabird to Johnson, August 12, 1854, "Statement A" J. Levins, October 15, 1854, "Statement B" L. Gerard, October 15, 1854, "Statement C" J. E. Gardner, October 16,

1854, and J. Plympton to Assistant Adjutant General, Department of Texas (hereafter cited as AAGDT), October 16, 1854, *Creek and Seminole,* 4-9.

36. *Texas State Times,* October 5, 1855.

37. Holabird to Johnson, August 12, 1854, and Plympton to AAGDT, October 16, 1854, *Creek and Seminole,* 4-6.

38. Frederick L. Olmsted, *Journey through Texas: A Saddle-trip on the Southwestern Frontier,* ed. by J. Howard (Austin: Von Boeckman-Jones Press, 1962 [1857]), 200.

39. *Boletín Oficial del Estado de Nuevo León y Coahuila,* July 19, 1859, January 5, 1862; Edward H. Moseley, "Indians from the Eastern United States and the Defence of Northeastern Mexico, 1855-1864," *Southwestern Social Science Quarterly* 46(1965): 279; Oates, *Rip Ford's Texas,* 196-97, 214-15; *Texas State Gazette,* June 2 and 23, 1855; *Texas State Times,* June 2, 1855; Ronnie C. Tyler, "The Callahan Expedition of 1855: Indians or Negroes?" *Southwestern Historical Quarterly* 70(April 1967): 576; Tyler, "Fugitive Slaves," 6-7.

40. *Boletín Oficial del Estado de Nuevo León y Coahuila,* October 24, 1855; Oates, *Rip Ford's Texas,* 215; Pingenot, *Paso del Aguila,* 71-72 n. 4; *Texas State Times,* October 6, 1855; Tyler, "Callahan Expedition," 577-79; Tyler, "Fugitive Slaves," 7-8.

41. P. F. Smith to C. S. Cooper, October 10, 1855, *Claims of the State of Texas,* 45 Cong., 2 Sess., Senate Exec. Doc. 19, 111; Smith to E. M. Pease, October 11, 1855, in Winfrey and Day, *Indian Papers of Texas,* vol. 3, 254-55; *El Siglo Diez y Nueve,* November 13, 1855; Foster, "Negro-Indian Relationships," 45; *San Antonio Herald,* October 16, 1855; Ernest Shearer, "The Callahan Expedition, 1855," *Southwestern Historical Quarterly* 54(1951): 439-42; Sumpter, "Oldest Citizen," 42; *Texas State Gazette,* October 13 and 20, 1855; *Texas State Times,* November 11 and 17, 1855.

42. Porter, "Lament for Wild Cat," 47.

43. Olmsted, *Journey through Texas,* 331-34; Sumpter, "Oldest Citizen," 40.

44. Tyler, "Callahan Expedition," 584.

45. Smith to Pease, October 11, 1855, in Winfrey and Day, *Indian Papers of Texas,* vol. 3, 254-55. See also Smith to L. Thomas, October 17, 1855, and Smith to Emilio Langberg, December 6, 1855, *Claims of the State of Texas,* 115-16, 119-20.

46. *Texas State Gazette,* October 20, 1855.

47. *Report of Committee of Investigation,* 191.

48. Porter, "Lament for Wild Cat," 47.

49. James Gadsden to M. M. Arrioja, November 29, 1855, in William R. Manning, ed., *Diplomatic Correspondence of the United States, Inter-American Affairs, 1831-1860,* 12 vols. (Washington, D.C.: Carnegie Endowment for International Peace, 1932-1939), vol. 9, 800-3.

50. LR from Colonel Emilio Langberg, October 22, 1855, LS to Langberg, October 25, 1855, Múzquiz Records; Smith, "Mamelukes," 80-81.

51. *Report of Committee of Investigation,* 410.

52. LR from Ignacio Galinda, November 27, 1855, LR from Jesús Garza González, May 11 and 24 (#172), 1856, December 18, 1857, and January 19, 1858, Múzquiz Records; Michael J. Box, *Captain James Box's Adventures in New and Old Mexico* (New York: J. Miller, 1869), 204; *El Restaurador de la Libertad,* May 20, 1856; *El Siglo Diez y Nueve,* May 27, 1856; Porter, "Seminole in Mexico," 163.

53. *El Restaurador de la Libertad,* May 20, 1856.

54. LR from T. T., May 19 and June 1, 1856, LR from González, May 24 (#172) and November 27 (#383), 1856, Múzquiz Records; Guajardo, "Historia de Coahuila," April 9 and 25, May 24, 1856.

55. Porter, "Seminole in Mexico," 154, 163, 165.

56. LR from T. T., May 26 and July 7, 1856, LR from González, June 2, 1856, LR from Salome de Garza, September 8, 1856, LS July [?], and August 4, 1856, Múzquiz Records; Guajardo, "Historia de Coahuila," May 5, 1856.

57. LS to Tesorero, November 5, 1856, LS to Secretario de Gobierno, November 5, 1856, LR from González, November 25, 1856, Múzquiz Records; Bancroft, *History of Mexico,* vol. 5, 698-99; Smith, "Mamelukes," 84.

58. LR from José María Jimenez, February 22, 1857, LR from González, February 23 and March 24, 1857, Múzquiz Records; Guajardo, "Historia de Coahuila," January 20, February 17, and September 6, 1857; *ARCIA 1870,* Doc. 123, Bliss to H. Clay Wood, July 14, 1870, 328-29; *El Restaurador de la Libertad,* January 23 and February 6, 1857; Foster, "Negro-Indian Relationships," 43-44; Porter, "Lament for Wild Cat," 48 and n. 1; Porter, "Seminole in Mexico," 155-56; Kenneth Wiggins Porter, "Wild Cat's Death and Burial," *Chronicles of Oklahoma* 21(1943): 41-43; *San Antonio Texan,* June 18, 1857.

59. Statement of Joe Philips in Foster, "Negro-Indian Relationships," 43-44.

60. Coe, *Red Patriots,* 169; *El Restaurador de la Libertad,* September 18 and November 27, 1857.

61. LR from González, March 25, April 21, September 8, and December 27, 1857, LS April 7, 1857, Múzquiz Records; *Boletín Oficial del Estado de Nuevo León y Coahuila,* January 19, 1858; *El Restaurador de la Libertad,* December 18, 1857; Guajardo, "Historia de Coahuila," July 8, August 3, 8, and 21, September 8, and December 14, 1857; Moseley, "Indians from the Eastern United States," 277; Porter, "Seminole in Mexico," 160.

62. LR from J. Felipe Ramón, September 13, 1858 [with enclosed complaint of Seminoles, dated Monterrey, August 29], 1858 (#172), March 14 (#50), and June 27, 1859, Múzquiz Records.

63. LS to Prefecto de Monclova, March 3 and 6, 1858, LS to Prefecto de Rio Grande, March 5, 1858, LR from Pablo Espinosa, March 9, 1858, LR from Ramón, April 8, 1858, Múzquiz Records; Porter, "Seminole in Mexico," 160.

64. Twiggs to Commissioner of Indian Affairs, December 28, 1858, M234-803, Seminole Agency 1859-1867, T339-58; Kappler, *Indian Affairs,* vol. 2, 569-76; Foreman, *Five Civilized Tribes,* 270.

65. Elias Rector to Charles E. Mix, August 21, 1858, and J. Thompson to Twiggs, September 13, 1858, M234-802, R897-58, F897-58; Twiggs to Commissioner of Indian Affairs, December 28, 1858, M234-803, T339-58.

66. LR from Ramón, February 17, 1859, Múzquiz Records; Report of L. Star, March 15, 1859, and Twiggs to Cooper, March 15, 1859, M234-803, 799-2, 799-2-10726; Twiggs, Special Order No. 12, copy to Governor H. R. Runnels, March 3, 1859, and Star to Runnels, March 12, 1859, in Winfrey and Day, *Indian Papers of Texas,* vol. 5, 319-20, 329.

67. "Reminiscences of Zenas R. Bliss, Major General United States Army 1854-1876," unpublished typescript, 5 vols., Manuscripts Division, Barker Texas History Center, University of Texas at Austin, Box 2Q411, vol. 2, 50-51. Bliss mistakenly dates this meeting as taking place in the fall of 1858.

68. Twiggs, Special Order No. 12, copy to Runnels, March 3, 1859, in Winfrey and Day, *Indian Papers of Texas,* vol. 5, 319-20.
69. LR from Ramón, March 31, 1859 (#66), Múzquiz Records.
70. LS to Prefecto de Monclova, May 21 and 25, 1859, Múzquiz Records; *ARCIA 1870,* Doc. 123, Bliss to Clay Wood, July 14, 1870, 328-29; Foster, "Negro-Indian Relationships," 43; "All the People Went Down to the Laguna" in Porter, "Freedom Over Me."
71. LR from Manuel Rejón, April 7 and 21, 1861, Múzquiz Records; Harris, *Mexican Family Empire,* 203.
72. W. C. Yeats to J. Buck Barry, n.d., James Buckner Barry Papers, Manuscripts Division, Barker Texas History Center, University of Texas at Austin; *ARCIA 1861,* E. H. Carruth to D. Hunter, November 26, 1861, 47; *ARCIA 1870,* Doc. 123, Bliss to Clay Wood, July 14, 1870, 328-29; *Daily Oklahoman,* January 16, 1921; Indian Pioneer Papers, vol. 58, no. 7011, Nina Tanyon, July 20, 1937, 395, vol. 74, Ponjo Harjo Guy, 266; James K. Greer, ed., *The Days of Buck Barry in Texas, 1845-1906* (Dallas: Southwest Press, 1932), 142; *The War of the Rebellion: A Compilation of the Official Records of the Union and Confederate Armies,* 4 ser., 130 vols. (Washington, D.C.: Government Printing Office, 1890-1901), ser. 4, vol. 1, 513-27; Muriel H. Wright, "Seal of the Seminole Nation," *Chronicles of Oklahoma* 34(1956): 266.

4. The Seminole Negro Indian Scouts

1. Mexican commissioners stated later that by the end of 1861, the "Black Muscogees, at Parras" numbered "from 40 to 60 persons," *Report of Committee of Investigation,* 411. This number probably referred to heads of household, for detailed calculations based upon contemporary reports and later censuses have determined that around 350 Seminole maroons in total must have been living in Coahuila by this time. The commissioners' figure, in fact, correlates well with the seventy-seven male Mascogos reported to be living in Mexico in 1891. See "Lista de los Negroes de la Tribu Mascogo Agraciada por el Gobierno General con Terrenos de la Colonia del Nacimiento," Seminoles y Mascogos, Número 94(1891), 44-12-60, Archivo de la Secretaria de Relaciones Exteriores, Colonización, Mexico City (hereafter cited as Seminoles y Mascogos).
2. "Thomas Factor," "They Could Outscheme the Indians," "The Women and Children Fleed (sic) to the Bushes," and "The Big Fight" in Porter, "Freedom Over Me"; Box, *Adventures and Explorations,* 203-4; Foster, "Negro-Indian Relationships," testimony of Joe Philips, July 1, 1930, 44, 46; James P. Newcomb, *History of Secession Times in Texas and Journal of Travel from Texas through Mexico to California* (San Francisco: n.p., 1863), 14-15.
3. Walter V. Scholes, *Mexican Politics During the Juárez Regime 1855-1872* (Columbia: University of Missouri Press, 1957), 8-9, 29, 89, 102-5; Richard N. Sinkin, *The Mexican Reform, 1855-1876: A Study in Liberal Nation-Building* (Austin: University of Texas Institute of Latin-American Studies, 1979), 105-9. The maroons later cited the revolution as being the main reason for their return to the United States. See Petition of Florida Seminole Negroes to President Grover Cleveland, n.d. but recd. by the Bureau of Indian Affairs February 9, 1888, National Archives Record Group 75, Letters Received by the Bureau of Indian Affairs 1881-1907 (hereafter cited as RG 75 LR 1881-1907), 3565-88.

4. "The French Burned El Burro" in Porter, "Freedom Over Me"; "Reminiscences of Zenas Bliss," vol. 5, 107; Jack A. Dabbs, *The French Army in Mexico 1861-1867: A Study in Military Government* (The Hague: Mouton and Co., 1963), 99; Porter, "Farewell to John Horse," 268, and biographical sketch of Rosa Fay, 270.

5. "They Did Not All Stick Together" and "Elijah Daniels" in Porter, "Freedom Over Me"; *ARCIA 1870,* Report 123, Bliss to Clay Wood, July 14, 1870, 328; *Depredations on the Frontiers of Texas,* Deposition 545, 22; United States, Records of the Bureau of the Census, National Archives Record Group 29, Ninth Census of the United States, 1870, Population Schedule, Uvalde County, Texas; John Kiveth, "Chief of the Seminole Negro Indians" to Brigadier General Christopher C. Augur, December 10, 1873, National Archives Microfilm Publications, Microcopy M619, Record Group 94, Letters Received by the Office of the Adjutant General, Main Series, 1780s-1917, 828 rolls (hereafter cited as M619), Roll 800, frames 117-19. Rolls 799 and 800 of M619 contain File 488-1870, "Papers relating to the return of the Kickapoo and the Seminole (Negro) Indians from Mexico to the United States, 1870-1885."

6. *ARCIA 1869,* Misc. 150, Edward Hatch to Ely S. Parker, August 9, 1869, 451; *Depredations on the Frontiers of Texas,* Deposition 545, 22; *Report of Committee of Investigation,* 411; Gibson, *Kickapoos,* 201; Latorre and Latorre, *Mexican Kickapoo,* 18-19.

7. George A. Root, ed., "No-ko-aht's Talk: A Kickapoo Chief's Account of a Tribal Journey from Kansas to Mexico and Return in the Sixties," *Kansas Historical Quarterly* 1 (1932): 156.

8. Guajardo, "Historia de Coahuila," November 29, 1866, and February 20, 1867; *Report of Committee of Investigation,* 411-12; Porter, "Seminole in Mexico," 164; Porter, "Wild Cat's Death," 43. Latorre and Latorre cite a decree of September 21, 1938, by President Lázaro Cárdenas stating that the Mascogos' ownership of land at Nacimiento dated back to 1866. See *Mexican Kickapoo,* 18, 123, 126. John Horse claimed later that he was in sole possession of the title to the Mascogos' land grant at the hacienda. See "Seminole Wild Cat Party," John Horse, "Colonel and Father of all the Seminole Indians, who rules all the Seminole Tribes," to C. C. Augur, December 10, 1873, M619-800, frames 121-24.

9. Ernest Wallace, *Ranald S. Mackenzie on the Texas Frontier* (Lubbock: West Texas Museum Assoc., 1965), 112 n. 21.

10. *Affairs of the Mexican Kickapoo Indians,* 60 Cong., 1 Sess., Senate Doc. 215, 3 vols., vol. 3, Appendix, 1886; *Depredations on the Frontiers of Texas,* Deposition 545, and Deposition 554, Thomas A. Napkins, 22; Foster, "Negro-Indian Relationships," 46.

11. Petition of Florida Seminole Negroes to President Cleveland, n.d. but recd. by BIA February 9, 1888, RG 75, LR 1881-1907, 3565-88.

12. *ARCIA 1868,* Doc. H, N. G. Taylor to O. H. Browning, July 14 and November 23, 1868, 87-88, 20; *ARCIA 1869,* Misc. 150, Hatch to Parker, August 9, 1869, and Parker to J. D. Cox, December 23, 1869, 451, 8.

13. Parker to Secretary of the Interior, April 26, 1870, M619-799, frames 592-95.

14. S. S. Brown to Victoria Cepada, dated incorrectly September 1, 1868, Cepada and T. Serapio Frajosa to Brown, June 15, 1868, Brown to M. Menchaca y Longoria, July 26, 1868, Menchaca to Brown, July 30, 1868, and Brown to Major General Joseph Reynolds, September 1, 1868, in Winfrey and Day, *Indian Papers of Texas,* vol. 4, 276-84.

15. Gibson, *Kickapoos,* 213.

16. *ARCIA 1870,* Report 123, Bliss to Clay Wood, July 14, 1870, 328-29. Laurence Foster states that a party of Mascogos from Nacimiento had visited the Seminole Nation earlier in 1866, but does not cite his source. See "Negro-Indian Relationships," 46.

17. Jacob C. De Gress to Clay Wood, March 17, 1870, "By order of Brevet Lieutenant Colonel J. C. De Gress" E. A. Rigg, post adjutant Fort Duncan, "to whom it may concern," March 17, 1870, Clay Wood to De Gress, March 25, 1870, and Parker to Secretary of the Interior, April 26, 1870, M619-799, frames 587-88, 585, 5, 592-95; "Brief of Papers in relation to the Seminole Negro Indians," and Philip Sheridan, endorsement to 217-1872, January 29, 1873, National Archives Record Group 393, Records of the United States Army Continental Commands, 1821-1920, Division of the Missouri, E2547, Special File Box 15, Seminole Negro Indians, 1872-1876 (hereafter cited as SF 15).

18. Parker to Secretary of the Interior, April 26, 1870, M619-799, frames 592-95; E. D. Townsend to Reynolds, May 10, 1870, M619-800, frame 766; Frank Perry to Clay Wood, May 15, 1870, "By command of Brevet Major General Reynolds" Clay Wood to Perry, May 21, 1870, and Henry Merriam to Commander of Fort Clark, August 5, 1872, SF 15; William Belknap to Secretary of the Interior, February 21, 1873, M234-805, Seminole Agency 1872-1876, I524-73 enc.

19. Perry to Clay Wood, May 15 and 29, 1870, SF 15.

20. Perry to Clay Wood, June 20, 1870, and "Brief of Papers in relation to the Seminole Negro Indians," SF 15.

21. John Kibbetts to AAGDT, February 8, 1874, SF 15; Petition of Florida Seminole Negroes to President Cleveland, n.d. but recd. by BIA February 9, 1888, RG 75, LR 1881-1907, 3565-88; Notes on the Mascogos' return to the United States from Mexico in 1870, Warren Perryman Collection, Archives Division, Texas State Library, Austin (hereafter cited as Perryman Collection); Foster, "Negro-Indian Relationships," 44, 47; Woodhull, "Scouts on the Border," Statement of Renty Grayson 1927, 123-24. Attempts to enter into such reciprocal agreements were a prominent feature of maroon diplomacy. See Sidney W. Mintz, *Caribbean Transformations* (Chicago: Aldine Publishing Co., 1974), 152-53.

22. William Warrior to Secretary of the Interior, February 20, 1894, RG 75, LR 1881-1907, 8296-94; D. M. Browning to Warrior, March 3, 1894, National Archives Record Group 75, Bureau of Indian Affairs Letters Sent and Letter Books 1881-1907 (hereafter cited as RG 75, LS and LB 1881-1907), Letter Book L 275, February 26, 1894 to March 21, 1894, 370. Warrior claimed that John Kibbetts had possessed a copy of "the treaty" but that it had been destroyed by fire after his death in 1878. In 1941, this was attested to by John Jefferson, who claimed that the treaty had been signed by John Kibbetts and Pompey Factor in Múzquiz. Kibbetts kept the document and would show it to nobody. His house burned down a year after his death, apparently destroying the agreement as well. See "John Kibbitts Made the Treaty," in Porter, "Freedom Over Me."

23. Townsend to Commanding General, Department of Texas, June 25, 1870, M619-799, frames 574-75; *ARCIA 1870,* Doc. 123, Bliss to Clay Wood, July 14, 1870, 328; National Archives Record Group 94, Records of the Adjutant General's Office, 1780s-1917, Records of the Record and Pension Office, 1784-1917, Medical Histories of Posts, New #83, vol. 1, Fort Duncan, Texas, April 1868-January 1873 (hereafter cited as Fort Duncan, Medical History), 2.

24. *ARCIA 1870,* Doc. 123, Bliss to Clay Wood, July 14, 1870, 328-29.

25. Ibid., Clay Wood to Bliss, July 20, 1870, 329.

26. Merriam to Commander at Fort Clark, August 5, 1872, SF 15.
27. United States War Department, Surgeon General's Office, *Circular No. 4: Report on Barracks and Hospitals with Descriptions of Military Posts* (New York: Sol Lewis, 1974 [1870]), 218; United States War Department, Surgeon General's Office, *Circular No. 8: Report on Hygiene of the United States Army with Descriptions of Military Posts* (New York: Sol Lewis, 1974 [1875]), 202 fig. 32; "Brief of Papers in relation to the Seminole Negro Indians," Muster Roll of Seminole Negro Indians as Scouts at Fort Duncan, Texas, from August 16, 1870, to December 16, 1870, War Department 15, 1207/76, SF 15; "Reminiscences of Zenas Bliss," vol. 2, 51, and vol. 5, 106. By early September, twelve had enlisted. This corresponds with the number listed in March 1872; see Bliss to Clay Wood, September 8, 1870, and Muster Roll of Seminole Negro Indian Scouts enrolled by Major Bliss at Fort Duncan, Texas, March 6, 1872, SF 15.
28. *ARCIA 1870,* Doc. 123, Bliss to Clay Wood, July 14, 1870, 328. See also "Reminiscences of Zenas Bliss," vol. 5, 108-9.
29. Bliss to Clay Wood, July 20, 1870, M619-799, frame 162; Bliss to Clay Wood, December 14, 1870, Muster Roll of Seminole Negro Indian Scouts enrolled by Major Bliss at Fort Duncan, Texas, March 6, 1872, and Merriam to AAGDT, June 17, 1872, SF 15; Bliss to Adjutant General, Department of Texas, August 26, 1884, M619-800, 720-25; Foster, "Negro-Indian Relationships," statement of Renty Grayson, 1927, 123-24. Some of the Seminole maroons apparently remained behind at Matamoros, a small community being reported there in the winter of 1875-76. See Charles M. Neal, Jr., "Incident on Las Moras Creek," *The Annals: Official Publication of the Medal of Honor Historical Society* 13(1990): 16.
30. There is no evidence that the main body of John Horse's followers ever crossed over into Texas. Indeed, over a hundred must have returned to Nacimiento, judging from later population statistics. By the time of Mackenzie's Remolino raid, in fact, most of the Parras Mascogos had relocated to the hacienda.
31. Lt. Col. W. Merritt to acting AAGDT, June 4, 1872, Merriam to AAGDT, June 17, 1872, Merriam to Commander at Fort Clark, July 18, 1872, 1st endorsement to last reference, Merritt to acting AAGDT, July 23, 1872, 2nd endorsement, J. A. Augur to Commander at Fort Clark, July 25, 1872, 3rd endorsement, Merritt to Merriam, August 2, 1872, Fort Duncan Special Orders No.96, August 3, 1872, Sections 7 and 8, issued by Post Adjutant H. F. Leggett, Merriam to Merritt, August 5, 1872, Merriam to AAGDT, August 5, 1872, Col. Ranald S. Mackenzie to acting AAGDT, April 23, 1873, and "Brief of Papers in relation to the Seminole Negro Indians," SF 15; Maj. Gen. J. F. Bell to Secretary of War, March 24, 1909, National Archives Record Group 393, Records of the United States Army Continental Commands, 1821-1920, Department of Texas, Seminole Negroes, Part 1, Entry 4882 (hereafter cited as DT 4882); James Parker, *The Old Army: Memories 1872-1918* (Philadelphia: Dorrance and Co., 1929), 99; Frank D. Reeve, ed., "Frederick E. Phelps: A Soldier's Memoirs," *New Mexico Historical Review* 25(1950): 203. For roughly contemporary descriptions of Las Moras Creek and its environs, see Robert G. Carter, "A Raid into Mexico," *Outing* 12(1888): 1; and John C. Reid, "Reid's Tramp: A Ten Months' Trip through Texas, New Mexico, Arizona, California and Mexico in 1857," *Frontier Times* 20(1943): 199-200.
32. Lt. John L. Bullis to AAGDT, May 28, 1875, SF 15; Col. William R. Shafter to Z. Chandler, December 28, 1875, and Brig. Gen. Edward O. C. Ord to T. G. Williams, June 15, 1876,

M234-805, S20-76, and S448-76; "A Negro Trooper of the Ninth Cavalry," *Frontier Times* 4(April 1927): 11; H. Conger Jones, "Old Seminole Scouts Still Thrive on Border," *Frontier Times* 11(1934): 327; Reeve, "Frederick Phelps," 215-17; Carlysle G. Raht, *The Romance of Davis Mountains and the Big Bend Country* (Odessa, TX: Rathbooks Co., 1963 [1919]), 206-7.

33. Fort Duncan, Medical History, 206; "Reminiscences of Zenas Bliss," vol. 5, 111-17.

34. Orsemus B. Boyd, *Cavalry Life in Tent and Field* (New York: Selwin Tait and Sons, 1894), 335-37.

35. For descriptions of the scouts' qualities and talents by contemporaries, see e.g. Maj. A. P. Morrow to AAGDT, May 15, 1875, SF 15; Florence Fenley, *Old Timers: Their Own Stories* (Uvalde, TX: Hornby Press, 1939), 187; Vinton L. James, *Frontier and Pioneer Recollections of Early Days in San Antonio and West Texas* (San Antonio: Artes Graficas Press, 1938), 26; Parker, *Old Army,* 99-100; and "Reminiscences of Zenas Bliss," vol. 5, 126-27.

36. Reeve, "Frederick Phelps," 203, 214.

37. Grace L. Bulter, "General Bullis: Friend of the Frontier," *Frontier Times* 12(1935): 360; Alexander E. Sweet and J. Armoy Knox, *On a Mexican Mustang, through Texas, from the Gulf to the Rio Grande* (Hartford, CT: S. S. Scranton and Co., 1883), 520-21; Woodhull, "Scouts on the Border," statement of Renty Grayson, 124-25.

38. "Brackettville and Old Fort Clark," *Frontier Times* 12(1935): 350.

39. "Reminiscences of Zenas Bliss," vol. 2, 51, and vol. 5, 109; Bullis to AAGDT, May 28, 1875, SF 15.

40. James, *Frontier and Pioneer Recollections,* 80.

41. "Negro Trooper," 11.

42. Quoted in Jack D. Foner, *Blacks and the Military in American History* (New York: Praeger, 1974), 53.

43. Merriam to AAGDT, June 17 and August 5, 1872, SF 15. For examples of routine patrols involving the scouts, 1870-1872, see Fort Duncan, Medical History, 201, 206, 217, 233, 241, 246, 249-50.

44. Francis B. Heitman, *Historical Register and Dictionary of the United States Army: From its Organization, September 29, 1789, to March 2, 1903,* 3 vols. (Washington, D.C.: Government Printing Office, 1903), vol. 2, 261; "Statement as to the military record in the United States Army of Brevet Major John L. Bullis, Captain 24th Infantry, U.S. Army," National Archives Record Group 94, Records of the Office of the Adjutant General, 1780s-1917, ACP for John L. Bullis, Box 79, 36719H, folder 1, F/W B191 CB1870 (hereafter cited as Bullis ACP), p.1; Edward S. Wallace, "General John Lapham Bullis, the Thunderbolt of the Texas Frontier," Part 1, *Southwestern Historical Quarterly* 54(1951): 457-60.

45. For information on the number of Seminole Negro Indian Scouts enlisted in the Department of Texas during the period of their greatest activity, see National Archives Record Group 393, Records of the United States Army Continental Commands, 1821-1920, Division of the Missouri, Special File Box 6, Indian Scouts Enlisted 1874-1877 (hereafter cited as SF 6), and National Archives Microfilm Publications, Microcopy M233, Record Group 94, United States Army Registers of Enlistments, Rolls 70-71, Indian Scouts 1866-1914. For official accounts of expeditions involving the scouts, see Heitman, *Historical Register,* vol. 2, 391-474; *Mexican Border Troubles,* 45 Cong., 1 Sess., House Exec. Doc. 13 (Serial 1773), 187-96; "Record of Engagements with Hostile Indians in

Texas 1868 to 1882," *West Texas Historical Association Yearbook* 9(1933): 101-18; *The Texas Border Troubles,* 45 Cong., 2 Sess., House Misc. Doc. 64 (Serial 1820), vol. 6, 186-205.

46. *ARCIA 1869,* Misc. 150, Hatch to Parker, August 9, 1869, and Parker to Cox, December 23, 1869, 451, 8; *Depredations on the Frontiers of Texas,* Report, 12-27, and Deposition 545, 22; *Report on the Relations of the United States with Mexico,* 45 Cong., 2 Sess., House Doc. 701 (Serial 1824), April 25, 1878, 13; Gibson, *Kickapoos,* 210; William C. Pool, "The Battle of Dove Creek," *Southwestern Historical Quarterly* 53(1950): 375-85; Wallace, *Mackenzie,* 93-95; Ernest Wallace, "Prompt in the Saddle: The Military Career of Ranald S. Mackenzie," *Military History of Texas and the Southwest* 9(1971): 166, 171; Ernest Wallace and Adrian N. Anderson, "R. S. Mackenzie and the Kickapoos: the Raid into Mexico in 1873," *Arizona and the West* 7(1965): 105-7.

47. *ARCIA 1873,* N, Report of H. M. Atkinson and T. G. Williams, October 8, 1873, 169; Affidavit of Jerome Strickland, April 21, 1873, and Mackenzie to AAGDT, April 22, 1873, in Ernest Wallace, ed., *Ranald S. Mackenzie's Official Correspondence Relating to Texas, 1871-1873* (Lubbock: West Texas Museum Association, 1967), 162-65; Department of Texas General Orders No.6, June 2, 1873, copy in Bullis ACP, 27; Robert G. Carter, *On the Border with Mackenzie or Winning the West from the Comanches* (New York: Antiquarian Press, 1961 [1935]), 424; Mrs. O. L. Shipman, *Taming the Big Bend: A History of the Extreme Western Portion of Texas from Fort Clark to El Paso* (n.p., 1926), 58.

48. Ernest R. Archambeau, ed., "Monthly Reports of the Fourth Cavalry, 1872-1874," *Panhandle-Plains Historical Review* 38(1965): 110-13.

49. Carter, *On the Border,* 421-24.

50. Mackenzie to Acting AAGDT, May 23, 1873, SF 15; *Depredations on the Frontiers of Texas,* Deposition 545, 22; *Texas Border Troubles,* vol. 6, Testimony of Bullis, 187-88; Latorre and Latorre, *Mexican Kickapoo,* 22; Wallace, *Mackenzie,* 97-98.

51. Mackenzie to AAGDT, May 23, 1873, in Wallace, ed., *Mackenzie's Correspondence, 1871-1873,* 167-68.

52. Ibid., and ed.'s n. 4; Department of Texas General Orders No. 6, June 2, 1873, copy in Bullis ACP, 27; Carter, *On the Border,* 429, 438; "Record of Engagements," 105.

53. Warren Perryman to Commissioner of Indian Affairs, February 27, 1929, Perryman to Merritt, March 25, 1929, and Perryman to G. M. Milburn, May 10, 1929, National Archives Record Group 75, Letters Received by the Bureau of Indian Affairs, 1907-1939 (hereafter cited as RG 75, LR 1907-1939), File 053, 11030-1929; Carter, "Raid into Mexico," 6; Carter, *On the Border,* 444; Porter, *Negro on the Frontier,* 479; Woodhull, "Scouts on the Border," statement of Charlie Daniels, 121.

54. J. K. Mizner to AAGDT, May 20, 1873, Sheridan to Belknap, May 22, 1873, and Mackenzie to AAGDT, May 23, 1873, in Wallace, ed., *Mackenzie's Correspondence, 1871-1873,* 165-70; Department of Texas General Orders No. 6, June 2, 1873, copy in Bullis ACP, 27; Archambeau, ed., "Monthly Reports," 113-14; *Texas Border Troubles,* Testimony of Bullis, 187; Carter, *On the Border,* 444-69; Joseph H. Dorst, "Ranald Slidell Mackenzie," *Armor, or Journal of the United States Cavalry Association* 10(1897): 375.

55. Mackenzie to AAGDT, May 23, 1873, in Wallace, ed., *Mackenzie's Correspondence, 1871-1873,* 169; "Statement as to the Military Record of John L. Bullis," Bullis ACP, enc. 1, 1; Atkinson and Williams to Smith, August 28, 1873, and Smith to Secretary of the Interior, September 10, 1873, M619-800, frames 64-69, 61-62; *ARCIA 1873,* N, Report

of Atkinson and Williams, October 8, 1873, 170-73; Grant Foreman, *The Last Trek of the Indians* (Chicago: University of Chicago Press, 1946), 210-11; *Galveston Daily News,* June 29, July 1, and September 5, 1873; Gibson, *Kickapoos,* 250-53, 265, 267; *Report of Committee of Investigation,* 416; Wallace, *Mackenzie,* 109.

56. Sheridan to General William T. Sherman, July 21, 1874, in Joe F. Taylor, ed., *The Indian Campaign on the Staked Plains, 1874-1875* (Canyon, TX: Panhandle-Plains Historical Society, 1962), 12; Archambeau, ed., "Monthly Reports," 114 n. 2; Carter, *On the Border,* 462.

57. *ARCIA 1874,* Report of Jno. D. Miles, Upper Arkansas Agency, Indian Territory, September 30, 1874, 233-34; *Sixth Annual Report of the Bureau of Indian Commissioners, 1874,* 79-88; William H. Leckie, "The Red River War," *Panhandle-Plains Historical Review* 29(1956): 78-82; Wilbur S. Nye, *Carbine and Lance: The Story of Old Fort Sill* (Norman: University of Oklahoma Press, 1937), 241-73.

58. Sherman to Sheridan, July 20, 1874, and Department of the Missouri, Special Orders 114, July 27, 1874, in Taylor, ed., *Indian Campaign,* 12, 14-16; Archambeau, ed., "Monthly Reports," 141-43; Robert G. Carter, *The Old Sergeant's Story: Winning the West from the Indians and Bad Men in 1870 to 1876* (New York: Fred H. Hitchcock, 1926), 103; Ernest Wallace, ed., *Ranald S. Mackenzie's Official Correspondence Relating to Texas, 1873-1879* (Lubbock: West Texas Museum Association, 1968), 80 n. 2.

59. Mackenzie's Expedition through the Battle of Palo Duro Canyon as described by a Special Correspondent of the New York Herald, published originally in *New York Herald,* October 16, 1874, reprinted in Wallace, ed., *Mackenzie's Correspondence, 1873-1879,* 113.

60. Mackenzie to C. C. Augur August 28, 1874, Mackenzie to AAGDT, September 19, 1874, Mackenzie's Expedition through the Battle of Palo Duro Canyon, and Mackenzie's Journal of Campaign: Part 1, in Wallace, ed., *Mackenzie's Correspondence, 1873-1879,* 83, 93, 113-14, 119; "Scouting on the 'Staked Plains' (Llano Estacado) with Mackenzie in 1874," by "One Who Was There," *The United Service(s)* 13(1885): 405; Donald J. Berthrong, *The Southern Cheyennes* (Norman: University of Oklahoma Press, 1963), 391-92; William H. Leckie, *The Military Conquest of the Southern Plains* (Norman: University of Oklahoma Press, 1963), 218.

61. Henry W. Strong, *My Frontier Days and Indian Fights on the Plains of Texas* (n.p., n.d., 122pp. typewritten and illustrated), 53.

62. Mackenzie to AAGDT, January 7, 1875, and see also Mackenzie to Townsend, August 31, 1875, 1st endorsement, Secretary of War, October 13, 1875, and 2nd endorsement, Townsend, October 19, 1875, in Wallace, ed., *Mackenzie's Correspondence, 1873-1879,* 193, 197-98; National Archives Microfilm Publications, Microcopy M929, Selected Records Relating to Black Servicemen (Record Groups 94, 107, 153), Documents Relating to the Military and Naval Service of Blacks Awarded the Congressional Medal of Honor from the Civil War to the Spanish American War, 4 rolls (hereafter cited as M929), Roll 2, Indian Campaigns—U.S. Regular Army, Target 10, Private Adam Paine.

63. Mackenzie's Expedition through the Battle of Palo Duro Canyon, Mackenzie's Journal of Campaign: Part 1, and Mackenzie to AAGDT October 1 and 26, 1874, in Wallace, ed., *Mackenzie's Correspondence, 1873-1879,* 115-17, 121-24, 146; R. C. Drum, AAGDT, and Sherman to Townsend, October 14, 1874, and Mackenzie to C. C. Augur, November 27 and December 2, 1874, in Taylor, ed., *Indian Campaign,* 75, 115, 119; *ARCIA 1874,* Report of Miles, September 30, 1874, 236; Archambeau, ed., "Monthly Reports," 144-53;

Carter, *Old Sergeant's Story,* 105-10; "Record of Engagements," 108; "Scouting on the Staked Plains," 408-12, 532-43; Strong, *Frontier Days,* 59, 102; William A. Thompson, "Scouting with Mackenzie," *Armor, or Journal of the United States Cavalry Association* 10(1897): 431-33.

64. Quoted in Wallace, *Mackenzie,* 166.

65. Bullis to Lieutenant G. W. Smith, April 27, 1875, quoted in Department of Texas General Orders No.10, J. H. Taylor to AAGDT, May 12, 1875, copy in Bullis ACP, 26; M929-2, Targets 4, 11, and 15, Private Pompey Factor, Trumpeter Isaac Payne, and Sergeant John Ward; John M. Carroll, ed., *The Medal of Honor: Its History and Recipients for the Indian Wars* (Bryan, TX: J. M. Carroll, 1979), 25-26, 70, 92; Foster, "Negro-Indian Relation-ships," Statement of Joseph Philips, 47-48; Robert E. Greene, *Black Defenders of America 1775-1973* (Chicago: Johnson Publishing Co., 1974), 117, 120; Woodhull, "Scouts on the Border," statement of Charlie Daniels, 122.

66. Martin L. Crimmins, "General Mackenzie and Fort Concho," *West Texas Historical Association Yearbook* 10(1934): 29; J. Evetts Haley, *Fort Concho and the Texas Frontier* (San Angelo, TX: San Angelo Standard Times, 1952), 231; William H. Leckie, *The Buffalo Soldiers: A Narrative of the Negro Cavalry in the West* (Norman: University of Oklahoma Press, 1967), 143.

67. Lt. Col. William R. Shafter to AAGDT, January 4, 1876, quoted in Martin L. Crimmins, ed., "Shafter's Explorations in Western Texas, 1875," *West Texas Historical Association Yearbook* 9(1933): 95. See also Bullis's report in Haley, *Fort Concho,* 235.

68. Woodhull, "Scouts on the Border," statement of Charlie Daniels, 122.

69. *Texas Border Troubles,* Testimony of Bullis, 188-89; Paul Howard Carlson, *"Pecos Bill": A Military Biography of William R. Shafter* (College Station: Texas A&M University Press, 1989), 94; Leckie, *Buffalo Soldiers,* 149-51; Theodore F. Rodenbough and William L. Haskin, *The Army of the United States: Historical Sketches of Staff and Line with Portraits of Generals-in-Chief* (New York: Maynard, Merrill and Co., 1896), 295; Edward S. Wallace, "General John Lapham Bullis: Thunderbolt of the Texas Frontier," Part 2, *Southwestern Historical Quarterly* 55(1951): 82.

70. Shafter to Ord, July 7, 1877, Bullis to 1st Lt. Helenus Dodt, July 9, 1877, 1st endorsement, Shafter, July 9, 1877, and Major G. W. Schofield to Acting Assistant Adjutant General, District of Nueces, n.d., *Mexican Border Troubles,* 172, 189-90, 195; *Texas Border Troubles,* testimony of Bullis, 191; Raht, *Romance of Davis Mountains,* 205.

71. *Texas Border Troubles,* 191-92. Bullis reported mistakenly that this action took place in late October, but then contradicted his own testimony by recounting that he had taken part in the Sierra del Carmen campaign at that same time, see Ibid., 194-95. See also Heitman, *Historical Register,* vol. 2, 443; Leckie, *Buffalo Soldiers,* 154; Rodenbough and Haskin, *Army,* 275.

72. Reeve, ed., "Frederick Phelps," 206-7; *Texas Border Troubles,* Testimony of Bullis, 195.

73. Burr G. Duval, "Journal of a Prospecting Trip to West Texas in 1879: Notes of an Exploring Expedition Organized by the Galveston, Houston and San Antonio Rail Road, the International and Great Northern Rail Road and the Texas and Pacific Rail Road for the Purpose of Examining the Mineral Resources East of the Rio Grande River in Presidio County, Texas," unpublished typescript, 116pp., J. C. and Burr G. Duval Papers, 1836-1937, Ms. 656, Manuscripts Division, Barker Texas History Center, University of Texas at Austin (hereafter cited as Duval, "Journal"), page 39. Selections from this journal have

been reproduced in Sam Woodford, ed., "The Burr G. Duval Diary," *Southwestern Historical Quarterly* 65(1962): 487-511.

74. Margaret Creel, "Gullah Attitudes Towards Life and Death," and Holloway, introduction to Holloway, ed., *Africanisms,* 85, xv.

75. *Texas Border Troubles,* Testimony of Bullis, 195. See also Heitman, *Historical Register,* 443; "Record of Engagements," 111; Reeve, ed., "Frederick Phelps," 209-14.

76. Mackenzie to AAGDT, June 23, 1878, Report of Expedition into Mexico, in Wallace, ed., *Mackenzie's Correspondence, 1873-1879,* 204-9 and n. 2 and 3; Wallace, *Mackenzie,* 176-82; Parker, *Old Army,* 109.

77. Shafter to AAGDT, January 4, 1876, in Crimmins, ed., "Shafter's Explorations," 82-96; Crimmins, "Mackenzie and Fort Concho," 29-30; Haley, *Fort Concho,* 232-38; Leckie, *Buffalo Soldiers,* 143, 147-48.

78. Captain John L. Rodgers, "Road Building on the Pecos River Texas, September, October, November 1878," Message from Bullis, presumably to Captain J. McNaught, commanding the expedition, received at Camp on the Pecos, October 14, 1879, Bullis to H. A. Greene, October 26, 1879, and 1st endorsement, McNaught, November 1, 1879, Fort Clark Records, Ms. 757, Box 2Q512, volume of photocopied correspondence and additional materials relating to period 1878-1881, Manuscripts Division, Barker Texas History Center, University of Texas at Austin; Duval, "Journal," 39 et. seq.; Herbert M. Hart, *Old Forts of the Far West* (New York: Bonanza Books, 1965), 147; *Houston Chronicle, Texas Magazine,* August 15, 1982; Raht, *Romance of Davis Mountains,* 207.

79. In October 1881, the scouts had one other brush with Indian raiders in West Texas, but this encounter is not listed in Heitman's *Historical Register* as an engagement. On the 21st, it was reported that a detachment of Seminole Negro Indian Scouts had come across a band of raiders "on the Rio Grande below the Rinconada near Antonia Cañón about 25 miles above Eagles Nest." The Indians escaped, but the scouts were able to capture thirteen head of stock, some of which had been stolen from settlers at Independence Creek on the Pecos. Captain James F. Randlett, Commanding Camp at Mayer Spring, Texas, to Post Adjutant, Fort Clark, October 21, 1881, RG 75, LR 1881-1907, 19982-81.

80. Major General John M. Schofield to Adjutant General, May 7, 1881, RG 75, LR 1881-1907, 7934-81; Lt. Col. Nelson B. Sweitzer to AAGDT, May 6, 1881, Stanley to C. C. Augur, May 6, 1881, Augur to Adjutant General, Military Division of the Missouri, September 27, 1881, and Stanley to Adjutant General, May 6, 1890, in Bullis ACP, 23-25, 13; Bulter, "General Bullis," 360-61; Frank S. Gray, *Pioneering in Southwest Texas: True Stories of Early Day Experiences in Edwards and Adjoining Counties,* ed. by Marvin J. Hunter (Austin: Steck Co., 1949), 241; "Last Indian Raid in Southwest Texas," *Frontier Times* 4(1927): 58-59; Andrew J. Sowell, *Early Settlers and Indian Fighters of Southwest Texas* (Austin: Ben C. Jones Co., 1900), 516-17; Andrew J. Sowell, "Last Indian Raid in Frio Canyon," *Frontier Times* 24(1947): 502; Woodhull, "Scouts on the Border," statement of Charlie Daniels, 123. For his role in this expedition and his earlier gallantry in action near Zaragoza, July 30, 1876, Bullis was breveted major on February 27, 1890.

81. James, *Frontier and Pioneer Recollections,* 26.

82. C. C. Augur to Bullis, October 25, 1882, Bullis ACP, 14; Carl C. Rister, *The Southwestern Frontier, 1861-1881* (Cleveland: Arthur H. Clark Co., 1928), 268-69; Wallace, "Thunderbolt," Part 2, 85.

5. Classifying Seminole Blacks

1. Belknap to Secretary of the Interior, April 19, 1870, Parker to Secretary of the Interior, April 26, 1870, and Merriam to AAGDT, August 12, 1872, M619-799, frames 592-95, 407-9; Townsend to Major General Joseph J. Reynolds, May 10, 1870, M619-800, frame 766; Clay Wood to Perry, May 21, 1870, SF 15; Belknap to Secretary of the Interior, February 21, 1873, M234-805, I524-73 enc.
2. Belknap to George Boutwell, September 29, 1870, Boutwell to Belknap, October 1, 1870, and 1st endorsement to last reference, Townsend, October 6, 1870, M619-799, frames 57-58, 577-79.
3. H. R. Clum to W. Otto, October 3, 1870, and see also Otto to Belknap, October 4, 1870, Ibid., frames 53-54, 50-51.
4. Merriam to AAGDT, August 12, 1872, Ibid., frames 407-9; Belknap to Secretary of the Interior, September 12, 1872, SF 15.
5. Samuel J. Cushing to AAGDT, August 5, 1872, endorsement to last reference, AAGDT, August 6, 1872, and Merriam to AAGDT, August 12, 1872, M619-799, frames 405-9; "Brief of Papers relative to the subsistence and c. at Fort Duncan Texas of the Seminole Negro Indians from Mexico in anticipation of their removal by the Interior Dept. to a reservation," M619- 800, frame 140.
6. It cost the army $540.39 to supply the Seminole maroons at Fort Duncan with rations of fresh beef, flour, coffee, brown sugar, and salt during August and September 1872. "Statement of the value of subsistence stores issued to the Seminole Negro Indians at Fort Duncan by Lt. J. M. Sturr 9th Cavalry in the Months of August and September 1872," Office of the Commissary General of Subsistence, January 14, 1873, M619-799, frame 545.
7. Belknap to Secretary of the Interior, September 12, 1872, SF 15; B. R. Cowen to F. A. Walker, September 25, 1872, M234-805, I183-72; Walker to Cowen, September 23, 1872, Cowen to Belknap, September 25, 1872, M619-799, frames 452-58, 460-61.
8. Walker to Secretary of the Interior, September 27, 1872, and see also endorsement to last reference, Cowen to Belknap, September 28, 1872, M619-799, frames 446-47.
9. Merriam, 4th endorsement, October 24, 1872, to his letter of August 12, 1872 to AAGDT, Ibid., frame 443; endorsement to last reference, Sheridan, November 15, 1872, in "Memoranda relative to Seminole Negro Indians," SF 15.
10. Walker to Secretary of the Interior, December 16, 1872, Cowen to Belknap, December 26, 1872, M619-799, frames 569-72, 565-66.
11. Sheridan to C. C. Augur, January 10, 1873, and C. C. Augur to Sheridan, January 14, 1873, reference in "Brief of Papers in relation to the Seminole Negro Indians" and "Memoranda relative to Seminole Negro Indians," SF 15.
12. Sheridan, Chicago, January 29, 1873, 1st endorsement to Cowen to Belknap, December 26, 1872, M619-799, frames 562-63.
13. Belknap to C. Delano, February 21, 1873, and Delano to Acting Commissioner of Indian Affairs, March 5, 1873, M234-805, I524-73.
14. Petition of Elijah Daniel(s), "Cife (chief) of the Simenoles (sic) negro Indians Scout," John Ward and James Bruner, Fort Clark, June 28, 1873, and endorsement, Col. Ranald S. Mackenzie, July 10, 1873, SF 15; second endorsement, Sheridan, July 22, 1873, M619-800, frame 110.

15. Major Alfred E. Latimer to AAGDT, December 22, 1873, and "Brief of Papers in relation to the Seminole Negro Indians," reference to communication from the Department of Texas to Latimer, December 27, 1873, SF 15.

16. John Kiveth (Kibbetts), "Chief of the Seminole Negro Indians," to C. C. Augur, December 10, 1873, M619-800, frames 117-19; "John Kibbetts Made the Treaty" in Porter, "Freedom Over Me."

17. "Seminole Wild Cat Party," John Horse, "Colonel and Father of all the Seminole Indians, who rules all the Seminole tribes," to C. C. Augur, December 10, 1873, and Kiveth to C. C. Augur, December 10, 1873, Ibid., frames 121-24, 117-19.

18. C. C. Augur to Adjutant General, February 21, 1874, Ibid., frames 101-6.

19. Latimer to AAGDT, January 1, 1874, SF 15; Kibbetts to AAGDT, February 8, 1874, M619-800, frames 113-15.

20. 1st endorsement to last reference, Bullis, February 9, 1874, and C. C. Augur to Adjutant General, February 21, 1874, M619-800, frames 112, 101-6.

21. Acting Commissary General, March 11, 1874, 4th endorsement to C. C. Augur, to Adjutant General, February 21, 1874, and Belknap to Secretary of the Interior, April 9, 1874, Ibid., frames 100, 146-47.

22. Col. John. M. Bacon to Commanding Officer at Fort Duncan, July 1, 1874, SF 15; Commanding Officer at Fort Duncan to AAGDT, July 13, 1874, 5th endorsement to last reference, Commissary General Subsistence, July 29, 1874, E. P. Smith to Secretary of the Interior, July 31, 1874, Belknap to Secretary of the Interior, August 7, 1874, Clum to Secretary of the Interior, August 20, 1874, and Cowen to Belknap, August 15 and 21, 1874, M619-800, frames 179-80, 177, 188, 182-83, 193, 185-86, 191.

23. H. M. Atkinson to Smith, November 16 and December 29, 1874, M234-805, A1085-74, A26-75.

24. Lt. Alfred C. Markley to Post Adjutant, Fort Duncan, March 12, 1875, Col. William R. Shafter to Atkinson, March 14, 1875, and Bullis to Lt. George H. Smith, May 1, 1875, M234-805, A408-75 and enc., B791-75; Department of Texas Special Orders 80, Section 3, April 28, 1875, M619-800, frame 262; Major Albert P. Morrow to AAGDT, May 3, 1875, "Brief of Papers in relation to the Seminole Negro Indians," reference to Ord's directive of May 5, 1875, to commanding officers at Forts Duncan and Clark, "List of Seminole Indian Negroes at Fort Duncan Texas, May 9, 1875," Compiled by Lt. Markley, Shafter to AAGDT, May 10, 1875, and Morrow to AAGDT, May 15, 1875, SF 15.

25. Cuffee Payne probably was the same "Cuffy" who had been involved in the Walking Joe incident at Wewoka in 1849, had accused Wild Cat of selling him into slavery in 1852, and had been recognized by the Mascogos as second-in-command to John Horse in Coahuila. This African's former association with a Seminole principal chief in Florida certainly suggests that he would have enjoyed such leadership status within the maroon community.

26. Markley to Post Adjutant, Fort Duncan, March 12, 1875, M234-805, A408-75 enc.; "List of Seminole Indian Negroes at Fort Duncan Texas, May 9, 1875," and Shafter to AAGDT, May 10, 1875, SF 15.

27. Shafter to AAGDT, May 10, 1875, SF 15.

28. Morrow to AAGDT, May 3 and 15, 1875, SF 15; Bullis to Smith, May 1, 1875, M234-805, B791-75.

29. Department of Texas Special Orders 80, Section 3, April 28, 1875, 2nd endorsement to last reference, A. Beckwith, Asst. Commissary General Subsistence, May 6, 1875,

Townsend to Secretary of War, May 7, 1875, Ord to Adjutant General, May 21, 1875, 1st endorsement to last reference, Sheridan, May 27, 1875, and 3rd endorsement, Townsend, June 2, 1875, Secretary of War's Chief Clerk to Secretary of the Interior, June 10, 1875, M619-800, frames 261-64, 267-68, 272-73; Townsend to Commanding General, Department of Texas, May 12, 1875, SF 15.

30. Bullis to AAGDT, May 28, 1875, 1st endorsement, Morrow, May 28, 1875, 2nd endorsement, Ord, May 28, 1875, and 3rd endorsement, Sheridan, June 4, 1875, M619-800, frames 285-86, 281-83.

31. Commissary General of Subsistence, June 15, 1875, 7th endorsement to Bullis to AAGDT, May 28, 1875, Belknap to Delano, June 19, 1875, Clum to Secretary of the Interior, June 23, 1875, Delano to Belknap, June 25, 1875, and Belknap to Secretary of the Interior, June 29, 1875, M619-800, frames 284, 288, 293-95, 290-91, 297-99; "Memoranda relative to Seminole Negro Indians," reference to July 9, 1875, SF 15.

32. Col. Edward Hatch to AAGDT, August 9, 1875, and endorsement, Ord, n.d., M619-800, 305-8, 300; 4th endorsement, Townsend, February 2, 1876, SF 15.

33. Senator Charles W. Jones to Smith, September 8, 1875, M619-800, frames 326-30.

34. Smith to Secretary of the Interior, September 20, 1875, Ibid., frames 319-24; Kappler, *Indian Affairs,* vol. 2, 695.

35. Cowen to Secretary of War, September 23, 1875, M619-800, frames 316-17. Copies of Cowen's communication were forwarded to Ord on October 16, 1875, and the commanding officers at Forts Duncan and Clark on November 16, 1875. See references in "Brief of Papers in relation to the Seminole Negro Indians," SF 15; *ARCIA 1875,* "Legislation Recommended," November 1, 1875, 30; Shafter to Z. Chandler, December 28, 1875, M234-805, S20-76.

36. Ord, "Report of Indian Scouts serving in the Department of Texas on January 31st 1877," SF 6, 925/77; "Blood on the Saddle" in Porter, "Freedom Over Me."

37. Mackenzie, commander at Fort Clark, July 10, 1873, endorsement to Petition of Elijah Daniels et al, June 28, 1873, Mackenzie to Adjutant General, March 28, 1875, Elizey Daniel (Elijah Daniels) to "General" (Mackenzie, commander at Fort Sill, Indian Territory), March 7, 1876, and 1st endorsement to last reference, Mackenzie, April 20, 1876, SF 15.

38. Austin Callan, "The End of the 'Seminoles'," *Frontier Times* 8(1930): 9-11.

39. Markley to Post Adjutant, Fort Duncan, March 12, 1875, M234-805, A408-75 enc.; "List of Seminole Indian Negroes at Fort Duncan Texas, May 9, 1875," SF 15; W. A. Bonnet, "King Fisher, a Noted Character," *Frontier Times* 3(1926): 36-37; O. Clark Fisher and J. C. Dykes, *King Fisher: His Life and Times* (Norman: University of Oklahoma Press, 1966), 45, 57; Porter, *Negro on the Frontier,* 485 and n. 45.

40. "John Creaton; an Autobiography, 1856-1932," unpublished typescript, 45pp., John Creaton Collection, Box 2Q490, Manuscripts Division, Barker Texas History Center, University of Texas at Austin, p. 33. Creaton did not date this event, but it must have taken place after 1881, while the author was in Eagle Pass, and before March 11, 1884, when Fisher was gunned down in San Antonio.

41. Petition of thirty-five citizens of Kinney County, Texas, to the Secretary of War, April 24, 1876, and 2nd endorsement, Ord, July 6, 1876, M619-800, frames 511-14.

42. Col. I Irvin Gregg to AAGDT, May 23, 1876, 1st endorsement to last reference, Ord, May 27, 1876, Gregg to AAGDT, May 25, 1876, and 1st endorsement to last reference,

Ord, May 29, 1876, Ibid., frames 500-501, 505-7; "Blood on the Saddle" in Porter, "Freedom Over Me"; Porter, "Farewell to John Horse," 266, 268.

43. Gregg to AAGDT, May 23 and 25, 1876, M619-800, frames 500-1, 505-6. Other episodes involving the Seminole maroons added to the air of tension. See District Court of Kinney County, Case Files 249, 263 (November term, 1876), 267, 268 (May term, 1877), Kinney Courthouse Records, Kinney County Courthouse, Brackettville, Texas (hereafter referred to as KCR). See also Neal, "Incident on Las Moras Creek," 16-19.

44. Gregg to AAGDT, May 23, 1876, 1st endorsement, Ord, May 27, 1876, 2nd endorsement, Sheridan, June 3, 1876, Gregg to AAGDT, May 25, 1876, 1st endorsement to last reference, Ord, May 29, 1876, and see also Gregg, July 6, 1876, 1st endorsement to Petition of thirty-five citizens of Kinney County, April 24, 1876, and 2nd endorsement, Ord, July 6, 1876, Ibid., frames 500-502, 505-7, 513-14.

45. J. Q. Smith to Secretary of the Interior, June 6, 1876, SF 15.

46. Ord to T. G. Williams, June 15, 1876, Williams to G. Schleicher, June 17, 1876, and John Hancock to J. Q. Smith, June 22, 1876, M234-805, S448-76, H472-76; Ord, July 6, 1876, 2nd endorsement to Petition of thirty-five citizens of Kinney County, April 24, 1876, M619-800, frame 514.

6. In Search of Home

1. District Court of Kinney County, Case File 276 (May term, 1877), and Minutes of Kinney County Commissioner's Court, Book 1, 150, 152, KRC; "Adam Payne Was a Bad Man" in Porter, "Freedom Over Me"; Neal, "Incident on Las Moras Creek," 16-19; Porter, "Farewell to John Horse," 266, 272 n.1; Taylor, ed., *Indian Campaign,* 227 n.

2. Bullis to AAGDT, June 14, 1880, M619-800, frames 618-19.

3. 1st endorsement to last reference, Stanley, June 15, 1880, 2nd endorsement, Ord, June 22, 1880, and E. J. Brooks to Secretary of the Interior, July 10, 1880, Ibid., frames 615, 623-24.

4. Stanley to Adjutant General, Department of Texas (hereafter cited as AGDT), May 19, 1882, Ibid., frames 627-29.

5. Stanley to AGDT, May 19, 24, and June 19, 1882, 1st endorsement to Stanley to AGDT, May 24, 1882, C. C. Augur, May 25, 1882, 2nd endorsement, Sheridan, June 1, 1882, and 2nd endorsement to Stanley to AGDT, June 19, 1882, Sheridan, June 28, 1882, Ibid., frames 627-629, 631, 639-640, 625-26, 638.

6. Lincoln to Secretary of the Interior, June 8, 1882, Ibid., frames 635-36. In 1874, the agencies in the Seminole, Creek, Cherokee, Choctaw, and Chickasaw Nations had been consolidated as the Union Agency. From then on, these nations were seved by a single Union Agent, based at Muskogee. Later, the name would change again to the Five Civilized Tribes Agency.

7. John Jumper to John Q. Tufts, August 2, 1882, Ibid., frames 651-52.

8. Tufts to H. Price, August 11, 1882, and Price to Secretary of the Interior, September 9, 1882, Ibid., frames 652, 647-49; Tufts to Price, March 26, 1884, National Archives Record Group 48, Records of the Department of the Interior, Indian Division, Special Files Box 48, Indian Territory Division, Choctaw Freedmen File (hereafter cited as SF 48), 6172-84, enc. with H. M. Teller to Commissioner of Indian Affairs, May 2, 1884, 8582-84.

9. Lt. Frederick H. French to AGDT, May 23, 1883, Secretary of War to Secretary of the Interior, June 20, 1883, 2nd endorsement to last reference, C. C. Augur, August 14, 1883, and Chief Clerk, War Department, to Secretary of the Interior, August 28, 1883, M619-800, frames 656-57, 667-68, 665, 730; Price to Tufts, September 6, 1883, RG 75, LS and LB 1881-1907, Letter Book 173, Miscellaneous, 665.

10. Jumper to Tufts, September 17, 1883, M619-800, frames 695-98. See also Sheridan to Adjutant General, October 27, 1883, Ibid., frames 703-4. Here Sheridan refuted the charge that he had described the Seminole maroons as "a turbulent lawless band," stating that he always had found them to be, on the contrary, "law abiding, well disposed and worthy of consideration."

11. Tufts to Price, October 13, 1883, Price to Secretary of the Interior, October 18, 1883, and Teller to Secretary of War, October 19, 1883, Ibid., frames 692-93, 686-90, 683-84.

12. Jumper to Tufts, March 1, 1884, and Tufts to Price, March 26, 1884, SF 48, 6172-84 and enc. A, enclosed with 8582-84.

13. Tufts to Price, March 26, 1884, Ibid.

14. Jumper to John F. Brown, March 31, 1884, Ibid., 6781-84 enc. 2, enclosed with 8582-84.

15. Price to Secretary of the Interior, April 25, 1884, RG 75, LS and LB 1881-1907, Letter Book L 124, 494.

16. Teller to Commissioner of Indian Affairs, May 2, 1884, SF 48, 8582-84.

17. E. L. Stevens to Tufts, May 17, 1884, RG 75, LS and LB 1881-1907, Letter Book L 125, 413; Brown to Commissioner of Indian Affairs, February 12, 1885, SF 48, 3139-85.

18. Brown to Commissioner of Indian Affairs, February 12, 1885, SF 48, 3139-85; Price to Tufts, February 18, 1885, RG 75, LS and LB 1881-1907, Letter Book L (February 1885), 133-35.

19. *ARCIA 1884,* Report of Union Agency, Tufts to Commissioner of Indian Affairs, August 29, 1884, 99; *Daily Oklahoman,* February 15, 1914; J. A. Newsom, *The Life and Practice of the Wild and Modern Indian, the Early Days of Oklahoma, Some Thrilling Experiences* (Oklahoma City: Harlow Publishing Co., 1922), 63-64. In addition to housing their fearsome residents, the towns of the Seminole freedmen also provided hideouts for an array of white, black, and Indian desperadoes. For a recent study of outlaws and lawmen in the Indian Territory during this period, see Arthur T. Burton, *Black, Red and Deadly: Black and Indian Gunfighters of the Indian Territory, 1870-1907* (Austin: Eakin Press, 1991).

20. "I Want to Go to My People and Settle in a Home" in Porter, "Freedom Over Me."

21. Listings of Joe Scippio and Caesar Bruner Bands, Seminole Census Records 1890, 64-81, 90-97, in C. Guy Cutlip Collection, Box 4, Manuscripts, Manuscripts Division, Western History Collections, University of Oklahoma, Norman; Ledger Book showing cash payments to Seminole Indians by bands, 1898, Seminole Volume 6, listings for Dosar Barkus and Caesar Bruner bands, 46-48, 81-90, and List of Headrights paid Seminole Indians by bands, J. F. Brown and Son, Headright 1901, Seminole Volume 7, listings for Dosar Barkus and Caesar Bruner bands, 47-69, 124-35, SMN 1, Microfilm, Indian Archives Division, Oklahoma Historical Society, Oklahoma City; U.S. Commission to the Five Civilized Tribes, *The Final Rolls of the Citizens and Freedmen of the Five Civilized Tribes in Indian Territory* (Washington, D.C.: Government Printing Office, 1907), Listings of Seminole freedmen, 627-34.

22. Stanley, May 16, 1885, 1st endorsement to Col. C. H. Smith to AGDT, May 9, 1885, M619-800, frames 786-88; Petition of Florida Seminole Negroes, recd. by BIA February

9, 1888, RG 75 LR 1881-1907, 3565-88; Army Discharge Papers of David Bowlegs of the Seminole Negro Indian Scouts, 1873-1880, Epton (Hicks) Collection, Manuscripts Division, Western History Collections, University of Oklahoma, Norman; "I Want to Go to My People and Settle in a Home" in Porter, "Freedom Over Me"; Porter, "Seminole in Mexico," 167-68 and n. 39.

23. Kappler, *Indian Affairs,* vol. 2, 695.

24. Jumper to Tufts, September 17, 1883, M619-800, frames 695-98; Jumper to Tufts, March 1, 1884, and Jumper to Brown, March 31, 1884, SF 48, 6172-84 enc. A, and 6781-84, both enclosed with 8582-84.

25. Col. Smith to AGDT, May 9, 1885, M619-800, frames 790-91.

26. R. Williams to Lt. General Commanding the Army, August 7, 1884, Williams to Adjutant General, August 7, 1884, Williams to Commanding General, Division of the Missouri, August 11, 1884, and Department of Texas Special Orders 104, Paragraph 3, August 18, 1884, M619-800, frames 705-6, 709-10, 714, 741.

27. Stanley, August 27, 1884, 1st endorsement to Bliss to AGDT, August 26, 1884, Ibid., frames 715-17.

28. Lt. Edward B. Ives to AGDT, August 24, 1884, Ibid., 727-28.

29. Ibid.; Bliss to AGDT, August 26, 1884, 1st endorsement to last reference, Stanley, August 27, 1884, 2nd endorsement, Major General John M. Schofield, September 1, 1884, and Secretary of War to Secretary of the Interior, September 19, 1884, Ibid., 720-25, 715-17, 783-85.

30. Col. Smith to AGDT, May 9, 1885, Ibid., 790-91.

31. 1st endorsement to last reference, Stanley, May 16, 1885, 2nd endorsement, Schofield, May 22, 1885, Ibid., frames 786-88, 793-94.

32. Sheridan to Commissioner of Indian Affairs, February 14, 1887, and see also Lt. Col. Sanford C. Kellogg to J. D. C. Atkins, March 25, 1886, RG 75 LR 1881-1907, 4313-87 and 8574-86.

33. Sergeant Bob Kibbit (Kibbetts), Papers presented to Bureau of Indian Affairs, n.d. but handed back March 17, 1886, Ibid., 7024-86; Acting Commissioner of Indian Affairs to John Jumper, March 17, 1886, and D. M. Browning to William Warrior, March 3, 1894, RG 75, LS and LB 1881-1907, Letter Book L 146, 8-9, and Letter Book L 275, 370.

34. Henry L. Dawes to Secretary of the Interior, March 20, 1886, RG 75, LR 1881-1907, 8066-86.

35. Acting Commissioner of Indian Affairs to Jumper, March 17, 1886, and Atkins to Sheridan, March 3, 1887, RG 75, LS and LB 1881-1907, Letter Book L 146, 8-9, and Letter Book L 156, 457-58.

36. Atkins to Secretary of the Interior, March 22, 1886, Ibid., Letter Book L 146, 107.

37. L. Q. C. Lamar to Dawes, March 23, 1886, National Archives Microfilm Publications, Microcopy M606, Record Group 48, Records of the Indian Division of the Office of the Secretary of the Interior, Letters Sent, 1849-1903, 127 rolls, Roll 44, February 8 to April 13, 1886, 340-41; Kellogg to Atkins, March 25, 1886, and Atkins to Kellogg, March 25, 1886, RG 75, LR 1881-1907, 8574-86 and enc.; Atkins to Sheridan, March 3, 1887, RG 75, LS and LB 1881-1907, Letter Book L 156, 457-58.

38. Petition of Florida Seminole Negroes, recd. by BIA February 9, 1888, RG 75, LR 1881-1907, 3565-88.

39. Brown to Major Edward M. Hayes, May 5, 1894, enc. with Warrior to Hoke Smith, May 15, 1894, Ibid., 19400-94. For background to this application, see Warrior to Secretary of the Interior, March 5, 1888, and February 20, 1894, Ibid., 6884-88, 8296-94; and Browning to Warrior, March 3, 1894, RG 75, LS and LB 1881-1907, Letter Book L 275, 370. John F. Brown typically was referred to as governor rather than principal chief of the Seminoles throughout his terms of office.

40. Interview with Miss Charles Emily Wilson, Brackettville, Texas, June 19, 1990; "Black Watch of Texas," *San Antonio Express*, November 16, 1924; "Both Sides of a Border" in Porter, "Freedom Over Me"; W. E. S. Dickerson, "Seminole Indians," in Walter Prescott Webb et al, *The Handbook of Texas*, 3 vols. (Austin: Texas State Historical Society, 1952), vol. 2, 592; Foster, "Negro-Indian Relationships," 48; James, *Frontier and Pioneer Recollections*, 79-80; Woodhull, "Scouts on the Border," 118; Miss Charles Emily Wilson, *History of the Seminole Indian Scout Cemetery*, leaflet printed by Cannon Graphics, Del Rio, TX, for the Seminole Indian Scout Cemetery Association, n.d., copy in possession of the author.

41. Major Henry O. S. Heistand, correspondence left at BIA, July 10, 1899, RG 75, LR BIA 1881-1907, 32063-99; Commissioner of Indian Affairs to Heistand, July 15, 1899, RG 75, LS and LB 1881-1907, Letter Book L 412, 33; *Annual Report of the War Department 1900*, Pt. 1, Report of Commander, Department of Texas, 251. The flood gave rise to renewed efforts to classify the maroons. For example, in 1903 the commander of the Department of Texas wrote: "At this time they can not be said to have any citizenship whatever. In the eyes of the law they are neither negroes, Indians, nor half-breeds." The commander recommended that the government purchase for this "interesting tribe of mongrel Americans," "these so-called Seminole Negroes," a tract of land in the Indian Territory. *Annual Report of the War Department 1903*, Vol. 3, Report of Commander, Department of Texas, 117-19.

42. Army Discharge Papers of Joseph Philips, 1893-1909, Perryman Collection; "Descriptive Book for a Detachment of Seminole Indians, 1889-1893," National Archives Record Group 391, Records of the United States Army Mobile Units, 1821-1942, Indian Scouts; AAGDT to Adjutant General, December 28, 1894, Assistant Adjutant General to AAGDT, December 29, 1894, Auditor for War Department to Assistant Adjutant General, December 6, 1895, and accompanying documentation, M929-2, Target 11; Muster Roll of 2nd Lieutenant Erubion H. Rubottom, Detachment Seminole Negro Indian Scouts, October 31, 1898, and Muster Roll of a Detachment of Seminole Negro Indian Scouts from December 31, 1910, reproduced in Greene, *Black Defenders of America*, 387; J. F. Bell to Secretary of War, March 24, 1909, DT 4882; Maclyn P. Burg, "Service on the Vanishing Frontier, 1887-1898," *Military History of Texas and the Southwest* 13(1976): 19; Arthur R. Gómez, *A Most Singular Country: A History of Occupation in the Big Bend* (Provo, UT: Charles Redd Center for Western Studies, Brigham Young University, 1990), 85-90; Porter, *Negro on the Frontier*, 471.

43. Brigadier General Albert L. Myer to Adjutant General, January 22, 1909, Colonel J. H. Dorst to AGDT, February 17 and 21, 1909, J. F. Bell to Secretary of War, March 24, 1909, Lieutenant R. N. Hayden to Commanding Officer Seminole Negro Indian Scouts, June 12 and 26, 1909, Morell Hall et al to Secretary of War, November 6, 1909, and Lieutenant Abbott Boone to AGDT, December 18, 1909 and accompanying 11 endorse-

ments, DT 4882; Captain Sterling P. Adams, Fort Clark, Texas, Order of July 10, 1914, copy in Old Guardhouse Museum, Fort Clark Springs, Texas.

44. Foster, "Negro-Indian Relationships," 48; Woodhull, "Scouts on the Border," 120.

45. J. F. Bell to Secretary of War, March 24, 1909, DT 4882.

46. Woodhull, "Scouts on the Border," 126-27.

47. *Affairs of the Mexican Kickapoo Indians,* 60 Cong., 1 Sess., Senate Doc. 215, 3 vols., vol. 3, Exhibit 129 (Goode), "Notes Regarding the Nacimiento lands held by the Federal Government of Mexico for the benefit of the Mexican Kickapoo and Muskogee Indians, numbering about 600," 2202; Latorre and Latorre, *Mexican Kickapoo,* 23-24.

48. Porter, "Farewell to John Horse," 265, 272 n. 2.

49. Ibid., 265-69, 273 n. 5; "He Was Going on Horseback to Mexico City," "Juan Caballo and Don Porfirio," "John Horse Went into Mexico and Died There," and "And... No Man Knoweth of his Sepulchre" in Porter, "Freedom Over Me"; Kenneth Porter to Kaye M. Teall, January 6, 1972, Porter Collection, Correspondence File, Box 1.

50. Alice Walker, *The Temple of My Familiar* (San Diego: Harcourt Brace Jovanovich, 1989), 185.

51. Latorre and Latorre , *Mexican Kickapoo,* 23-24, 123-29; "Juan Caballo and Don Porfirio" in Porter, "Freedom Over Me"; Porter, "Farewell to John Horse," 272-73 nn. 3 and 5.

52. *Affairs of the Mexican Kickapoo,* vol. 3, 2201-2. The Senate document's figure of "300 Muskogees" ties in well with Mexican census figures of roughly the same period. For example, an 1891 Mexican census (see Seminoles y Mascogos) listed 46 Seminole maroon families, including 123 males. Sixty-seven of the males were living at Nacimiento, 10 in other parts of Mexico, and 46 in Texas. Interestingly, the census reported that 97 of the males understood Spanish while 26 did not. All spoke "English," but only some spoke Spanish, and the bilingual males spoke both languages "incorrectly." Clearly, Afro-Seminole remained the first language of the maroons on both sides of the border.

7. Either Side of a Border

1. Interview with Miss Charles Emily Wilson, June 19, 1990; Jones, "Old Seminole Scouts," 329; Foster, "Negro-Indian Relationships," 48; Porter, "Farewell to John Horse," 273 n. 18.

2. "Both Sides of a Border" in Porter, "Freedom Over Me"; Interview with Miss Charles Emily Wilson, June 19, 1990; *El Paso Herald-Post,* January 20, 1962; *Houston Chronicle, Texas Magazine,* August 15, 1982; *San Antonio Express-News,* April 29, 1989; Woodhull, "Scouts on the Border," 118.

3. "Both Sides of a Border" in Porter, "Freedom Over Me."

4. Richard Price, *First-Time: the Historical Vision of an Afro-American People* (Baltimore: Johns Hopkins University Press, 1983), 5.

5. For a discussion of the importance of the past in the construction of identity among the Seminole freedmen of Oklahoma, see Bateman, "We're Still Here," 15-16, 29, 303.

6. *San Antonio Express News,* April 29, 1989.

7. Creel, "Gullah Attitudes," 90.

8. Interview with Miss Charles Emily Wilson, June 19, 1990; Interview with William "Dub" Warrior, Brackettville, Texas, September 15, 1990; Interview with Billy Joe Pierce,

Brackettville, Texas, September 14, 1990; Olatunde B. Lawuyi, "Why I am Afro-Seminole: the Search for Identity Among a Brackettville Ethnic Group," unpublished M.A. thesis, University of Illinois at Urbana-Champaign, 1983, 36-37.

9. Interview with Miss Charles Emily Wilson, June 19, 1990; Interview with Charles "Shelley" Best, Brackettville, Texas, September 14, 1990; "Black Watch of Texas," *San Antonio Express,* November 16, 1924; Porter, "Freedom Over Me," photo caption for Mount Gilead Church. For a discussion of a related African-Christian syncretism among the Gullahs of South Carolina, see Margaret Washington Creel, *"A Peculiar People": Slave Religion and Community Culture Among the Gullahs* (New York: New York University Press, 1988), Chapter 8.

10. Interview with Miss Charles Emily Wilson, June 19, 1990; Interview with Charles Best, September 15, 1990; Personal observations during Juneteenth weekend celebration, 1990; L. M. Haynes, "Candid Chimaera: Texas Seminole," unpublished paper read at the Southwest Area Linguistics Workshop, San Antonio, Texas, 1976; *San Angelo Standard,* April 5, 1982.

11. Molefi Kete Asante, "African Elements in African-American English," in Holloway, ed., *Africanisms,* 25. See also Sidney W. Mintz and Richard Price, *An Anthropological Approach to the Afro-American Past: A Caribbean Perspective* (Philadelphia: Institute for the Study of Human Issues Occasional Papers in Social Change No. 2, 1976), 27; and Ernie A. Smith, "Ebonics," *Western Journal of Black Studies* 2(1978): 202-7. Price has argued convincingly that the uniqueness of the more developed maroon communities rests firmly on their adherence to African cultural principles rather than isolated retentions. See *Maroon Societies,* 28-29.

12. On naming patterns among the Seminole freedmen of Oklahoma, see Bateman, "We're Still Here," 343-54.

13. *San Antonio Express-News,* April 29, 1989.

14. For other examples of "exclusive and inclusive ideas," including group members' use of the terms *cousin, slick, dumb,* and *buckra,* see Lawuyi, "Why I am Afro-Seminole," 26-34.

15. "They Stopped at Las Moras Springs" in Porter, "Freedom Over Me."

16. Bateman, "Africans and Indians," 9, 19 n. 2.

17. Carolyn T. Foreman, *Indian Women Chiefs* (Muskogee, OK: Star Printery, Inc., Pubs., 1954), 63; Robert E. Trevathan, "School Days at Emahaka Academy," *Chronicles of Oklahoma* 38(1960): 273; "Tribute to Alice Brown Davis: Delivered by Mrs. William S. Key," *Chronicles of Oklahoma* 42(1965): 98.

18. Indian Pioneer Papers, vol. 105, Int. 13865, W. Gray, 457; Foreman, *Indian Women Chiefs,* 64-66; *Indian Republican,* March 3, 1905; *Tulsa Democrat,* March 17, 1905.

19. *Daily Oklahoman,* January 16 and 23, 1921; Indian Pioneer Papers, vol. 77, Louis C. Brown, 312.

20. *Daily Oklahoman,* January 16, 1921.

21. Ibid., February 6, 1921.

22. Ibid., January 30, 1921.

23. Ibid., February 6, 1921, and see also Ibid., March 6, 1921.

24. Indian Pioneer Papers, vol. 52, Int. 12115, Marchey Yetchie, 79, and vol. 58, Int. 7011, Nina Tanyon, July 20, 1937, 395-96; "The Tribesmen Back the Stars and Bars," unpublished typescript, n.d., 1p., C. Guy Cutlip Collection, Manuscripts Division, Western History Collections, University of Oklahoma, Norman, Box 2, Mss; Unidentified press

clipping relating to the Seminoles' mission to Mexico in June 1937, Seminole Indian File, Grant Foreman Collection, Library Division, Oklahoma Historical Society, Oklahoma City.

25. Indian Pioneer Papers, vol. 58, Int. 7011, Nina Tanyon, 395-96.

26. Ibid., vol. 46, Int. 12475, Wesley Tanyon, 201-2.

27. *Daily Oklahoman,* June 12 and November 1, 1938.

28. Interview with William C. Wantland, Oklahoma City, January 12, 1979; Interview with Richmond Tiger, principal chief of the Seminole Nation, Wewoka, Oklahoma, January 25, 1979.

29. Conversations, meetings, and correspondence with William Dawson, attorney for the Seminole freedmen and Oklahoma State Senator, spring 1984; Bateman, "Africans and Indians," 21 n.13.

30. William Phillips to Secretary of the Interior, July 17 and August 7, 1918, and S. G. Hopkins to Secretary of State, July 29, 1918, RG 75, LR BIA 1907-1939, 60332-18, File 53 and encs.; *Odessa American,* September 17, 1983.

31. Foster, "Negro-Indian Relationships," 49, 56.

32. Bateman, "We're Still Here," 11-13, 21-22; Interview with Miss Charles Emily Wilson, June 19, 1990; Personal observations during Juneteenth and Seminole Day weekend celebrations, 1990; Lawuyi, "Why I am Afro-Seminole," 41-43; *San Antonio Express-News,* April 29, 1989. For a survey of similar festivities, see William H. Wiggins, Jr., *O Freedom! Afro-American Emancipation Celebrations* (Knoxville: University of Tennessee Press, 1987).

33. *On Campus* (University of Texas at Austin student newspaper), March 16-29, 1981; Interview with Ben Warrior, Dosar Barkus band leader, Sasakwa, Oklahoma, March 1, 1983; Interview with William Warrior, September 15, 1990.

Bibliography

Archival and Manuscript Collections

Barry, James Buckner. Papers. Manuscripts Division, Barker Texas History Center, University of Texas at Austin.

Bliss, Zenas R. "Reminiscences of Zenas R. Bliss, Major General United States Army 1854-1876." Unpublished typescript, 5 vols. Manuscripts Division, Barker Texas History Center, University of Texas at Austin.

Creaton, John. Collection. Manuscripts Division, Barker Texas History Center, University of Texas at Austin.

Cutlip, C. Guy. Collection. Manuscripts Division, Western History Collections, University of Oklahoma, Norman.

Duval, J. C., and Burr G. Duval Papers, 1836-1937, Manuscripts Division, Barker Texas History Center, University of Texas at Austin.

Epton (Hicks). Collection. Manuscripts Division, Western History Collections, University of Oklahoma, Norman.

Foreman, Grant. Collection. Seminole Indian File. Library Division, Oklahoma Historical Society, Oklahoma City.

———. Papers. Manuscripts Division, Thomas Gilcrease Institute of American History and Art, Tulsa, Oklahoma.

Fort Clark, Texas. Records. Manuscripts Division, Barker Texas History Center, University of Texas at Austin.

Guajardo, General Luis Alberto, comp. "Apuntes Datos y Noticias para la Historia de Coahuila," circa 1613-1911. Western Americana Collections, Beinecke Rare Book and Manuscript Library, Yale University, New Haven, Connecticut.

Indian Pioneer Papers. 116 vols. Indian Archives Division, Oklahoma Historical Society, Oklahoma City.

Kinney County, Texas. Records. Kinney County Courthouse, Brackettville, Texas.

Lilley, Mary Ann. "The Autobiography of Mary Ann Lilley." Unpublished typescript, 64pp. Indian Archives Division, Oklahoma Historical Society, Oklahoma City.

Mexico. Archivo de la Secretaria de Relaciones Exteriores. Colonización. Seminoles y Mascogos, Número 94 (1891), 44-12-60. Mexico City.

Múzquiz, Coahuila. Records. Western Americana Collections, Beinecke Rare Book and Manuscript Library, Yale University, New Haven, Connecticut.

Perryman, Warren. Collection. Archives Division, Texas State Library, Austin.

Porter, Kenneth Wiggins. Papers. Archives Division, Schomburg Center for Research in Black Culture, New York City.

Saltillo, Coahuila. Archivo de la Secretaria de Gobierno, 1848-1876. Volume 44. Legajo
    Número 45, 1853 (photocopy). Manuscripts Division, Bancroft Library, University
    of California, Berkeley.
Seminole Nation. Records. Seminole Volume 6 and Seminole Volume 7. SMN 1,
    Microfilm. Indian Archives Division, Oklahoma Historical Society, Oklahoma City.
Sumpter, Jesse. "Life of Jesse Sumpter, the Oldest Citizen of Eagle Pass, Texas."
    Unpublished typescript, 70pp., 1906. Manuscripts Division, Barker Texas History
    Center, University of Texas at Austin.
Texas. Governors' Papers. Peter Hansborough Bell. Archives Division, Texas State Library,
    Austin.
United States. Records of the Bureau of Indian Affairs. National Archives Record Group
    75.
    Letters Received, 1824-1881. National Archives Microfilm Publications, Microcopy
        M234.
        Creek Agency, 1843-1852 (Rolls 227-28).
        Florida Superintendency, 1838-1850 (Roll 289).
        Seminole Agency, 1824-1876 (Rolls 800-5).
        Seminole Agency Emigration, 1827-1859 (Rolls 806-7).
        Texas Agency, 1847-1859 (Roll 858).
        Western Superintendency, 1840-1851 and Western Superintendency Emigration,
            1836-1842 (Rolls 923-24).
    Letters Received, 1881-1907, 1907-1939.
    Letters Sent and Letter Books, 1881-1907.
    Miscellaneous Muster Rolls 1832-1846: Seminole.
    Records of the Southern Superintendency, 1832-1870. National Archives Microfilm
        Publications, Microcopy M640.
        Western Superintendency, Letters Received, 1849-1851 (Roll 7).
    Seminole Annuity Rolls, 1860-1898.
    Seminoles and Seminole Immigration, 1823-1860.
    Special Files, 1807-1904. National Archives Microfilm Publications, Microcopy M574.
        File 96. "Seminole Claims to Certain Negroes 1841-1849" (Roll 13).
——. Records of the Bureau of the Census. National Archives Record Group 29. Ninth
    Census of the United States, 1870. Population Schedule, Uvalde County, Texas.
——. Records of the Department of the Interior, Indian Division. National Archives
    Record Group 48.
    Letters Received, 1881-1907.
    Letters Sent, 1849-1903. National Archives Microfilm Publications, Microcopy M606.
        Roll 44, Feb. 8–Apr. 13, 1886.
    Special Files Box 48. Indian Territory Division, Choctaw Freedmen File.
——. Records of the Office of the Adjutant General, 1780s-1917. National Archives
    Record Group 94.
    ACP for John Lapham Bullis.
    General Jesup's Papers. Letters Sent.
    Letters Received. National Archives Microfilm Publications, Microcopy M619. File
        488-70, "Papers relating to the return of the Kickapoo and the Seminole (Negro)
        Indians from Mexico to the United States, 1870-1885," (Rolls 799, 800).

Records of the Record and Pension Office, 1784-1917. Medical Histories of Posts. Fort Duncan and Fort Clark.

Tabular Statement of Expeditions and Scouts Against Indians etc. Made in the Department of Texas During the Year Ending 31 August 1875.

United States Army Registers of Enlistments. Indian Scouts 1866-1914. National Archives Microfilm Publications, Microcopy M233, Rolls 70, 71.

———. Records of the United States Army Continental Commands, 1821-1920. National Archives Record Group 393.

Department of Texas. Seminole Negroes. Part 1. Entry 4882.

Division of the Missouri. Special Files. Box 6, Indian Scouts Enlisted 1874-1877. Box 15, Seminole Negro Indians, 1872-1876.

Fort Gibson. Letters Received, Letters Sent, and Volume "Indian Affairs."

Second and Seventh Military Departments, Letters Received and Letters Sent.

———. Records of the United States Army Mobile Units, 1821-1942. National Archives Record Group 391. Indian Scouts.

———. Selected Records Relating to Black Servicemen. National Archives Record Groups 94, 107, 153. National Archives Microfilm Publications, Microcopy M929.

Documents Relating to the Military and Naval Service of Blacks Awarded the Congressional Medal of Honor from the Civil War to the Spanish American War. Roll 2, Indian Campaigns—U.S. Regular Army.

Government Documents and Publications

Carter, Clarence Edwin, comp. and ed. *The Territorial Papers of the United States.* 28 vols. Washington, D.C.: Government Printing Office, 1934-1975.

Heitman, Francis B. *Historical Register and Dictionary of the United States Army: From its Organization, September 29, 1789, to March 2, 1903.* 3 vols. Washington, D.C.: Government Printing Office, 1903.

Informe de la Comisión Pesquisidora de la Frontera del Norte. Mexico City: Imprenta del Gobierno en Palacio, 1877.

Kappler, Charles J., comp. *Indian Affairs, Laws and Treaties.* 3 vols. Washington, D.C.: Government Printing Office, 1904-1913.

Maza, Francisco F. de la. *Código de Colonización y Terrenos Baldíos de la República Mexicana 1451-1892.* Mexico City: Oficina de la Secretaria de Fomento, 1893.

Mexico. Secretaria de Estado. *Memoria de la Secretaria de Estado y del Despacho de Guerra y Marina.* Mexico, 1851.

Report of the Committee of Investigation Sent in 1873 by the Mexican Government to the Frontier of Texas. Translated from the Official Edition Made in Mexico. New York: Baker and Godwin Printers, 1875.

Swanton, John R. "Early History of the Creek Indians and Their Neighbors." United States. Bureau of American Ethnology. *Bulletin* 73. Washington, D.C.: Government Printing Office, 1922.

———. "Religious Beliefs and Medical Practices of the Creek Indians." In United States. Bureau of American Ethnology. Forty-Second *Annual Report.* Washington, D.C.: Government Printing Office, 1928, 473-672.

——. "Social Organization and the Social Usages of the Creek Confederacy." In United States. Bureau of American Ethnology. Forty-Second *Annual Report.* Washington, D.C.: Government Printing Office, 1928, 23-472.

United States. Bureau of Indian Commissioners. Sixth *Annual Report,* 1874.

——. Commission to the Five Civilized Tribes. *The Final Rolls of the Citizens and Freedmen of the Five Civilized Tribes in Indian Territory.* Washington, D.C.: Government Printing Office, 1907.

——. Commissioner of Indian Affairs. *Annual Report,* 1838-1915. Washington, D.C.: Government Printing Office.

——. War Department. *Annual Report,* 1900, 1903. Washington, D.C.: Government Printing Office.

——. War Department. *Exploration of the Red River of Louisiana in the Year 1852.* Washington, D.C.: Robert Armstrong, Public Printer, 1853.

——. War Department. Surgeon General's Office. *Circular No. 8: Report on Hygiene of the United States Army with Descriptions of Military Posts.* New York: Sol Lewis, 1974 [1875].

——. War Department. Surgeon General's Office. *Circular No. 4: Report on Barracks and Hospitals with Descriptions of Military Posts.* New York: Sol Lewis, 1974 [1870].

United States Congress. *American State Papers.* 38 vols. Washington, D.C.: Government Printing office, 1832-1861.

——. *U.S. Statutes at Large, 1789-1863.* Boston, 1852-1867.

——. House. *Depredations on the Frontiers of Texas.* 43 Congress, 1 Session, Hse. Ex. Doc. 257.

——. House. *Indians—Creek and Seminole.* 33 Congress, 2 Session, Hse. Ex. Doc. 15.

——. House. *Mexican Border Troubles.* 45 Congress, 1 Session, Hse. Ex. Doc. 13.

——. House. *Negroes, &c., Captured from Indians in Florida.* 25 Congress, 3 Session, Hse. Doc. 225.

——. House. *Report on the Relations of the United States with Mexico.* 45 Congress, 2 Session, Hse. Doc. 701.

——. House. *Report on the United States and Mexican Boundary Survey.* By William H. Emory. 2 vols. 34 Congress, 1 Session, Hse. Ex. Doc. 135.

——. House. *The Texas Border Troubles.* 45 Congress, 2 Session, Hse. Misc. Doc. 64.

——. Senate. *Affairs of the Mexican Kickapoo Indians.* 3 vols. 60 Congress, 1 Session, Sen. Doc. 215.

——. Senate. *Claims of the State of Texas.* 45 Congress, 2 Session, Sen. Ex. Doc. 19.

The War of the Rebellion: A Compilation of the Official Records of the Union and Confederate Armies. 4 ser., 130 vols. Washington, D.C.: Government Printing Office, 1890-1901.

Interviews

Charles "Shelley" Best. Brackettville, Texas, September 14, 1990.
William Dawson. Conversations, Meetings, and Correspondence, Oklahoma, Spring 1984.
Billy Joe Pierce. Brackettville, Texas, September 14, 1990.
Richmond Tiger. Wewoka, Oklahoma, January 25, 1979.
William C. Wantland. Oklahoma City, January 12, 1979.

Ben Warrior. Sasakwa, Oklahoma, March 1, 1983.
William "Dub" Warrior. Brackettville, Texas, September 15, 1990.
Miss Charles Emily Wilson. Brackettville, Texas, June 19, 1990.

Theses, Dissertations, and Unpublished Papers

Bateman, Rebecca B. "We're Still Here: History, Kinship, and Group Identity Among the Seminole Freedmen of Oklahoma." Ph.D. Dissertation, Johns Hopkins University, 1990.

Berringer, Dieter G. "Mexican Attitudes Towards Immigration 1821-1857." Ph.D. Dissertation, University of Wisconsin, 1972.

Duffner, Michael Paul. "The Seminole-Black Alliance in Florida: An Example of Minority Co-operation." M.A. Thesis, George Mason University, 1973.

Foster, Laurence. "Negro-Indian Relationships in the Southeast." Ph.D. Dissertation, University of Pennsylvania, 1935.

Gallaher, Arthur, Jr. "A Survey of the Seminole Freedmen." M.A. Thesis, University of Oklahoma, 1951.

Haynes, L. M. "Candid Chimaera: Texas Seminole." Paper read at the Southwest Area Linguistics workshop, San Antonio, Texas, 1976.

Landers, Jane. "Black Society in Spanish St. Augustine, 1784-1821." Ph.D. Dissertation, University of Florida, 1988.

Lawuyi, Olatunde Bayo. "Seminole Freedmen's Identity in Plural Setting." Ph.D. Dissertation, University of Illinois at Urbana-Champaign, 1985.

———. "Why I am Afro-Seminole: The Search for Identity Among a Brackettville Ethnic Group." M.A. Thesis, University of Illinois at Urbana-Champaign, 1983.

Miller, Susan A. "A New Border for an Old Use: Seminole Indians at the Rio Grande." Paper read at the annual conference of the Western History Association, Austin, Texas, October 1991.

———. "Wild Cat and the Origins of the Seminole Migration to Mexico." M.A. Thesis, University of Oklahoma, 1988.

Mulroy, Kevin. "Classifying the Texas Seminole Maroons, 1870-1886: Seminoles, Freedmen, 'Negro-Indians,' or Just Plain Mexicans?" Paper read at the annual conference of the American Society for Ethnohistory, Toronto, Canada, November 1990, and at the annual convention of the Pacific Coast Branch of the American Historical Association, Kona, Hawaii, August 1991.

———. "Either Side of a Border: The Seminole Maroons in Coahuila and Texas." Paper read at the annual conference of the Western History Association, Austin, Texas, October 1991.

———. "Ethnogenesis and Ethnohistory of the Seminole Maroons." Paper read at the Eleventh Oklahoma Symposium on Comparative Frontier Studies, "Ethnogenesis, A Frontier Phenomenon?" University of Oklahoma, Norman, March 1992.

———. "Relations Between Blacks and Seminoles After Removal." Ph.D. Thesis, University of Keele (England), 1984.

Nunley, Mary Christopher. "Foraging the Border: The Binational Adaptation of the Kickapoo Indians." Paper read at the annual conference of the Western History Association, Austin, Texas, October 1991.

Roethler, Michael D. "Negro Slavery Among the Cherokee Indians 1540-1866." Ph.D. Dissertation, Fordham University, 1964.

Sameth, Sigmund. "Creek Negroes: A Study of Race Relations." M.A. Thesis, University of Oklahoma, 1940.

Sattler, Richard A. "Siminoli Italwa: Socio-Political Change Among the Oklahoma Seminoles Between Removal and Allotment." Ph.D. Dissertation, University of Oklahoma, 1987.

Welsh, Michael E. "The Road to Assimilation: The Seminoles in Oklahoma, 1839-1936." Ph.D. Dissertation, University of New Mexico, 1983.

Articles, Essays, Newspapers, and Periodicals

Anderson, Robert L. "The End of an Idyll." *Florida Historical Quarterly* 42(1963): 35-47.

Aptheker, Herbert. "Maroons Within the Present Limits of the United States." *Journal of Negro History* 24(1939): 167-184.

Archambeau, Ernest R., ed. "Monthly Reports of the Fourth Cavalry, 1872-1874." *Panhandle-Plains Historical Review* 38(1965): 95-153.

Arkansas Intelligencer, 1844-1846.

Asante, Molefi Kete. "African Elements in African-American English." In *Africanisms in American Culture,* ed. by Joseph E. Holloway. Bloomington: Indiana University Press, 1990, 19-33.

Bateman, Rebecca B. "Africans and Indians: A Comparative Study of the Black Carib and Black Seminole." *Ethnohistory* 37(1990): 1-24.

Billington, Monroe. "Black Slavery in Indian Territory: The Ex-Slave Narratives." *Chronicles of Oklahoma* 60 (1982): 56-65.

"Black Watch of Texas." *San Antonio Express,* November 16, 1924.

Boletín Oficial del Estado de Nuevo León y Coahuila, 1855, 1858, 1859, 1862.

Bonnet, W. A. "King Fisher, a Noted Character." *Frontier Times* 3(1926): 36-37.

Boyd, Mark F. "Events at Prospect Bluff on the Apalachicola River, 1808-1818." *Florida Historical Quarterly* 16(1937): 55-96.

——. "The Seminole War, Its Background and Onset." *Florida Historical Quarterly* 30 (1951): 3-115.

"Brackettville and Old Fort Clark." *Frontier Times* 12(1935): 349-51.

Bulter, Grace L. "General Bullis: Friend of the Frontier." *Frontier Times* 12(1935): 358-63.

Burg, Maclyn P. "Service on the Vanishing Frontier, 1887-1898." *Military History of Texas and the Southwest* 13 (1976): 5-21.

Bushnell, Amy Turner. "Ruling 'the Republic of Indians' in Seventeenth-Century Florida." In *Powhatan's Mantle: Indians in the Colonial Southeast,* ed. by Peter H. Wood, Gregory A. Waselkov and M. Thomas Hatley. Lincoln: University of Nebraska Press, 1989, 134-50.

Callan, Austin. "The End of the 'Seminoles'." *Frontier Times* 8(1930): 9-11.

Carter, Robert G. "A Raid into Mexico." *Outing* 12(1888): 1-9.

Cherokee Advocate, 1845, 1846, 1850.

Cody, Cheryll Ann. "There Was No 'Absolom' on the Ball Plantations: Slave-Naming Practices in the South Carolina Low Country, 1720-1865." *American Historical Review* 92(1987): 563-96.

Craton, Michael. "From Caribs to Black Caribs: The Amerindian Roots of Servile Resistance in the Caribbean." In *In Resistance: Studies in African, Caribbean, and Afro-American History,* ed. by Gary Y. Okihiro. Amherst: University of Massachusetts Press, 1986.

Creel, Margaret. "Gullah Attitudes Towards Life and Death." In *Africanisms in American Culture,* ed. by Joseph E. Holloway. Bloomington: Indiana University Press, 1990, 69-97.

Crimmins, Martin L. "General Mackenzie and Fort Concho." *West Texas Historical Association Yearbook* 10(1934): 16-31.

———., ed. "Old Fort Duncan: A Frontier Post." *Frontier Times* 15(1938): 379-85.

———., ed. "Shafter's Explorations in Western Texas, 1875." *West Texas Historical Association Yearbook* 9(1933): 82-96.

Crowe, Charles. "Indians and Blacks in White America." In *Red, White and Black: Symposium on Indians in the Old South,* ed. by Charles M. Hudson. Athens: University of Georgia Press, 1971, 148-69.

Daily Oklahoman, 1914, 1921, 1938.

Dickerson, W. E. S. "Seminole Indians." In Walter Prescott Webb et al. *The Handbook of Texas.* 3 vols. Austin: Texas State Historical Society, 1952.

Doran, Michael F. "Negro Slaves of the Five Civilized Tribes." *Annals of the Association of American Geographers* 68(1978): 335-50.

Dorst, Joseph H. "Ranald Slidell Mackenzie." *Armor, or Journal of the United States Cavalry Association* 10(1897): 367-82.

Dundes, Alan. "African Tales Among the North American Indians." *Southern Folklore Quarterly* 29(1965): 207-19.

Edwards, Bryan. "Observations on [the] Maroon Negroes of the Island of Jamaica." In *Maroon Societies: Rebel Slave Communities in the Americas,* ed. by Richard Price. Rev. ed. Baltimore: Johns Hopkins University Press, 1979, 230-45.

El Paso Herald-Post, 1962.

Faulk, Odie B. "Projected Mexican Colonies in the Borderlands, 1852." *Journal of Arizona History* 10(1969): 115-28.

———. "Projected Mexican Military Colonies for the Borderlands, 1848." *Journal of Arizona History* 9(1968): 39-47.

Foreman, Carolyn T. "The Jumper Family of the Seminole Nation." *Chronicles of Oklahoma* 34(1956): 272-85.

Foreman, Grant, ed. "The Journal of Elijah Hicks." *Chronicles of Oklahoma* 13(1935): 68-99.

Fort Smith Herald, 1850.

Galveston Daily News, 1873.

Goggin, John M. "The Mexican Kickapoo Indians." *Southwestern Journal of Anthropology* 7(1951): 314-27.

——. "The Seminole Negroes of Andros Island, Bahamas." *Florida Historical Quarterly* 24(1946): 201-6.

Halliburton, Janet. "Black Slavery in the Creek Nation." *Chronicles of Oklahoma* 56(1978): 298-314.

Hancock, Ian F. "Creole Features in the Afro-Seminole Speech of Brackettville, Texas." *Society for Caribbean Linguistics Occasional Papers* 3(1975).

——. "Further Observations on Afro-Seminole Creole." *Society for Caribbean Linguistics Occasional Papers* 7(1977).

——. "Texas Gullah: the Creole English of the Brackettville Afro-Seminoles." In *Perspectives on American English,* ed. by Joseph L. Dillard. The Hague: Mouton, 1980, 305-33.

Hatfield, Charles A. P. "The Comanche, Kiowa and Cheyenne Campaign in Northwest Texas and Mackenzie's Fight in the Palo Duro Canyon September 26, 1874." *West Texas Historical Association Yearbook* 5(1928): 118-23.

Helms, Mary. "Black Carib Domestic Organization in Historical Perspective: Traditional Origins of Contemporary Patterns." *Ethnology* 20(1981): 77-86.

——. "Negro or Indian? The Changing Identity of a Frontier Population." In *Old Roots in New Lands: Historical and Anthropological Perspectives on Black Experiences in the Americas,* ed. by Ann M. Pescatello. Westport, CT: Greenwood Press, 1977, 155-72.

Holloway, Joseph E. Introduction. In *Africanisms in American Culture,* ed. by Joseph E. Holloway. Bloomington: Indiana University Press, 1990, ix-xxi.

Houston Chronicle, 1982.

Hunter, John W. "Old Amy, the Seminole Squaw." *Frontier Times* 3(1926): 14-15.

"'I'm in the Wewoka Switch': Heard in the Oil Fields over the World." *Chronicles of Oklahoma* 41(1963): 455-58.

Indian Republican, 1905.

Inscoe, John C. "Carolina Slave Names: An Index to Acculturation." *Journal of Southern History* 49(1983): 527-54.

Johnson, Michael. "Runaway Slaves and the Slave Communities in South Carolina, 1799-1830." *William and Mary Quarterly* 38(1981): 418-41.

Jones, H. Conger. "Old Seminole Scouts Still Thrive on Border." *Frontier Times* 11(1934): 327-32.

Kersey, Harry A., Jr. "The Seminole Negroes of Andros Island Revisited: Some New Pieces of an Old Puzzle." *Florida Anthropologist* 34(1981): 169-76.

Klos, George. "Black Seminoles in Territorial Florida." *Southern Historian* 10(1989): 26-42.

——. "Blacks and the Seminole Removal Debate, 1821-1835." *Florida Historical Quarterly* 68(1989): 55-78.

Köbben, A.J.F. "Unity and Disunity: Cottica Djuka Society as a Kinship System." In *Maroon Societies: Rebel Slave Communities in the Americas,* ed. by Richard Price. Rev. ed. Baltimore: Johns Hopkins University Press, 1979, 320-69.

Landers, Jane. "African Presence in Early Spanish Colonization of the Caribbean and the Southeastern Borderlands." In *Archaeological and Historical Perspectives on the Spanish Borderlands East. Columbian Consequences vol. 2,* ed. by David Hurst Thomas. Washington, D.C.: Smithsonian Institution, 1990, 315-27.

——. "Gracia Real de Santa Teresa de Mose: A Free Black Town in Spanish Colonial Florida." *American Historical Review* 95(1990): 9-30.

——. "Spanish Sanctuary; Fugitive Slaves in Florida, 1687-1790." *Florida Historical Quarterly* 62(1984): 296-313.

"Last Indian Raid in Southwest Texas." *Frontier Times* 4(1927): 58-59.

Leckie, William H. "The Red River War." *Panhandle-Plains Historical Review* 29(1956): 78-100.

Littlefield, Daniel F., Jr. and Lonnie E. Underhill. "Slave 'Revolt' in the Cherokee Nation, 1842." *American Indian Quarterly* 3(1977): 121-31.

Littlefield, Daniel F., Jr. and Mary Ann Littlefield. "The Beams Family: Free Blacks in Indian Territory." *Journal of Negro History* 61(1976): 16-35.

McLoughlin, William G. "Red Indians, Black Slavery and White Racism: America's Slaveholding Indians." *American Quarterly* 26(1974): 367-85.

——. "Red, White and Black in the Antebellum South." *Baptist History and Heritage* 7(1972): 69-75.

Milligan, John D. "Slave Rebelliousness and the Florida Maroon." *Prologue* 6(1974): 4-18.

Mistletoe Leaves (Newsletter of the Oklahoma Historical Society) 21, No. 10 (Oct. 1990): 8.

Moseley, Edward H. "Indians from the Eastern United States and the Defence of Northeastern Mexico, 1855-1864." *Southwestern Social Science Quarterly* 46(1965): 273-80.

Neal, Charles M., Jr. "Incident on Las Moras Creek." *The Annals: Official Publication of the Medal of Honor Historical Society* 13(1990): 16-19.

"A Negro Trooper of the Ninth Cavalry." *Frontier Times* 4(April 1927): 9-11.

Niles Weekly Register, 1838.

Odessa American, 1983.

On Campus. University of Texas at Austin student newspaper. March 16-29, 1981.

La Patria, 1851.

Perdue, Theda. "Cherokee Planters, Black Slaves and African Colonization." *Chronicles of Oklahoma* 60(1982): 322-31.

——. "Cherokee Planters: the Development of Plantation Slavery Before Removal." In *The Cherokee Nation: A Troubled History,* ed. by Duane H. King. Knoxville: University of Tennessee Press, 1979, 110-28.

Peterson, Jacqueline, and Jennifer S. H. Brown. Introduction. In *The New Peoples: Being and Becoming Métis in North America,* ed. by Jacqueline Peterson and Jennifer S. H. Brown. Lincoln: University of Nebraska Press, 1985.

Pool, William C. "The Battle of Dove Creek." *Southwestern Historical Quarterly* 53(1950): 367-85.

Porter, Kenneth Wiggins. "Billy Bowlegs (Holata Micco) in the Seminole Wars." *Florida Historical Quarterly* 45(1967): 210-43.

——. "The Cowkeeper Dynasty of the Seminole Nation." *Florida Historical Quarterly* 30 (1952): 341-49.

——. "Davy Crockett and John Horse: A Possible Origin of the Coonskin Story." *American Literature* 15(1943): 10-15.

——. "Farewell to John Horse: An Episode of Seminole Negro Folk History." *Phylon* 8 (1947): 265-73.

——. "The Hawkins Negroes go to Mexico." *Chronicles of Oklahoma* 24(1946): 55-58.

——. "Lament for Wild Cat." *Phylon* 4(1943): 39-48.

——. "A Legend of the Biloxi." *Journal of American Folklore* 59(1946): 168-73.

——. "Louis Pachecho: The Man and the Myth." *Journal of Negro History* 28(1943): 65-72.

——. "Negro Guides and Interpreters in the Early Stages of the Seminole War, 28 December 1835–6 March 1837." *Journal of Negro History* 35(1950): 174-82.

——. "Negroes and Indians on the Texas Frontier, 1834-1874." *Southwestern Historical Quarterly* 53(1949): 151-63.

——. "Negroes and Indians on the Texas Frontier, 1831-1876: A Study in Race and Culture." *Journal of Negro History* 41(1956): 185-214.

——. "Notes on the Seminole Negroes in the Bahamas." *Florida Historical Quarterly* 24 (1945): 56-60.

——. "Seminole Flight from Fort Marion." *Florida Historical Quarterly* 22(1944): 112-33.

——. "Seminole in Mexico, 1850-1861." *Chronicles of Oklahoma* 29(1951): 153-68.

——. "Wild Cat's Death and Burial." *Chronicles of Oklahoma* 21(1943): 41-43.

Porter, Kenneth Wiggins and Edward S. Wallace. "Thunderbolt of the Frontier." *Westerners New York Posse Brand Book* 8(1961): 73-75, 82-86.

Price, Richard. "Introduction: Maroons and Their Communities." In *Maroon Societies: Rebel Slave Communities in the Americas,* ed. by Richard Price. Rev. ed. Baltimore: Johns Hopkins University Press, 1979, 1-30.

"Record of Engagements with Hostile Indians in Texas 1868 to 1882." *West Texas Historical Association Yearbook* 9(1933): 101-18.

Reeve, Frank D., ed. "Frederick E. Phelps: A Soldier's Memoirs." *New Mexico Historical Review* 25(1950): 187-221.

Reid, John C. "Reid's Tramp: a Ten Months' Trip through Texas, New Mexico, Arizona, California and Mexico in 1857." *Frontier Times* 20(1943): 197-208.

El Restaurador de la Libertad, 1856, 1857.

Rippy, James Fred. "Border Troubles Along the Rio Grande, 1848-1860." *Southwestern Historical Quarterly* 23(1919): 91-111.

——. "The Indians of the Southwest in the Diplomacy of the United States and Mexico, 1848-1853." *Hispanic American Historical Review* 2(1919): 363-96.

Root, George A., ed. "No-ko-aht's Talk: A Kickapoo Chief's Account of a Tribal Journey from Kansas to Mexico and Return in the Sixties." *Kansas Historical Quarterly* 1 (1932): 153-59.

San Angelo Standard, 1982.

San Antonio Express-News, 1989.

San Antonio Herald, 1855.

San Antonio Texan, 1857.

San Antonio Western Texas, 1850-1852.

"Scouting on the 'Staked Plains' (Llano Estacado) with Mackenzie in 1874." By "One Who Was There." *The United Service(s)* 13(1885): 400-412.

Sefton, James E. "Black Slaves, Red Masters, White Middlemen: A Congressional Debate of 1852." *Florida Historical Quarterly* 51(1972): 113-28.

Shearer, Ernest. "The Callahan Expedition, 1855." *Southwestern Historical Quarterly* 54 (1951): 430-51.

——. "The Carvajal Disturbances." *Southwestern Historical Quarterly* 55 (1951): 201-30. *El Siglo Diez y Nueve,* 1850, 1852, 1855, 1856.

Smith, Ernie A. "Ebonics." *Western Journal of Black Studies* 2(1978): 202-7.

Smith, Ralph A. "The Mamelukes of West Texas and Mexico." *West Texas Historical Association Year Book* 39(1963): 65-88.

Southall, E. P. "Negroes in Florida Prior to the Civil War." *Journal of Negro History* 19 (1934): 16-86.

Sowell, Andrew J. "Last Indian Raid in Frio Canyon." *Frontier Times* 24(1947): 500-3.

Spoehr, Alexander. "Camp, Clan and Kin Among the Cow Creek Seminole of Florida." *Publications of the Field Museum of Natural History,* Anthropological Series 33, No. 1 (1941): 1-27.

——. "Changing Kinship Systems." *Publications of the Field Museum of Natural History,* Anthropological Series 33, No. 4 (1947): 159-235.

——. "The Florida Seminole Camp." *Publications of the Field Museum of Natural History,* Anthropological Series 33, No. 3 (1944): 115-50.

——. "Kinship System of the Seminole." *Publications of the Field Museum of Natural History,* Anthropological Series 33, No. 2 (1942): 29-113.

——. "Oklahoma Seminole Towns." *Chronicles of Oklahoma* 19(1941): 377-80.

Sturtevant, William C. "Creek Into Seminole." In *North American Indians in Historical Perspective,* ed. by Eleanor B. Leacock and Nancy O. Lurie. New York: Random House, 1971, 92-128.

——. "The Medicine Bundles and Busks of the Florida Seminoles." *Florida Anthropologist* 7(1954): 31-70.

——. Review of *Africans and Seminoles: From Removal to Emancipation,* by Daniel F. Littlefield, Jr. *American Anthropologist* 81(1979): 916-17.

——. "Seminole Myths of the Origin of Races." *Ethnohistory* 10(1963): 80-85.

TePaske, John J. "The Fugitive Slave: Intercolonial Rivalry and Spanish Slave Policy, 1687-1764." In *Eighteenth-Century Florida and Its Borderlands,* ed. by Samuel Proctor. Gainesville: University of Florida Press, 1975.

Texas Monument, 1850.

Texas State Gazette, 1855.

Texas State Times, 1855.

Thomas, Robert K. "Afterword." In *The New Peoples: Being and Becoming Métis in North America,* ed. by Jacqueline Peterson and Jennifer S. H. Brown. Lincoln: University of Nebraska Press, 1985.

Thompson, William A. "Scouting with Mackenzie." *Armor, or Journal of the United States Cavalry Association* 10(1897): 429-33.

Thybony, Scott. "Against All Odds, Black Seminole Won Their Freedom." *Smithsonian* 22(1991): 90-101.

Trevathan, Robert E. "School Days at Emahaka Academy." *Chronicles of Oklahoma* 38 (1960): 265-73.

"Tribute to Alice Brown Davis: Delivered by Mrs. William S. Key." *Chronicles of Oklahoma* 42 (1965): 96-101.

Tulsa Democrat, 1905.

Tyler, Ronnie C. "The Callahan Expedition of 1855: Indians or Negroes?" *Southwestern Historical Quarterly* 70(April 1967): 574-85.

———., ed. "Exploring the Rio Grande: Lieutenant Duff C. Green's Report of 1852." *Arizona and the West* 10(1968): 43-60.

———. "Fugitive Slaves in Mexico." *Journal of Negro History* 57(1972): 1-12.

Wallace, Edward S. "General John Lapham Bullis, the Thunderbolt of the Texas Frontier." Parts 1 and 2. *Southwestern Historical Quarterly* 54(1951): 452-62; 55(1951): 77-85.

Wallace, Ernest. "Prompt in the Saddle: the Military Career of Ranald S. Mackenzie." *Military History of Texas and the Southwest* 9(1971): 161-89.

Wallace, Ernest, and Adrian N. Anderson. "R. S. Mackenzie and the Kickapoos: The Raid into Mexico in 1873." *Arizona and the West* 7(1965): 105-26.

Watts, Jill M. "'We Do Not Live for Ourselves Only': Seminole Black Perceptions and the Second Seminole War." *UCLA Historical Journal* 7(1986): 5-28.

White, Lonnie J. "The First Battle of the Palo Duro Canyon." *Texas Military History* 6(1967): 222-35.

———. "Indian Battles in the Texas Panhandle 1874." *Journal of the West* 6(1967): 278-309.

Willis, William S., Jr. "Divide and Rule: Red, White and Black in the South East." In *Red, White and Black: Symposium on Indians in the Old South,* ed. by Charles M. Hudson. Athens: University of Georgia Press, 1971, 99-115.

Willson, Walt. "Freedmen in Indian Territory During Reconstruction." *Chronicles of Oklahoma* 49(1971): 230-44.

Wood, Peter H. "The Changing Population of the Colonial South: An Overview by Race and Region, 1685-1790." In *Powhatan's Mantle: Indians in the Colonial Southeast,* ed. by Peter H. Wood, Gregory A. Waselkov and M. Thomas Hatley. Lincoln: University of Nebraska Press, 1989, 35-103.

Woodford, Sam, ed. "The Burr G. Duval Diary." *Southwestern Historical Quarterly* 65(1962): 487-511.

Woodhull, Frost. "The Seminole Indian Scouts on the Border." *Frontier Times* 15(1937): 118-27.

Wright, Irene. "Dispatches of Spanish Officials Bearing on the Free Negro Settlement of Gracia Real de Santa Teresa de Mose, Florida." *Journal of Negro History* 9(1924): 144-95.

Wright, James Leitch, Jr. "Blacks in British East Florida." *Florida Historical Quarterly* 54(1976): 425-42.

———. "A Note on the First Seminole War as seen by the Indians, Negroes, and their British Advisers." *Journal of Southern History* 34(1968): 565-75.

Wright, Muriel H. "Seal of the Seminole Nation." *Chronicles of Oklahoma* 34(1956): 262-71.

Books

Abel, Annie H. *The American Indian as Slaveholder and Secessionist: An Omitted Chapter in the Diplomatic History of the Southern Confederacy.* Cleveland: Arthur H. Clark Co., 1925.

Aptheker, Herbert. *American Negro Slave Revolts.* New York: Columbia University Press, 1943.

Bancroft, Hubert Howe. *History of Mexico.* 6 vols. Works of Hubert Howe Bancroft v. 9-14. San Francisco: History Company, 1886-1888.

Barr, Alwyn. *Black Texans: A History of Negroes in Texas.* Austin: Jenkins Pub. Co., 1973.

Bartram, William. *Travels Through North and South Carolina, Georgia, East and West Florida.* Philadelphia, 1794.

Berry, Brewton. *Almost White.* New York: Macmillan, 1963.

Berthrong, Donald J. *The Southern Cheyennes.* Norman: University of Oklahoma Press, 1963.

Blassingame, John W. *The Slave Community: Plantation Life in the Antebellum South.* Rev. and enl. ed. New York: Oxford University Press, 1979.

Box, Michael J. *Captain James Box's Adventures in New and Old Mexico.* New York: J. Miller, 1869.

Boyd, Orsemus B. *Cavalry Life in Tent and Field.* New York: Selwin Tait and Sons, 1894.

Brown, John H. *History of Texas from 1685-1892.* 2 vols. St. Louis: L. E. Daniell, 1892-1893.

Burton, Arthur T. *Black, Red and Deadly: Black and Indian Gunfighters of the Indian Territory, 1870-1907.* Austin: Eakin Press, 1991.

Bushnell, Amy Turner. *The King's Coffer: Proprietors of the Spanish Florida Treasury 1565-1702.* Gainesville: University Presses of Florida, 1981.

Campbell, Randolph B. *An Empire for Slavery: The Peculiar Institution in Texas, 1821-1865.* Baton Rouge: Louisiana State University Press, 1989.

Carlson, Paul Howard. *"Pecos Bill": A Military Biography of William R. Shafter.* College Station: Texas A&M University Press, 1989.

Carroll, John M., ed. *The Black Military Experience in the American West.* New York: Liveright, 1971.

——., ed. *The Medal of Honor: Its History and Recipients for the Indian Wars.* Bryan, TX: J.M. Carroll, 1979.

Carter, Robert G. *The Old Sergeant's Story: Winning the West from the Indians and Bad Men in 1870 to 1876.* New York: Fred H. Hitchcock, 1926.

——. *On the Border with Mackenzie or Winning the West from the Comanches.* New York: Antiquarian Press, 1961 [1935].

Chatelain, Verne Elmo. *The Defenses of Spanish Florida, 1565 to 1763.* Washington, D.C.: Carnegie Institute of Washington Publication 511, 1941.

Clifford, James. *The Predicament of Culture: Twentieth-Century Ethnography, Literature, and Art.* Cambridge: Harvard University Press, 1988.

Cline, Howard F. *Notes on Colonial Indians and Communities in Florida, 1700-1821.* Vol. 1 of *Florida Indians,* 3 vols. Garland American Indian Ethnohistory Series. New York: Garland, 1974.

Coe, Charles H. *Red Patriots: The Story of the Seminoles.* Cincinnati: Editor Publishing Co., 1898.

Coffman, Edward M. *The Old Army: A Portrait of the American Army in Peacetime, 1784-1898.* New York: Oxford University Press, 1986.

Cohen, Myer M. *Notices of East Florida and the Campaigns.* Charleston: Burges and Honour; New York: B.B. Hussey, 1836.

Coker, William S., and Thomas D. Watson. *Indian Traders of the Southeastern Spanish Borderlands: Panton, Leslie and Company and John Forbes and Company, 1783-1847.* Pensacola: University of West Florida Press, 1986.

Craton, Michael. *Testing the Chains: Resistance to Slavery in the British West Indies.* Ithaca: Cornell University Press, 1982.

Crawford, Michael H., ed. *Black Caribs: A Case Study in Biocultural Adaptation.* New York: Plenum Press, 1984.

Creel, Margaret Washington. *"A Peculiar People": Slave Religion and Community Culture Among the Gullahs.* New York: New York University Press, 1988.

Dabbs, Jack A. *The French Army in Mexico 1861-1867: A Study in Military Government.* The Hague: Mouton and Co., 1963.

Dillard, Joseph L. *Black English: Its History and Usage in the United States.* New York: Random House, 1972.

Domenech, E. H. D. *Missionary Adventures in Texas and Mexico. A Personal Narrative of Six Years' Sojourn in Those Regions.* London: Longmans and Roberts, 1858.

Ellison, Ralph. *Going to the Territory.* New York: Random House, 1986.

Everett, Dianna. *The Texas Cherokees: A People Between Two Fires.* Norman: University of Oklahoma Press, 1990.

Fabila, Alfonso. *La Tribu Kickapoo de Coahuila.* Mexico: Biblioteca Enciclopedica Popular de la Secretaria de Education Pública, Número 50, 1945.

Fairbanks, Charles H. *Ethnohistorical Report on the Florida Indians.* Vol. 3 of *Florida Indians,* 3 vols. Garland American Indian Ethnohistory Series. New York: Garland, 1974.

Fenley, Florence. *Old Timers: Their Own Stories.* Uvalde, TX: Hornby Press, 1939.

Fisher, O. Clark, and J. C. Dykes. *King Fisher: His Life and Times.* Norman: University of Oklahoma Press, 1966.

Foner, Jack D. *Blacks and the Military in American History.* New York: Praeger, 1974.

Forbes, J. G. *Sketches, Historical and Topographical of the Floridas, more particularly of East Florida.* Gainesville: University of Florida Press, 1964 [1821].

Foreman, Carolyn T. *Indian Women Chiefs.* Muskogee, OK: Star Printery, Inc., 1954.

Foreman, Grant. *Advancing the Frontier 1830-1860.* Norman: University of Oklahoma Press, 1933.

——, ed. *Adventure on Red River by Captain Randolph B. Marcy and Captain G. B. McClellan.* Norman: University of Oklahoma Press, 1937.

——. *The Five Civilized Tribes.* Norman: University of Oklahoma Press, 1934.

——. *Indian Removal.* Norman: University of Oklahoma Press, 1932.

——. *The Last Trek of the Indians.* Chicago: University of Chicago Press, 1946.

——, ed. *A Traveller in Indian Territory: The Journal of Ethan Allen Hitchcock, Late Major-General in the United States Army.* Cedar Rapids, IA: Torch Press, 1930.

Fowler, Arlen L. *The Black Infantry in the West, 1869-1891*. Westport, CT: Greenwood Press, 1971.

Fröbel, Julius. *Aus Amerika, Efrahungen, Reisen und Studien*. 2 vols. Leipzig: J. J. Weber, 1857-1858.

Genovese, Eugene D. *Roll, Jordan, Roll: The World the Slaves Made*. New York: Pantheon Books, 1974.

Gibson, Arrell Morgan. *The Kickapoos: Lords of the Middle Border*. Norman: University of Oklahoma Press, 1963.

Giddings, Joshua R. *The Exiles of Florida*. Columbus, OH: Follett, Foster and Co., 1858.

Glisan, Rodney. *Journal of Army Life*. San Francisco: A. L. Bancroft and Co., 1874.

Gómez, Arthur R. *A Most Singular Country: A History of Occupation in the Big Bend*. Provo, UT: Charles Redd Center for Western Studies, Brigham Young University, 1990.

González, Nancie L. Solien. *Sojourners of the Caribbean: Ethnogenesis and Ethnohistory of the Garífuna*. Urbana: University of Illinois Press, 1988.

Gray, Frank S. *Pioneering in Southwest Texas: True Stories of Early Day Experiences in Edwards and Adjoining Counties,* ed. by Marvin J. Hunter. Austin: Steck Co., 1949.

Green, Michael D. *The Politics of Indian Removal: Creek Government and Society in Crisis*. Lincoln: University of Nebraska Press, 1982.

Greene, Robert E. *Black Defenders of America 1775-1973*. Chicago: Johnson Publishing Co., 1974.

Greer, James K., ed. *The Days of Buck Barry in Texas, 1845-1906*. Dallas: Southwest Press, 1932.

Gregg, Josiah. *Commerce of the Prairies*. 2 vols. New York: H. G. Langley, 1844.

Halatsz, Nicholas. *The Rattling Chains: Slave Unrest and Revolt in the Antebellum South*. New York: McKay, Van Rees, 1966.

Haley, J. Evetts. *Fort Concho and the Texas Frontier*. San Angelo, TX: San Angelo Standard Times, 1952.

Hancock, Ian F. *The Texas Seminoles and Their Language*. Austin: University of Texas African and Afro-American Studies and Research Center, 1980.

Harper, F., ed. *The Travels of William Bartram, Naturalists' Edition*. New Haven: Yale University Press, 1958 [1791].

Harris, Charles H., III. *A Mexican Family Empire: The Latifundio of the Sánchez Navarros, 1765-1867*. Austin: University of Texas Press, 1975.

Hart, Herbert M. *Old Forts of the Far West*. New York: Bonanza Books, 1965.

Herskovits, Melville Jean. *The Myth of the Negro Past*. New York and London: Harper and Bros., 1941.

Hitchcock, Ethan Allen. *Fifty Years in Camp and Field: The Diary of Major General Ethan Allen Hitchcock*. Ed. by W. A. Croffut. New York: G.P. Putnam's Sons, 1909.

Holloway, Joseph E., ed. *Africanisms in American Culture*. Bloomington: Indiana University Press, 1990.

Hughes, William J. *Rebellious Ranger: Rip Ford and the Old Southwest*. Norman: University of Oklahoma Press, 1964.

James, Vinton L. *Frontier and Pioneer Recollections of Early Days in San Antonio and West Texas*. San Antonio: Artes Graficas Press, 1938.

Jones, Mrs. John M., Jr. (Rosemary Whitehead), ed. *La Hacienda*. Del Rio, TX: Whitehead Memorial Museum and Val Verde County Historical Commission, 1976.

Jordan, Terry G. *Texas Graveyards: A Cultural Legacy*. Austin: University of Texas Press, 1982.

Joyner, Charles. *Down by the Riverside: A South Carolina Slave Community*. Urbana: University of Illinois Press, 1984.

Katz, William Loren. *Black Indians: A Hidden Heritage*. New York: Atheneum, 1986.

———. *The Black West*. 3rd ed., rev. and expanded. Seattle: Open Hand, 1987.

Kerns, Virginia. *Women and the Ancestors: Black Carib Kinship and Ritual*. Urbana: University of Illinois Press, 1983.

Krogman, Wilton M. *The Physical Anthropology of the Seminole Indians of Oklahoma*. Rome: Failli, 1935.

Latorre, Felipe A., and Dolores L. LaTorre. *The Mexican Kickapoo Indians*. Austin: University of Texas Press, 1976.

Laumer, Frank. *Massacre!* Gainesville: University of Florida Press, 1968.

Leckie, William H. *The Buffalo Soldiers: A Narrative of the Negro Cavalry in the West*. Norman: University of Oklahoma Press, 1967.

———. *The Military Conquest of the Southern Plains*. Norman: University of Oklahoma Press, 1963.

Levine, Lawrence W. *Black Culture and Black Consciousness: Afro-American Folk Thought from Slavery to Freedom*. New York: Oxford University Press, 1977.

Littlefield, Daniel C. *Rice and Slaves: Ethnicity and the Slave Trade in Colonial South Carolina*. Baton Rouge: Louisiana State University Press, 1981.

Littlefield, Daniel F., Jr. *Africans and Creeks: From the Colonial Period to the Civil War*. Westport, CT: Greenwood Press, 1979.

———. *Africans and Seminoles: From Removal to Emancipation*. Westport, CT: Greenwood Press, 1977.

———. *The Cherokee Freedmen: From Emancipation to American Citizenship*. Westport, CT: Greenwood Press, 1978.

———. *The Chickasaw Freedmen: A People Without a Country*. Westport, CT: Greenwood Press, 1980.

McCall, George A. *Letters from the Frontiers*. Philadelphia: J.B. Lippincott and Co., 1868.

McReynolds, Edwin C. *The Seminoles*. Norman: University of Oklahoma Press, 1957.

Mahon, John K. *History of the Second Seminole War, 1835-1842*. Gainesville: University of Florida Press, 1967.

Manero, Vicente E., comp. *Documentos Interesantes, sobre Colonización: Los ha reunido, puesto en orden Cronológico y los Pública*. Mexico: Imprenta de Hijos de Murguia, 1878.

Manning, William R., ed. *Diplomatic Correspondence of the United States, Inter-American Affairs, 1831-1860*. 12 vols. Washington, D.C.: Carnegie Endowment for International Peace, 1932-1939.

Marcy, Randolph B. *Thirty Years of Army Life on the Border*. New York: Harper and Bros., 1866.

Mintz, Sidney W. *Caribbean Transformations*. Chicago: Aldine Publishing Co., 1974.

Mintz, Sidney W., and Richard Price. *An Anthropological Approach to the Afro-American Past: A Caribbean Perspective.* Philadelphia: Institute for the Study of Human Issues Occasional Papers in Social Change No. 2, 1976.

Montgomery, Cora. *Eagle Pass; Or, Life on the Border.* New York: Putnam's Semi-monthly Library for Travellers and the Fireside, 1852.

Morse, Jedidiah. *Report to the Secretary of War of the United States on Indian Affairs.* New Haven: S. Converse, 1822.

Motte, Jacob R. *Journey Into Wilderness; an Army Surgeon's Account of Life in Camp and Field During the Creek and Seminole Wars, 1836-1838.* Ed. by James F. Sunderman. Gainesville: University of Florida Press, 1953.

Nash, Gary B. *Red, White and Black: The Peoples of Early America.* Englewood Cliffs, NJ: Prentice-Hall, 1974.

Newcomb, James P. *History of Secession Times in Texas and Journal of Travel from Texas through Mexico to California.* San Francisco, 1863.

Newsom, J. A. *The Life and Practice of the Wild and Modern Indian, the Early Days of Oklahoma, Some Thrilling Experiences.* Oklahoma City: Harlow Publishing Co., 1922.

Nye, Wilbur S. *Carbine and Lance: The Story of Old Fort Sill.* Norman: University of Oklahoma Press, 1937.

Oates, Stephen B., ed. *Rip Ford's Texas by John Salmon Ford.* Austin: University of Texas Press, 1963.

O'Beirne, Harry S. and E. S. O'Beirne, comps. *The Indian Territory; Its Chiefs, Legislators and Leading Men.* St. Louis: C. B. Woodward Co., 1892.

Olmsted, Frederick L. *Journey through Texas: A Saddle-trip on the Southwestern Frontier.* Ed. by J. Howard. Austin: Von Boeckman-Jones Press, 1962 [1857].

Opala, Joseph A. *A Brief History of the Seminole Freedmen.* Norman: Dept. of Anthropology, University of Oklahoma, 1980.

Parker, James. *The Old Army: Memories 1872-1918.* Philadelphia: Dorrance and Co., 1929.

Patrick, Rembert W. *Florida Fiasco: Rampant Rebels on the Georgia-Florida Frontier, 1810-1815.* Athens: University of Georgia Press, 1954.

Perdue, Theda. *Slavery and the Evolution of Cherokee Society, 1540-1866.* Knoxville: University of Tennessee Press, 1979.

Peters, Virginia. *The Florida Wars.* Hamden, CT: Archon Books, 1979.

Peterson, Jacqueline, and Jennifer S. H. Brown, eds. *The New Peoples: Being and Becoming Métis in North America.* Lincoln: University of Nebraska Press, 1985.

Pingenot, Ben E. *Paso del Aguila: A Chronicle of Frontier Days on the Texas Border as Recorded in the Memoirs of Jesse Sumpter, 1827-1910.* Austin: Encino Press, 1969.

Pirtle, Caleb, III, and Michael F. Cusack. *The Lonely Sentinel. Fort Clark: On Texas's Western Frontier.* Austin: Eakin Press, 1985.

Porter, Kenneth Wiggins. *The Negro on the American Frontier.* New York: New York Times and Arno Press, 1971.

Potter, Woodburne. *The War in Florida.* Baltimore: Lewis and Coleman, 1836.

Pratt, J. W. *Expansionists of 1812.* New York: Macmillan, 1925.

Price, Richard. *First-Time: The Historical Vision of an Afro-American People.* Baltimore: Johns Hopkins University Press, 1983.

——, ed. *Maroon Societies: Rebel Slave Communities in the Americas.* Rev. ed. Baltimore: Johns Hopkins University Press, 1979.

Prucha, Francis Paul. *The Great Father: The United States Government and the American Indian.* 2 vols. Lincoln: University of Nebraska Press, 1984.

——. *Indian Policy in the United States: Historical Essays.* Lincoln: University of Nebraska Press, 1981.

Raht, Carlysle G. *The Romance of Davis Mountains and the Big Bend Country.* Odessa, TX: Rathbooks Co., 1963 [1919].

Rawick, George P., ed. *The American Slave: A Composite Autobiography.* 19 vols. Westport, CT: Greenwood Press, 1972. Texas Narratives, v. 4-5; Oklahoma and Mississippi Narratives, v. 7; Florida Narratives, v. 17.

——., ed. *The American Slave: A Composite Autobiography.* Supplement Series 1. 12 vols. Westport, CT: Greenwood Press, 1977. Oklahoma Narratives, v. 12.

——., ed. *The American Slave: A Composite Autobiography.* Supplement Series 2. 10 vols. Westport, CT: Greenwood Press, 1979. Oklahoma and Florida Narratives, incl. in v. 1; Texas Narratives, v. 2-10.

Record of Engagements with Hostile Indians in the Military Division of the Missouri, from 1868-82, Lieutenant General P. H. Sheridan, Commanding, Compiled from Official Records. Chicago, 1882.

Richardson, Rupert N. *The Comanche Barrier to South Plains Settlement: A Century and a Half of Savage Resistance to the Advancing White Frontier.* Glendale, CA: Arthur H. Clark Co., 1933.

Rickey, Don. *Forty Miles a Day on Beans and Hay: The Enlisted Soldier During the Indian Wars.* Norman: University of Oklahoma Press, 1963.

Rippy, J. Fred. *The United States and Mexico.* New York: Knopf, 1926.

Rister, Carl C. *The Southwestern Frontier, 1861-1881.* Cleveland: Arthur H. Clark Co., 1928.

Ritzenthaler, Robert E., and Frederick A. Peterson. *The Mexican Kickapoo Indians.* Milwaukee: Milwaukee Public Museum Publications in Anthropology No. 2, 1956.

Rodenbough, Theodore F., and William L. Haskin. *The Army of the United States: Historical Sketches of Staff and Line with Portraits of Generals-in-Chief.* New York: Maynard, Merrill and Co., 1896.

Scholes, Walter V. *Mexican Politics During the Juárez Regime 1855-1872.* Columbia: University of Missouri Press, 1957.

Shipman, O. L. (Mrs.). *Taming the Big Bend: A History of the Extreme Western Portion of Texas from Fort Clark to El Paso.* n.p., 1926.

Simmons, William Hayne. *Notices of East Florida, with an account of the Seminole Nation of Indians.* Gainesville: University of Florida Press, 1973 [1822].

Sinkin, Richard N. *The Mexican Reform, 1855-1876: A Study in Liberal Nation-Building.* Austin: University of Texas Institute of Latin-American Studies, 1979.

Sivad, Doug. *The Black Seminole Indians of Texas.* Boston: American Press, 1984.

Sowell, Andrew J. *Early Settlers and Indian Fighters of Southwest Texas.* Austin: Ben C. Jones Co., 1900.

——. *Rangers and Pioneers of Texas.* New York: Argosy Antiquarian, 1964 [1884].

Spickard, Paul R. *Mixed Blood: Intermarriage and Ethnic Identity in Twentieth-Century America.* Madison: University of Wisconsin Press, 1989.

Sprague, John T. *The Origin, Progress and Conclusion of the Florida War.* New York: Appleton and Co., 1848.

Stout, Joseph A., Jr. *The Liberators: Filibustering Expeditions into Mexico, 1848-1862, and the Last Thrust of Manifest Destiny.* Los Angeles: Westernlore Press, 1973.

Strong, Henry W. *My Frontier Days and Indian Fights on the Plains of Texas.* n.p., n.d. 122pp. typewritten and illustrated.

Sweet, Alexander E., and J. Armoy Knox. *On a Mexican Mustang, through Texas, from the Gulf to the Rio Grande.* Hartford, CT: S. S. Scranton and Co., 1883.

Taylor, Joe F., ed. *The Indian Campaign on the Staked Plains, 1874-1875.* Canyon, TX: Panhandle-Plains Historical Society, 1962.

Teall, Kaye M. *Black History in Oklahoma: A Resource Book.* Oklahoma City: Oklahoma City Public Schools, 1971.

Thompson, Richard A. *Crossing the Border With the 4th Cavalry: Mackenzie's Raid into Mexico, 1873.* Waco, TX: Texian Press, 1986.

Thompson, Robert Farris. *Flash of the Spirit: African and Afro-American Art and Philosophy.* New York: Random House, 1983.

Turner, Lorenzo Dow. *Africanisms in the Gullah Dialect.* Chicago: University of Chicago Press, 1949.

Tyler, Ronnie C. and L.R. Murphy, eds. *The Slave Narratives of Texas.* Austin: Encino Press, 1974.

Utley, Robert M. *Frontier Regulars: the United States Army and the Indian 1866-1891.* New York: Macmillan, 1973.

Vass, Winifred. *The Bantu Speaking Heritage of the United States.* Los Angeles: UCLA Center for Afro-American Studies, 1979.

Walker, Alice. *The Temple of My Familiar.* San Diego: Harcourt Brace Jovanovich, 1989.

Wallace, Ernest. *Ranald S. Mackenzie on the Texas Frontier.* Lubbock: West Texas Museum Assoc., 1965.

——, ed. *Ranald S. Mackenzie's Official Correspondence Relating to Texas, 1871-1873.* Lubbock: West Texas Museum Association, 1967.

——, ed. *Ranald S. Mackenzie's Official Correspondence Relating to Texas, 1873-1879.* Lubbock: West Texas Museum Association, 1968.

Waring, Antonio J., ed. *Laws of the Creek Nation.* Athens: University of Georgia Press, 1960.

Weisman, Brent Richards. *Like Beads on a String: A Culture History of the Seminole Indians in North Peninsular Florida.* Tuscaloosa: University of Alabama Press, 1989.

Wiggins, William H., Jr. *O Freedom! Afro-American Emancipation Celebrations.* Knoxville: University of Tennessee Press, 1987.

Williams, John L. *The Territory of Florida.* Gainesville: University of Florida Press, 1962 [1837].

Wilson, Miss Charles Emily. *History of the Seminole Indian Scout Cemetery.* Leaflet printed by Cannon Graphics, Del Rio, TX, for the Seminole Indian Scout Cemetery Association, n.d.

Winfrey, Dorman H., and James M. Day, eds. *The Indian Papers of Texas and the Southwest 1825-1916.* 5 vols. Austin: Pemberton Press, 1966.

Wood, Peter. *Black Majority; Negroes in Colonial South Carolina from 1670 through the Stono Rebellion.* New York: Knopf, 1974.

Wright, James Leitch, Jr. *Creeks and Seminoles: The Destruction and Regeneration of the Muscogulge People.* Lincoln: University of Nebraska Press, 1986.

———. *The Only Land They Knew: The Tragic Story of the American Indians in the Old South.* New York: Macmillan, 1981.

Yoakum, Henderson K. *History of Texas from Its First Settlement in 1685 to Its Annexation to the United States in 1846.* 2 vols. New York: Refield, 1855.

Movie and Television Productions

Bogart, Paul, director. *Skin Game.* Warner Bros. 1971.

Mathews, Denise, producer and writer. "Black Warriors of the Seminole." WUFT-TV, Channel 5 Production. Gainesville, Florida, 1989.

Index